Reginald Bosworth Smith

Rome and Carthage, the Punic Wars

Reginald Bosworth Smith

Rome and Carthage, the Punic Wars

ISBN/EAN: 9783744781466

Printed in Europe, USA, Canada, Australia, Japan

Cover: Foto ©ninafisch / pixelio.de

More available books at **www.hansebooks.com**

Epochs of Ancient History

EDITED BY

Rev. SIR G. W. COX, Bart., M.A. and C. SANKEY, M.A.

ROME and CARTHAGE

R. BOSWORTH SMITH, M.A.

EPOCHS OF ANCIENT HISTORY.

Edited by Rev. G. W. Cox and CHARLES SANKEY, M.A. Eleven volumes, 16mo, with 41 Maps and Plans. Price per vol., $1.00. The set, Roxburgh style, gilt top, in box, $11.00.

Troy—Its Legend, History, and Literature. By S. G. W. Benjamin.
The Greeks and the Persians. By G. W. Cox.
The Athenian Empire. By G. W. Cox.
The Spartan and Theban Supremacies. By Charles Sankey.
The Macedonian Empire. By A. M. Curteis.
Early Rome. By W. Ihne.
Rome and Carthage. By R. Bosworth Smith.
The Gracchi, Marius and Sulla. By A. H. Beesley.
The Roman Triumvirates. By Charles Merivale.
The Early Empire. By W. Wolfe Capes.
The Age of the Antonines. By W. Wolfe Capes.

EPOCHS OF MODERN HISTORY.

Edited by EDWARD E. MORRIS. Eighteen volumes, 16mo, with 77 Maps, Plans, and Tables. Price per vol., $1.00. The set, Roxburgh style, gilt top, in box, $18.00.

The Beginning of the Middle Ages. By R. W. Church.
The Normans in Europe. By A. H. Johnson.
The Crusades. By G. W. Cox.
The Early Plantagenets. By Wm. Stubbs.
Edward III. By W. Warburton.
The Houses of Lancaster and York. By James Gairdner.
The Era of the Protestant Revolution. By Frederic Seebohm.
The Early Tudors. By C. E. Moberly.
The Age of Elizabeth. By M. Creighton.
The Thirty Years' War, 1618-1648. By S. R. Gardiner.
The Puritan Revolution. By S. R. Gardiner.
The Fall of the Stuarts. By Edward Hale.
The English Restoration and Louis XIV. By Osmund Airy.
The Age of Anne. By Edward E. Morris.
The Early Hanoverians. By Edward E. Morris.
Frederick the Great. By F. W. Longman.
The French Revolution and First Empire. By W. O'Connor Morris. Appendix by Andrew D. White.
The Epoch of Reform, 1830-1850. By Justin Macarthy.

EPOCHS OF ANCIENT HISTORY

ROME AND CARTHAGE

THE PUNIC WARS

BY

R. BOSWORTH SMITH, M.A.

*Assistant-Master in Harrow School: formerly Fellow of Trinity College, Oxford.
Author of " Mohammed and Mohammedanism," and
" Carthage and the Carthaginians."*

NEW YORK:
CHARLES SCRIBNER'S SONS,
1889.

MATRI MEÆ

CUJUS NOMEN VIVÆ

HUIC OPUSCULO PRÆTEXI DEBUERAT

QUOD MATERNO AMORE INCEPTUM FOVEBAT

MORTUÆ PERACTUM

AMANTISSIMUS DEDICO

PREFACE.

THE PAGES which follow are an abbreviation, specially authorized by me for Messrs. Scribner, of my larger work on "Carthage and the Carthaginians." I have made no attempt to alter the language of the larger work, except where it appeared to me that I could alter it for the better. Indeed, any attempt to write down to the capacities of younger readers seems to me quite unnecessary in dealing with an "epoch of history" which, in the unique interest and importance of its subject, and in the simple grandeur of its leading characters, appeals with almost equal force to young and old. And if I have been led to dwell at greater length, and with apparently more genuine enthusiasm, on the elements of greatness which are to be found in Carthage, and on the genius of her two greatest sons, than on the qualities of her successful rival, it is not because I would suggest any doubt that Rome was the fitter of the two for empire, or that her victory was on the whole the victory of progress and of civilization; but because, owing to the conditions under which the history of Carthage has come down to us, and the distorted medium through which we must needs view it, it is, in my judgment, the proper business of the historian, so far as in him lies, to restore the balance. Multitudinous voices of the past, of the present, and in a sense, even of the future, attest, in language that cannot be mistaken by anyone, the greatness of the "Eternal City;" but the mournful and solitary silence which weighs upon the traveller as he stands upon the deserted site of Carthage, while it attests how thoroughly the Romans carried out their hateful work of obliteration, calls upon him in tones which to him, at least, are equally unmistakable, to lay stress on what may be fairly said for the city and the civilization which have never spoken, and can now, unfortunately, no longer speak for themselves.

One chapter only of this volume seems to require special comment here. In the spring of 1877, after I had finished the first draft of my larger work, I was enabled to pay a visit to the site of Carthage and its neighbourhood. It was a short visit, but was full of deep and varied interest. It was my first sight of an eastern city, and it brought me for the first time into direct personal contact with that vast religious system which is one of the greatest facts of human history, and which from causes deep as human nature itself, seems destined, whatever the upshot of the present Eastern difficulties always to maintain its hold on the Eastern world. I was able several times to visit the site of the Phœnician city, and to study, as far as my limited time would permit me, on the spot those questions of its topography and history with the general bearings of which I had been so long familiar in books. I walked round the harbours of Carthage, bathed in water which half preserves and half conceals its ruins, explored the Byrsa and the cisterns, traced for many miles the course of the aqueduct, crossed the river Bagradas, and examined, amongst other spots renowned in ancient story, the site of the still more ancient city, the parent city of Utica. In the concluding chapter of this volume, I have endeavoured to gather up some of the impressions which I derived from these varied sights and scenes; and I hope I have been able by these means, as well as by various touches which I have inserted subsequently in other portions of the book, to communicate to my readers in

America, what I think I gained for myself, a more "vivid" mental picture of that ancient city whose chequered fortunes in connection with her great antagonist, I have endeavoured to relate.

THE KNOLL, HARROW,
December, 1880.

CONTENTS.

CHAPTER I.

CARTHAGE.

PAGE

Characteristics of Phœnicians—Their defects—Size of their territory—Their relations to Israelites—Early commerce in Mediterranean—Pre eminence of Phœnicians—Origin of Carthage—its position and population—its relation to Sicily—Our knowledge of Carthage, whence derived—Its early history—Rapid growth of its empire—Its dealings with the Native Africans—with the Phœnician cities in Africa—with Tyre—with Sicilian Greeks—Constitution of Carthage—The Suffetes—The Senate—Deterioration of constitution—The "Hundred" Judges—Close oligarchy—General contentment—Social life of Carthaginians—Their commercial principles—Their agriculture—Merits of Mago's work on Agriculture—Carthaginian religion—Worship of Baal-Moloch—of Tanith or Astarte—Inferior divinities—Worship of Melcarth—Carthaginian literature—The Army—The mercenaries and the Numidian Cavalry—Condition of the masses—Colonization—Periplus of Hanno—Disaffection of subject races—Was Rome or Carthage best fitted for empire? 1

CHAPTER II.

CARTHAGE AND ROME.

Rome and Carthage compared—Contrasted—Origin and growth of Rome—Constitutional progress—Military progress—Conquest of Etruscans - of Gauls—of Latins, B.C. 390—of Samnites—Roman methods in war—War with Pyrrhus—Rome brought face to face with Carthage . 23

CHAPTER III.

FIRST PUNIC WAR.

MESSANA AND AGRIGENTUM.

(264-262 B. C.)

PAGE

Relations of Sicily to Carthage and Rome—Appeal of Mamertines for aid—The question at issue—Importance of the decision—Romans occupy Messana—They attack Syracuse—Results of first campaign—Romans ally themselves with Hiero—Carthaginians unprepared for war—Agrigentum—Its siege—Its fate 30

CHAPTER IV.

FIRST ROMAN FLEET. BATTLES OF MYLÆ AND ECNOMUS.

(262-256 B.C.)

Carthaginian naval supremacy—Roman naval affairs—Commercial treaties with Carthage—Difficulties of Romans—Want of ships of war—Want of sailors—The new fleet—Its first ventures—Naval science and tactics of the Ancients—The Corvus—Battle of Mylæ—Honours paid to Duillius—Egesta—The Romans attack Sardinia and Corsica—Energy of Carthaginians—Romans resolve to invade Africa—Enormous naval armaments—Route taken by the Romans—order of battle—Battle of Ecnomus . 39

CHAPTER V.

INVASION OF AFRICA. REGULUS AND XANTHIPPUS.

(256-250 B.C.)

Invasion of Africa—Romans overrun Carthaginian territory—Shortsightedness of Carthaginians—Changes necessary in Roman military system—Recall of Manlius—Victory of Regulus—Desperate plight of Carthaginians—Terms of peace rejected—Arrival of Xanthippus—He is given the command—His great victory near Adis—Joy of Carthaginians—Thank-offerings to Moloch—Departure of Xanthippus—The survivors at Clypea—Roman fleet destroyed in a storm—Carthaginian reinforcements for Sicily—Romans build a new fleet—Take Panormus—Second Roman fleet destroyed in a storm—Carthaginians threaten Panormus—Romans build a third fleet—Battle of Panormus—Part played by elephants in first Punic War Story of embassy and death of Regulus—How far true? . . 54

CHAPTER VI.

HAMILCAR BARCA AND THE SIEGE OF LILYBÆUM.

(250–241 B.C.)

Fortresses remaining to Carthaginians in Sicily – Siege of Lilybæum—Its origin and situation—Early siege operations—Carthaginians run the blockade—Hannibal the Rhodian—Carthaginian sortie—Distress of Romans—The Consul Claudius—Battle of Drepanum – Claudian family – Roman reinforcements for siege of Lilybæum lost at sea—Romans seize Eryx—Hamilcar Barca—He occupies Mount Ercte—Exhaustion of Romans—Culpable conduct of Carthaginians—Genius of Hamilcar—His plans—His enterprises—He transfers his camp from Ercte to Eryx—Romans build one more fleet—Lutatius Catulus—The Carthaginian plan—Battle of Ægatian Isles—Magnanimity of Hamilcar—Terms of peace—Roman gains and losses—Carthaginian losses and prospects—Contests only deferred 74

CHAPTER VII.

HAMILCAR BARCA AND THE MERCENARY WAR.

(241-238 B.C.)

Events between First and Second Punic War –Significance of Mercenary War—Weakness of Carthaginian Government

                                                              PAGE
—Symptoms of mutiny—Revolt of mercenaries and native
Africans—Hanno and Hamilcar Barca—The Truceless
War—Its atrocities and termination 96

CHAPTER VIII.

HAMILCAR BARCA IN AFRICA AND SPAIN.

(238-219 B.C.)

Conduct of Romans during Mercenary War—They appropriate Sardinia and Corsica—Peace and war parties at Carthage—Hamilcar's command—He crosses to Spain—Advantages of his position there—His administration and death—His character—Administration of Hasdrubal—New Carthage founded—Early career of Hannibal—Remissness of Romans—Rising of Gauls in Italy—Its suppression—Hannibal besieges Saguntum—War declared between Rome and Carthage 102

CHAPTER IX.

SECOND PUNIC WAR.

(218-201 B.C.)

PASSAGE OF THE RHONE AND THE ALPS, B.C. 218

Preparations of Hannibal—He determines to go by land—Numbers of his army—His march through Gaul—His passage of the Rhone—Vagueness of ancient writers in geographical matters—Passage over Alps selected by Hannibal—Route by which he approached it—The first ascent—Valley of the Isère—The main ascent—The summit—Hannibal addresses his troops—The descent—Interest attaching to the passage of the Alps—Its cost and results—The "War of Hannibal" 114

CHAPTER X.

BATTLES OF TREBIA AND TRASIMENE.

(218-217 B. C.)

PAGE

P. Scipio returns from Italy to Gaul—Sempronius recalled from Sicily—Battle of the Ticinus—Hannibal crosses the Po—He is joined by the Gauls—Retreat of Scipio to the Trebia—Hannibal selects his ground and time—Battle of the Trebia—Results of the victory—Hannibal crosses the Apennines—The marshes of the Arno—Position of the Roman armies—Flaminius and his antecedents—Despondency at Rome—Resolution of Flaminius—He follows Hannibal from Arretium—Livy and Polybius compared—Position chosen by Hannibal—Battle of the Trasimene lake—Death of Flaminius. 126

CHAPTER XI.

HANNIBAL OVERRUNS CENTRAL ITALY.

(217-216 B. C.)

News of the Trasimene defeat reaches Rome—Measures of the Roman Senate—Hannibal marches into Picenum—Sends despatches to Carthage—He arms his troops in the Roman fashion—Advance of the Dictator Fabius—His policy—Discontent of his troops—Hannibal ravages Samnium and Campania—Beauty and wealth of Campania—Continued inaction of Fabius—He tries to entrap Hannibal but fails—Minucius left in command—Is raised to equal rank with Fabius—Is saved from disaster by him—Services of Fabius to Rome. 142

CHAPTER XII.

BATTLE OF CANNÆ. CHARACTER OF HANNIBAL.

(216 B. C.)

Energy and spirit of the Romans—The rival armies face each other at Cannæ—Nature of the ground—The double command of Æmilius Paullus and Varro—Anxiety at Rome—Dispositions of Hannibal for the battle—Battle of Cannæ—Number of the slain—Panic at Rome—Measures of the Senate—Course of the war—Was Hannibal right or wrong in not advancing on Rome now?—Greatness of Hannibal and of Rome—Character and genius of Hannibal—His ascending series of successes—His influence over men—Sources of our knowledge of him—Charges against him—Roman feeling towards him—Change in character of war after Cannæ. . 152

CHAPTER XIII.

REVOLT OF CAPUA. SIEGE OF SYRACUSE.

(216–212 B. C.)

Capua revolts—Marcellus—Hannibal winters at Capua—Latin colonies still true to Rome—Great exertions of Rome—Hannibal negotiates with Syracuse, Sardinia, and Macedon—His position at Tifata—Fabius and Marcellus Consuls—The tide turns against Hannibal—He gains possession of Tarentum—The war in Sicily—Importance of Syracuse—Its siege and capture—Its fate. . . 171

CHAPTER XIV.

SIEGE OF CAPUA AND HANNIBAL'S MARCH ON ROME.

(212–208 B. C.)

Importance of war in Spain—Successes and death of the two Scipios—Renewed activity of Hannibal—Siege of Capua—Hannibal attempts to relieve it—His march on Rome—

Fate of Capua—Continued superiority of Hannibal in the field—Death of Marcellus—Influence of family traditions at Rome—Patriotism of Romans—Latin colonies show symptoms of exhaustion. 182

CHAPTER XV.
BATTLE OF THE METAURUS.
(207 B.C.)

The approach of Hasdrubal from Spain—His messengers fail to find Hannibal—Brilliant march of Nero—Battle of the Metaurus—Triumph and brutality of Nero . . . 193

CHAPTER XVI.
P. CORNELIUS SCIPIO.
(210-206 B.C.)

Scipio in Spain—His early history—His character and influence—Made proconsul—Takes New Carthage Carthaginians finally driven out of Spain 199

CHAPTER XVII.
THE WAR IN AFRICA; BATTLE OF ZAMA.
(206-202 B.C.)

Scipio returns to Rome and is elected Consul—Receives leave to invade Africa—Goes to Sicily—His doings and difficulties there—Sails for Africa—Massinissa and Syphax—Roman ignorance of Carthage—The fall of Carthage, how far a matter of regret—Siege of Utica—Scipio's command longed—He burns the Carthaginian camps—Sophonisba—The Carthaginian peace party—Sons of Hamilcar recalled to Africa—Mago obeys the summons—Hannibal obeys it—Joy in Italy—First operations of Hannibal in Africa—Battle of Zama—Dignity of Hannibal—Terms of peace—Results of the war—Alternative policies open to Rome 207

CHAPTER XVIII.

CARTHAGE AT THE MERCY OF ROME.

(201–150 B.C.)

PAGE

Deterioration of Roman character—Condition of Italy—Condition of Rome—Condition of Roman provinces—Rapid conquest of the East—Reforms introduced by Hannibal at Carthage—Romans demand his surrender—His exile and wanderings—His schemes, his sufferings, and his death—Death of Scipio—Treatment of Carthage by Romans and Massinissa 229

CHAPTER XIX.

DESTRUCTION OF CARTHAGE.

(149–146 B.C.)

Topography of Carthage—Causes of its obscurity—Changes made by nature and man—The peninsula—The fortifications—The Tænia—The harbours—Resolve of Rome respecting Carthage—Treachery of Romans—Scene at Utica—Scene at Carthage—The Roman attack fails—Repeated failures and losses—Scipio Æmilianus—His character and connections—He takes the Megara—Siege of the city proper—Scipio's mole and the new outlet—Contradictions in Carthaginian character—Scipio attacks the harbour quarter—He takes Nepheris—The final assault—The three streets—The Byrsa—Fate of the city and its inhabitants—Curse of Scipio—Unique character of the fall of Carthage—Its consequences—Subsequent cities on its site—Final destruction by the Arabs 239

CHAPTER XX.

CARTHAGE AS IT IS.

Interest of a visit to Carthage—Nature of impressions thence derived—Its topography—The Goletta and the Tænia—Djebel Khawi and the Necropolis—Sanctity of burying-place among Semitic races—Râs Sidi Bu Said and its sanctity—Scene of misadventure of Mancinus—Hill of St. Louis the ancient Byrsa—Gulf of Tunis and Peninsula of the Dakhla—Lake of Tunis and plain of Carthage—The aqueduct—Utica—Obliteration of Punic City—The "smaller cisterns"—The larger cisterns—Excavations of Dr. Davis—Excavations of M. Beulé—Remains of ancient harbours—Buildings beneath the sea—Oriental character of Tunis—The neighbourhood of Tunis—Characteristics of the Arab—Conclusion 263

MAPS.

	PAGE
THE CARTHAGINIAN EMPIRE AND DEPENDENCIES	9
SICILY, TO ILLUSTRATE THE FIRST PUNIC WAR	30
BATTLE OF ECNOMUS	51
ITALY, TO ILLUSTRATE THE SECOND PUNIC WAR	114
BATTLE OF TREBIA	131
BATTLE OF TRASIMENE	139
BATTLE OF CANNÆ	159
CARTHAGE AND ITS NEIGHBOURHOOD	239
PLAN OF HARBOURS AT CARTHAGE	243

ROME AND CARTHAGE: THE PUNIC WARS.

CHAPTER I.

CARTHAGE.

IT was well for the development and civilization of the ancient world that the Hebrew fugitives from Egypt were not able to drive at once from the whole coast of Syria its old inhabitants; for the accursed race of the Canaanites whom, for their licentious worship and cruel rites, they were bidden to extirpate from Palestine itself, were no other than those enterprizing mariners and those dauntless colonists who, sallying from their narrow roadsteads, committed their fragile barks to the mercy of unknown seas, and, under their Greek name of Phœnicians, explored island and promonotory, creek and bay, from the coast of Malabar even to the lagunes of the Baltic. From Tyre and Sidon issued those busy merchants who carried, with their wares, to distant shores the rudiments of science and of many practical arts which they had ob-

Characteristics of the Phœnicians.

tained from the far East, and which, probably, they but half understood themselves. It was they who, at a period antecedent to all contemporary historical records, introduced written characters, the foundation of all high intellectual development, into that country which was destined to carry intellectual and artistic culture to the highest point which humanity has yet reached. It was they who learned to steer their ships by the sure help of the Polar Star, while the Greeks still depended on the Great Bear; it was they who rounded the Cape of Storms, and earned the best right to call it the Cape of Good Hope, 2,000 years before Vasco de Gama. Their ships returned to their native shores bringing with them sandal wood from Malabar, spices from Arabia, fine linen from Egypt, ostrich plumes from the Sahara. Cyprus gave them its copper, Elba its iron, the coast of the Black Sea its manufactured steel. Silver they brought from Spain, gold from the Niger, tin from the Sicily Isles, and amber from the Baltic. Where they sailed, there they planted factories which opened a caravan trade with the interior of vast continents hitherto regarded as inaccessible, and which became inaccessible for centuries again when the Phœnicians disappeared from history. They were as famous for their artistic skill as for their enterprize and energy. Did the greatest of the Jewish kings desire to adorn the Temple which he had erected to the Most High in the manner least unworthy of Him? A Phœnician king must supply him with the well-hewn cedars of his stately Lebanon, and the cunning hand of a Phœnician artisan must shape the pillars and the lavers, the oxen and the lions of brass, which decorated the shrine. Did the King of Persia himself, in the intoxication of his pride, command miracles to be performed, boisterous straits to be bridged, or a peninsula to become an island? It was Phœnician architects who lashed together the boats that were to connect Asia with Europe, and it was Phœnician workmen who knew best how to economize their toil in digging the canal that was to transport the fleet of Xerxes through dry land, and save it from the winds and waves of Mount Athos. The merchants of Tyre were, in truth, the princes, and her traffickers the honourable men, of the earth. Wherever a ship could penetrate, a factory be planted, a trade developed or created, there we find these ubiquitous, these irrepressible Phœnicians.

We know well what the tiny territory of Palestine has done for the religion of the world, and what the tiny Greece has done for its intellect and its art; but we are apt to forget that what the Phœnicians did for the development and intercommunication of the world was achieved by a state confined within narrower boundaries still. In the days of their greatest prosperity, when their ships were to be found on every known and on many unknown seas, the Phœnicians proper of the Syrian coast remained content with a narrow strip of fertile territory, squeezed in between the mountains and the sea, of the length of some thirty and of the average breadth of only a single mile! And if the existence of a few settlements beyond these limits entitles us to extend the name of Phœnicia to some 120 miles of coast, with a plain behind it which sometimes broadened out into a sweep of a dozen miles, was it not sound policy, even in a community so enlarged, to keep for themselves the gold they had so hardly won, rather than lavish it on foreign mercenaries in the hope of extending their sway inland, or in the vain attempt to resist by force of arms the mighty mon-

Size of their territory.

archs of Egypt, of Assyria, or of Babylon? Their strength was to sit still, to acknowledge the titular supremacy of anyone who chose to claim it, and then, when the time came, to buy the intruder off.

The land-locked sea, the eastern extremity of which washes the shores of Phœnicia proper, connecting as it does three continents, and abounding in deep gulfs, in fine harbours, and in fertile islands, seems to have been intended by Nature for the early development of commerce and colonization. By robbing the ocean of half its mystery and of more than half its terrors, it allured the timid mariner, even as the eagle does its young, from headland on to headland, or from islet to islet, till it became the highway of the nations of the ancient world; and the products of each of the countries whose shores it laves became the common property of all.

Extent of their commerce and colonization.

But in this general race of enterprise and commerce among the nations which bordered on the Mediterranean, it is to the Phœnicians that unquestionably belongs the foremost place. In the dimmest dawn of history, many centuries before the Greeks had set foot in Asia Minor or in Italy, before even they had settled down in secure possession of their own territories, we hear of Phœnician settlements in Asia Minor and in Greece itself, in Africa, in Macedon, and in Spain. There is hardly an island in the Mediterranean which has not preserved some traces of these early visitors: Cyprus, Rhodes, and Crete in the Levant; Malta, Sicily, and the Balearic Isles in the middle passage; Sardinia and Corsica in the Tyrrhenian Sea; the Cyclades, as Thucydides tells us in the mid-Ægean; and even Samothrace and Thasos at its northern extremity, where Herodotus, to use his own forcible expression, himself saw a whole mountain "turned upside down" by their mining energy; all have either yielded Phœnician coins and inscriptions, have retained Phœnician proper names and legends, or possess mines, long, perhaps, disused, but which were worked as none but Phœnicians ever worked them.

And among the Phœnician factories which dotted the whole southern shore of the Mediterranean, from the east end of the greater Syrtis even to the Pillars of Hercules, there was one which, from a concurrence of circumstances, was destined rapidly to outstrip all the others, to make herself their acknowledged head, to become the Queen of the Mediterranean, and, in some sense, of the Ocean beyond, and, for a space of over a hundred years, to maintain a deadly and not unequal contest with the future mistress of the world. The history of that great drama, its antecedents, and its consequences, forms the subject of this volume. *They found Carthage.*

The rising African factory was known to its inhabitants by the name of Kirjath-Hadeschath, or New Town, to distinguish it from the much older settlement of Utica, of which it may have been, to some extent, an offshoot. The Greeks, when they came to know of its existence, called it Karchedon, and the Romans, Carthago. The date of its foundation is uncertain; but the current tradition refers it to a period about a hundred years before the founding of Rome. The fortress that was to protect the young settlement was built upon a peninsula projecting eastwards from the inner corner of what is now called the Gulf of Tunis, the largest and most beautiful roadstead of the North African coast. The topography of Carthage will be described in detail at a later period of this history. At present it will be sufficient to remark that the city *Position, topography, and population.*

proper, at the time at which it is best known to us, the period of the Punic wars, consisted of the Byrsa or Citadel quarter, a Greek word corrupted from the Canaanitish Bozra, or Bostra, that is, a fort, and of the Cothon, or harbour quarter, so important in the history of the final siege. To the north and west of these, and occupying all the vast space between them and the isthmus behind, were the Megara (Hebrew, Magurim), that is, the suburbs and gardens of Carthage, which, with the city proper, covered an area twenty-three miles in circumference. Its population must have been fully proportionate to its size. Just before the third Punic war, when its strength had been drained by the two long wars with Rome and by the incessant depredations of that chartered brigand Massinissa, it contained 700,000 inhabitants, and towards the close of the final siege the Byrsa alone was able to give shelter to a motley multitude of 50,000 men, women, and children.

Facing the Hermæan promontory (Cape Bon), the north-eastern horn of the Gulf of Tunis, at a distance of only ninety miles, was the Island of Sicily, *Its relation to Sicily.* which, as a glance at the map, and as the sunken ridge extending from one to the other still clearly show, must have once actually united Europe to Africa. This fair island it was which, crowded, even in those early days, with Phœnician factories, seemed to beckon the chief of Phœnician cities onwards towards an easy and a natural field of foreign conquest. This it was which proved to be the apple of fierce discord for centuries between Carthage and the Greek colonies, which soon disputed its possession with her. This, in an ever chequered warfare, and at the cost of torrents of the blood of her mercenaries, and of untold treasures of her citizens, enriched Carthage with the most splendid trophies — stolen trophies though they were — of Greek art. This, finally, was the chief battle-field of the contending forces during the whole of the first Punic war — in the beginning that is, of her fierce struggle for existence with all the power of Rome.

Such, very briefly, was the city, and such the race whose varied fortunes, so far as our fragmentary materials allow us, we are about to trace. What were the causes of the rapid rise of Carthage; what was the extent of her African and her foreign dominions, and the nature of her hold upon them; what were the peculiar excellences and defects of her internal constitution, and what the principles on which she traded and colonized, conquered and ruled;—to these and other questions some answer must be given, as a necessary preliminary to that part of her history which alone we can trace consecutively. Some answer we must give; but how are we to give it? No native poet, whose writings have come down to us, has sung of the origin of Carthage, or of her romantic voyages; no native orator has described, in glowing periods which we can still read, the splendour of her buildings and the opulence of her merchant princes. No native annalist has preserved the story of her long rivalry with Greeks and Etruscans, and no African philosopher has moralized upon the stability of her institutions or the causes of her fall. All have perished. The text of three treaties with Rome, made in the days of her prosperity; the log-book of an adventurous Carthaginian admiral, dedicated on his return from the Senegal or the Niger as a votive offering in the temple of Baal; some fragments of the practical precepts of a Carthaginian agriculturist, translated by the order of the utilitarian Roman Senate; a speech or two of a vagabond

Meagreness of Carthaginian records.

Carthaginian in the Pænulus of Plautus, which has been grievously mutilated in the process of transcribing it into Roman letters; a few Punic inscriptions buried twenty feet below the surface of the ground, entombed and preserved by successive Roman, and Vandal, and Arab devastations, and now at length revealed and deciphered by the efforts of French and English archæologists; the massive substructions of ancient temples; the enormous reservoirs of water; and the majestic procession of stately aqueducts which no barbarism has been able to destroy—these are the only native or semi-native sources from which we can draw the outlines of our picture, and we must eke out our narrative of Carthage in the days of her prosperity, as best we may, from a few chapters of reflections by the greatest of the Greek philosophers, from the late Roman annalists who saw everything with Roman eyes, and from a few but precious antiquarian remarks in the narrative of the great Greek historian, Polybius, who, with all his love of truth and love of justice, saw Carthage only at the moment of her fall, and was the bosom friend of her destroyer.

In her origin, at least, Carthage seems to have been like other Phœnician settlements, a mere commercial factory. Her inhabitants cultivated friendly relations with the natives, looked upon themselves as tenants at will rather than as owners of the soil, and, as such, cheerfully paid a rent to the African Berbers for the ground covered by their dwellings. It was the instinct of self-preservation alone which dictated a change of policy, and transformed this peace-loving mercantile community into the warlike and conquering state, of which the whole of the Western Mediterranean was so

Spread of Carthaginian influence in the Western Mediterranean.

soon to feel the power. The result of this change of policy was that the western half of the Mediterranean became—what, at one time, the whole of it had bidden fair to be—a Phœnician lake, in which no foreign merchantmen dared to show themselves. It was a vast preserve, to be caught trespassing upon which, so Strabo tells us, on the authority of Eratosthenes, ensured the punishment of instant death by drowning. No promontory was so barren, no islet so insignificant, as to escape the jealous and ever-watchful eye of the Carthaginians. In Corsica, if they could not get any firm or extensive foothold themselves, they at least prevented any other state from doing the like. Into their hands fell, in spite of the ambitious dreams of Persian kings and the aspirations of patriot Greeks, that "greatest of all islands," the island of Sardinia; theirs were the Ægatian and the Liparæan, the Balearic and the Pityusian Isles; theirs the tiny Elba, with its inexhaustible supply of metals; theirs, too, Malta still remained, an outpost pushed far into the domain of their advancing enemies, a memorial of what once had been, and, perhaps, to the sanguine Carthaginian temperament, an earnest of what might be again hereafter. Above all, the Phœnician settlements in Spain, at the innermost corner of the great preserve, with the adjacent silver mines which gave to these settlements their peculiar value, were now trebly safe from all intruders.

Elated, as it would seem, by their naval successes, which were hardly of their own seeking, the Carthaginians thought that they might now at last become the owners of the small strip of African territory which they had hitherto seemed to occupy *In Africa.* on sufferance only, and they refused the ground-rent which, up till now, they had paid to the adjoining tribes.

Step by step they enlarged their territories at the expense of the natives, till the whole of the rich territory watered by the Bagradas became theirs. The nomadic tribes were beaten back beyond the river Triton into the country named, from the roving habits of its inhabitants, Numidia, or into the desert of Tripolis. The agricultural tribes were forced to pay tribute to the conquerors for the right of cultivating their own soil, or to shed their blood on the field of battle in the prosecution of further conquests from the tribes beyond. Nor did the kindred Phœnician settlements in the adjoining parts of Africa escape unscathed. Utica alone, owing probably to her antiquity and to the semi-parental relation in which she stood to Carthage, was allowed to retain her walls and full equality of rights with the rising power; but Hippo Zarytus, and Adrumetum, the greater and the lesser Leptis, were compelled to pull down their walls and acknowledge the supremacy of the Carthaginian city. All along the northern coast of Africa the original Phœnician settlers, and probably to some extent, the Carthaginians themselves, had intermarried with the natives. The product of these marriages was that numerous class of Liby-Phœnicians which proved to be so important in the history of Carthaginian colonization and conquest; a class which, equi-distant from the Berbers on the one hand and from the Carthaginians proper on the other, and composed of those who were neither wholly citizens nor yet wholly aliens, experienced the lot of most half-castes, and were alternately trusted and feared, pampered and oppressed, loved and hated by the ruling state.

One enterprize which was undertaken by the Carthaginians in obedience to the fiat of the king of Persia, to the lasting good of humanity, failed of its object.

Xerxes (B. C. 480), advancing with his millions of barbarians upon Athens from the east, bade, so it is said, Hamilcar advance with his 300,000 mercenaries upon Syracuse from the west. The torch of Greek learning and civilization was to be extinguished at the most opposite ends of the Greek world at one and the same moment; but, happily for mankind at large, both attempts were foiled. The efforts of Xerxes ended in the destruction of the Persian fleet at Salamis, and the disgraceful flight of the king to Asia; the efforts of Hamilcar ended in his defeat and death at Himera, and in the destruction of 150,000 of his army; and by a dramatic propriety which is not common in history, whatever it may be in fiction, this double victory of Greek civilization is said to have taken place in the same year and on the very same day. *Attack on Greeks in Sicily fails.*

Let us now turn to the political organization of the city which achieved so rapid and marvellous a development, and inquire how far it was the effect and how far the cause of her prosperity. The constitution of Carthage was not the work of a single legislator, as that of Sparta is said to have been, nor of a series of legislators like that of Athens; it was rather, like that of England, the growth of circumstances and of centuries. It obtained the praise of Aristotle for its judicious admixture of the monarchical, the oligarchical, and the democratical elements. The original monarchical constitution—doubtless inherited from Tyre—was represented by two supreme magistrates called by the Romans Suffetes. Their name is the same as the Hebrew Shofetim, mistranslated in our Bible, Judges. The Hamilcars and Hannos of Carthage were, like their prototypes, the Gideons and the Samsons of the Book of Judges, not so *Constitution of Carthage.*

much the judges, as the protectors and the rulers of their respective states. They are compared by Greek writers to the two kings of Sparta, and by the Romans to their own consuls. Beneath these kings came, in the older constitution, a council, called by the Greeks the Gerusia, or Council of Ancients, consisting of twenty-eight members, over which the Suffetes presided. This council declared war, ordered levies of troops, appointed generals, sent out colonies. If the council and Suffetes agreed, their decision was final; if they disagreed, the matter was referred to the people at large. In this and in other ways each element of the body politic had its share in the administration of the State.

But the Carthaginian constitution described and praised by Aristotle is not the same as that of the Punic wars. In the interval which separates the two epochs, short as it is, a great change which must have been long preparing, had been completed. The Suffetes had gradually become little more than an honorary magistracy. The Senate over which they presided had allowed the main part of their power to slip out of their hands into those of another body, called the Judges, or "The Hundred," which, if it seemed to be more liberal in point of numbers and in conformation, was much more exclusive in policy and in spirit. The appeal to the people was only now resorted to in times of public excitement, when the rulers, by appearing to share power, tried to lessen envy, and allowed the citizens to go through the form of registering what, practically, they had already decreed. The result was an oligarchy, like that of Venice, clear-sighted and consistent, moderate, nay, often wise in its policy, but narrow in its views, and often suspicious alike of its opponents and of its friends. By the old constitu-

The growth of power of the Hundred Judges.

tion the Senate had the right to control the magistrates; but this new body of Judges controlled the Senate, and therefore, in reality, the magistrates also. Nor was it content to control the Senate; it practically superseded it. Its members did not, as a rule, appropriate the offices of State to themselves; but they could summon their holders before them, and so draw their teeth. No Shofete, no senator, no general, was exempt from their irresponsible despotism. The Shofetes presided, the senators deliberated, the generals fought, as it were, with a halter round their necks. The sentences passed by the Hundred, if they were often deserved, were often also, like those of the dreaded "Ten" at Venice, to whom they bore a striking resemblance, arbitrary and cruel. The unsuccessful general, whether his ill-success was the result of uncontrollable circumstances or of culpable neglect, might be condemned to crucifixion; indeed, he often wisely anticipated his sentence by committing suicide.

Within the ranks of this close oligarchy first-rate ability would seem to have been at a discount. Indeed, the exact equality of all within the privileged ranks is as much a principle of oligarchy as is the equal suppression of all that *Narrowness of oligarchy.* is outside of it. Language bears testimony to this in the name given alike to the Homoioi of Sparta and the "Peers" of England. It was jealousy, for instance, of the superior abilities of the family of Mago, and their prolonged pre-eminence in the Carthaginian State, which had in the fifth century B.C. cemented the alliance between other and less able families of the aristocracy, and so had first given rise to this very institution of the Hundred Judges; and it was the same mean jealousy of all that is above itself, which, afterwards, in the time of the Punic wars, united, as one man, a large part of the ruling oligarchs in the vain effort to control and to thwart, and to annoy with a thousand petty annoyances, the one family of consummate ability which Carthage then possessed, that noble-minded Barcine gens, that "lion's brood," who were brought to the front in those troublous times by the sheer force of their genius, and who, for three generations, ruled by the best of all rights—the right Divine—that of unswerving devotion to their country, of the ability to rule, and the will to use that ability well.

If we try, as we cannot help trying, to picture to ourselves the daily life and personal characteristics of the people whose political organization we have just described, and to ask, not what the Carthaginians did—for that we know—but what they were, we are confronted by the provoking blank in the national history which has been already noticed. Such few indications as we have are in thorough keeping with the view we have taken of the political exclusiveness of the ruling clique. There were public baths; but since no member of the Senate would bathe where the people bathed, a special class of baths were set apart for their use. There were public messes, as they were called; but these were not, as Aristotle supposed, analogous to the Spartan Syssitia, an institution intended to foster manliness and simplicity of life. The black broth of the heroes of Sparta would not have suited the Carthaginian nobles, who, clad in their famous cloth, dyed twice over with the purple dye of their African, their Spanish, or their Tyrian fisheries, and decorated with the finely-cut glass beads, the invention of their Phœnician forefathers, fared sumptuously on their abounding flocks and herds, or on such delicious fruits as those with which

Social life at Carthage.

Cato moved the astonishment and the envy of the senators of Rome. The Carthaginian Syssitia were incentives to luxury, not checks upon it; they were clubs formed originally for social gatherings, and afterwards applied to the purposes of political gossip or corruption. Dining-tables of the costly citron wood, a single specimen of which, Pliny tells us, in the time of the Roman Empire cost as much as a broad estate, must have been common amongst those who monopolized the commerce of the countries where alone the citron-tree grows. Gold and silver plate cannot have been rare amongst those who controlled the rich mines of Spain, and to whom their ambassadors reported, with a touch of scorn, upon their return from Rome, that they had been hospitably entertained by senator after senator, but that one service of plate had done duty for all. Objects of fine art—statues, and paintings, and embroideries—there were in abundance at Carthage; but they were the work of Greek, not of Phœnician artists, and their abundance indicated not so much the genius, critical or creative, of the Carthaginian community, as the number of Greek towns—Selinus and Himera, Gela and Agrigentum—sacked in the Sicilian wars.

Carthage was, beyond doubt, the richest city of antiquity. Her ships were to be found on all known seas, and there was probably no important product, animal, vegetable, or mineral, of the ancient world, which did not find its way into her harbours and pass through the hands of her citizens. But it is remarkable, that while in no city then known did commerce rank so high, the noblest citizens even of Carthage seem to have left commercial enterprize to those who came next below them in the social scale. They preferred to live on their estates as agri-

Wealth and agriculture.

culturists or country gentlemen, and derived their princely revenues from their farms or their mines, which were worked by prodigious gangs of slaves. The cultivation of the soil was, probably, nowhere carried on with such astonishing results as in the smiling country which surrounded Carthage.

Those members of the Carthaginian aristocracy who did not find a sufficient field for their ability in agriculture or in politics, in literature or in commerce, took refuge in the profession of arms, and formed always the chief ornament, and often the chief strength of the Punic armies. And military spirit. At one period, at least, of the history of the state, they formed a so-called "Sacred Band," consisting of 2,500 citizens, who, clad in resplendent armour, fought around the person of their general-in-chief, and, feasting from dishes of the costliest gold and silver plate, commemorated in their pride the number of their campaigns by the number of rings on their fingers.

But the most important factor in the history of a people—especially if it be a Semitic people—is its religion. The religion of the Carthaginians was what their race, their language, and their history would lead us to expect. It was, with slight modifications, the religion of the Canaanites, the religion, that is, which, in spite of the purer monotheism of the Hebrews and the higher teachings of their prophets, so long exercised a fatal fascination over the great bulk of the Hebrew race. Religion of Carthage. Baal-Moloch was a malignant deity; he was the fire-god, rejoicing in "human sacrifices and in parents' tears." His worshippers gashed and mutilated themselves in their religious frenzy. Like Kronos or Saturn—to whom the Greeks and Romans aptly enough compared him—he was the devourer of his own children. In times of unbroken security the Carthaginians neglected or forgot him; but when they were elated by an unlooked-for victory, or depressed by a sudden reverse, that fanaticism which is often dormant but never altogether absent from the Semitic breast, burst forth into a devouring flame, which gratified to the full his thirst for human blood. Tanith or Astarte, in the nobler aspects which she sometimes presented, as the goddess of wedded love or war, of the chase or of peaceful husbandry, was identified by the Romans, now with Juno, now with Diana, and now again with Ceres; but, unfortunately, it was when they identified her with their Venus Cœlestis that they came nearest to the truth. Her worship, like that of the Babylonian Mylitta, required immorality, nay, consecrated it. The "abomination of the Sidonians" was also the abomination of the Carthaginians.

But there was one god who stood in such a peculiar relation to Carthage, and whose worship seems to have been so much more genial and so much more spiritual than the rest, that we are fain to dwell upon it as a foil to what has preceded. *Worship of Melcarth.* This god was Melcarth, that is Melech-Kirjath, or the king of the city; he is called by the Greeks "the Phœnician Hercules," and his name itself has passed, with a slight alteration, into Greek mythology as Melicertes. The city of which he was pre-eminently the god was Tyre. There he had a magnificent temple which was visited for antiquarian purposes by Herodotus. It contained two splendid pillars, one of pure gold, the other, as Herodotus believed, of emerald, which shone brilliantly at night, but there was no image of the god to be seen. The same was the case in his famous temple at Thasos, and the still more famous one at

Gades, which contained an oracle, a hierarchy of priests, and a mysterious spring which rose and fell inversely with the tide, but still no image. At Carthage, Melcarth had not even a temple. The whole of the city was his temple, and he refused to be localized in any particular part of it. He received, there is reason to believe, no sacrifices of blood; and it was his comparatively pure and spiritual worship which, as we see repeatedly in Carthaginian history, formed a chief link in the chain that bound the parent to the various daughter-cities scattered over the coasts and islands of the Mediterranean.

The Carthaginian proper names which have come down to us form one among many proofs of the depth of their religious feelings; for they are all, *Proper names.* or nearly all, compounded with the name of one or other of their chief gods. Hamilcar is he whom Melcarth protects; Hasdrubal is he whose help is in Baal; Hannibal, the Hanniel of the Bible, is the grace of Baal; and so on with Bomilcar, Himilco, Ethbaal, Maherbal, Adherbal, and Mastanabal.

A considerable native literature there must have been at Carthage, for Mago, a Carthaginian Shofete, did not *Literature.* disdain to write a treatise of twenty-eight books upon the agricultural pursuits which formed the mainstay of his order; and when the Roman Senate, in their fatuous disregard for intellect, gave over with careless profusion to their friends, the Berber chiefs, the contents of all the libraries they had found in Carthage, they reserved for this work the especial honour of an authorized translation into Latin, and of a formal recommendation of its practical maxims to the thrifty husbandmen of Rome.

It was the one fatal weakness of the Carthaginian

State for military purposes that the bulk of their vast
armies consisted not of their own citizens,
nor even of attached and obedient subjects, <small>Mercenaries.</small>
but of foreign mercenaries. There were few countries
and few tribes in the western world which were not represented in a Carthaginian army. Money or superior
force brought to Carthage samples of every nation
which her fleets could reach. Native Libyan and Liby-
Phœnicians, Gauls and Spaniards, slingers from the
far-famed Balearic Isles, Greeks and Ligurians, Volscians and Campanians, were all to be found within its
ranks.

But it was the squadrons of light horsemen drawn
from all the nomad tribes lying between the Altars of
the Phileni on the east and the Pillars of
Hercules on the west, which formed its <small>Numidian cavalry.</small>
heart. Mounted on their famous barbs,
with a shield of elephant's hide on their arm and a
lion's skin thrown over their shoulders, the only rai-
ment they ever wore by day and the only couch they
ever cared to sleep on at night; without a saddle and
without a bridle, or with a bridle only of twisted reeds
which they rarely needed to touch; equally remarkable
for their fearlessness, their agility, and their cunning;
equally formidable, whether they charged or made believe to fly; they were, at once, the strength and the
weakness, the delight and the despair of the Carthaginian State. Under the mighty military genius of Hannibal—with the ardour which he breathed into the feeblest
and the discipline which he enforced on the most undis-
ciplined of his army—they faced without shrinking the
terrors of the Alps and the malaria of the marshes, and
they proved invincible against all the power of Rome,
at the Ticinus and the Trebia, at Thrasimene and at

Cannæ; but, as more often happened, led by an incompetent general, treated by him, as not even Napoleon treated his troops, like so many beasts for the slaughter, and sometimes even basely deserted or betrayed into the enemies' hand, they naturally proved a two-edged weapon, piercing the hand that leaned upon it, faithless and revengeful, learning nothing and forgetting nothing, finding once and again in the direst extremity of Carthage their own deadliest opportunity.

But if the life of the great capitalists of Carthage was as brilliant as we have described it, how did it fare with the poorer citizens, with those whom we call the masses, till we sometimes forget that they are made up of individual units? If we know little of the rich, how much less do we know of the poor of Carthage and her dependencies. The city population, with the exception—a large exception doubtless —of those engaged in commerce, well contented, as it would seem, like the Romans under the Empire, if nothing deprived them of their bread and of their amusements, went on eating and marrying and multiplying till their numbers became excessive, and then they were shipped off by the prudence of their rulers to found colonies in other parts of Africa or in Spain. Their natural leaders, or, as, probably, more often happened, the bankrupt members of the aristocracy, would take the command of the colony, and obtain free leave, in return for their services, to enrich themselves by the plunder of the adjoining tribes. To so vast an extent did Carthage carry out the modern principle of relieving herself of a superfluous population, and at the same time of extending her empire, by colonization, that, on one occasion, the admiral, Hanno, whose "Periplus" still remains, was despatched with sixty ships of war of

Condition of the poor.

fifty oars each, and with a total of not less than 30,000 half-caste emigrants on board, for the purpose of founding colonies on the shores of the ocean beyond the Pillars of Hercules.

To defray the expenses of this vast system of exploration and colonization, as well as of their enormous armies, the most ruinous tribute was imposed and exacted with unsparing rigour from the subject native states, and no slight one from the cognate Phœnician cities. *Sources of weakness.* The taxes paid by the natives sometimes amounted to a half of their whole produce, and among the Phœnician dependent cities themselves we know that the lesser Leptis alone paid into the Carthaginian treasury the sum of a talent daily. The tribute levied on the conquered Africans was paid in kind, as is the case with the Rayahs of Turkey to the present day, and its apportionment and collection were doubtless liable to the same abuses and gave rise to the same enormities as those of which Europe has lately heard so much. Hence arose that universal disaffection, or rather that deadly hatred, on the part of her foreign subjects, and even of the Phœnician dependencies, towards Carthage, on which every invader of Africa could safely count as his surest support. Hence the ease with which Agathocles, with his small army of 15,000 men, could overrun the open country, and the monotonous uniformity with which he entered, one after another, two hundred towns, which Carthaginian jealousy had deprived of their walls, hardly needing to strike a blow. Hence, too, the horrors of the revolt of the outraged Libyan mercenaries, supported as it was by the free-will contributions of their golden ornaments by the Libyan women, who hated their oppressors as perhaps women only can, and which is known in history by the name of the "War without Truce," or the "Inexpiable War."

It must, however, be borne in mind that the inherent differences of manners, language and race between the native of Africa and the Phœnician incomer were so great; the African was so unimpressible, and the Phœnician was so little disposed to understand, or to assimilate himself to his surroundings, that, even if the Carthaginian government had been conducted with an equity, and the taxes levied with a moderation which we know was far from being the case, a gulf profound and impassable must probably have always separated the two peoples. This was the fundamental, the ineradicable weakness of the Carthaginian Empire, and in the long run outbalanced all the advantages obtained for her by her navies, her ports, and her well-stocked treasury; by the energies and the valour of her citizens; and by the consummate genius of three, at least, of her generals. It is this, and this alone, which in some measure reconciles us to the melancholy, nay the hateful termination of the struggle, on the history of which we are about to enter. But if, under the conditions of ancient society, and the savagery of the warfare which it tolerated, there was an unavoidable necessity for either Rome or Carthage to perish utterly, we must admit, in spite of the sympathy which the brilliancy of the Carthaginian civilization, the heroism of Hamilcar and Hannibal, and the tragic catastrophe itself, call forth, that it was well for the human race that the blow fell on Carthage rather than on Rome. A universal Carthaginian Empire could have done for the world, as far as we can see, nothing comparable to that which the Roman universal Empire did for it. It would not have melted down national antipathies; it would not have given a common literature or language; it would not have prepared the way for a higher civilization and an infinitely purer religion. Still less would it have built up that majestic fabric of law which forms the basis of the legislation of all the states of modern Europe and America.

CHAPTER II.

ROME.

IT is time now to take a glance at the origin and rise of the younger city on the banks of the Tiber, whose progress towards the dominion of the world Carthage, and Carthage alone of the states of antiquity, was able seriously to delay. *Rome and Carthage compared.* The history of Rome is like, and yet unlike, that of Carthage. It is like it, for we see in each the growth of a civic community which, from very small beginnings, under an aristocratic form of government, and with slight literary or artistic tastes, acquired first, by the force of circumstances, the leadership of the adjoining cities, which were akin to her in blood, and subsequently, by a far-sighted policy, or by a strong arm, became mistress, not only of them, but, by their aid, of all the tribes whom Nature had not cut off from them by the sea, the mountains, or the desert.

But Roman history is intrinsically unlike the Carthaginian, for the greatness of Rome rested not, as did the greatness of Carthage, on her wealth, or her commerce, or her colonies, or her narrow *Contrasted.* oligarchy, but on the constitutional progress which, after a long struggle, obliterated the mischievous privileges of an aristocracy of birth, and raised the commonalty to a complete social and political equality with their former lords. It rested on the grand moral qualities which formed the ground-work of the Roman character in its best times, earnestness and simplicity of life, reverence for the sanctities of the family relations, reverence for the law, reverence for the gods. It rested on the extraordinary concentration of all these qualities, together with the soundest practical ability which the state contained, in the Senate, perhaps when taken at its best, the noblest deliberative assembly which the world has ever seen. And when the two orders in the State had become united, and Rome was fairly launched in her career as a conquering power her greatness rested (how unlike to Carthage!) on the real community of interest and of blood which united her to the greater number of the Italian tribes that she absorbed; on the self-sacrifice which bade her then, and for a long time to come, tax not her subjects but herself; on the wise precautions which she took to secure their permanent allegiance, partly by isolating them from one another, partly by leaving them in some sense to govern themselves, or by admitting them to a share, actual or prospective, in the Roman citizenship.

It belongs not to our purpose here to trace the vicissitudes of the long and eventful struggle between the privileged Patricians and the unenfranchised Plebs. It is incumbent upon us only to note the result of that long constitutional conflict; and that grand result was that the two orders became indissolubly united, socially and politically, into one nation, and were thus prepared, whether for good or for evil, to assert their natural supremacy over the rest of Italy, and then to conquer the world. Nor, again, does it fall within our scope to follow with any degree of minuteness the early progress of the Roman arms. It must suffice to trace only so much of its outline as may enable us to judge of the true position of the conquering city, where a wider field opened before her, and she had to face, no longer the petty warfare of bordering townships, nor even the collective strength of Samnite and Etruscan confederations, but Carthage, Macedon, and the East.

The expulsion of the kings left Rome still a prey to internal discord, a circumstance of which her nearest neighbours, the Etruscans, wholly alien as they were to her in race, were not slow to avail themselves. The Etruscan nation, with its gloomy and mysterious religion, the solemn trifling of its augural science, and the cruelty of its gladiatorial games, was just then at the height of its power by land and sea. Now was its opportunity; the fond but soul-stirring romances of the ballad singers and annalists of early Rome have not been able wholly to disguise the fact that the city itself fell before the arms of Porsena. But the triumph of Etruria was not long lived. A protracted warfare of 150 years succeeded, in which the star of Rome came gradually into the ascendant, and the fall of Veii after a ten years' siege, and still more perhaps, the hurricane of Northern barbarians, which just then burst over the fairest plains of Italy, set Rome forever free from danger on the side of Etruria.

Conquest of Etruscans. B. C. 509.

But Rome was delivered from the Etruscans only (B. C. 390) to find that the Gaul was thundering at her gates. The city was burned to the ground, her temples desecrated, her historical records destroyed, her inhabitants dispersed or slain; but no such ephemeral calamity could shatter the traditions or shake the resolution of the Roman people. Rome rose, like the phœnix, from her ashes, and started afresh on her career of conquest. Her ancient enemies, the

And Latins.

Æquians and Volscians, who, according to the patriotic narrative of Livy, had for so many years in the early history of the Republic been annually exterminated, and had annually revived to be exterminated again, had long since died their last death as independent nations. The Etruscans were now powerless. The last desperate effort of the Latins to restore, when it was too late (B. C. 340–338), the equality of their ancient league, was crushed in two campaigns, and Rome now found herself face to face with the worthiest antagonists she had yet met, the brave and hardy Sabellian race, which was akin to herself in blood, which had lately almost annexed Campania, and which clung with desperate tenacity and with manners that never changed to the rugged mountains and the inaccessible defiles of the Central and Southern Apennines. The struggle is memorable for the deeds of heroism which mark its course on either side, for the stubborn resistance and chivalrous bravery of the weaker, and, on more than one occasion, for the perfidy and the meanness of the stronger combatant. But it is yet more remarkable, in the eye of him who would read the story of the Punic Wars aright, for the light it throws upon the true secret of the Roman strength in war.

Never did the iron resolution and devotion of her citizens, never did the unbending consistency of purpose and the marvellous self-restraint of the Senate, display itself more brilliantly. Without haste, but without a pause, never elated by victory, never depressed by defeat, not caring to overrun what they could not hold by force of arms, or to obtain by treaty what they could not take without it, willing to employ years instead of months, and to conquer by inches where they might have conquered by leagues,

Irresistible advance of Rome.

the Roman Senate, slow but sure, held on the even tenour of their course, determined only that where the Roman eagles had once set down their talons, there they should remain, till the time came to plunge them more deeply into the vitals of the foe. Did Samnium at the close of the great twenty-two years' struggle lie, to all appearance, prostrate at the feet of Rome, the last of her fortresses, Bovianum, in the grasp of the conqueror? That conqueror concluded an equitable peace, on terms of all but equal alliance, not because she liked to spare the conquered—that maxim is to be found only in the patriotic imagination of the author of the "Æneid"— but simply because she did not choose to be brought face to face with Southern Italy before she had made quite sure of Central. To build a new fortress, to found a new military colony, to complete a stage or two more of a great military road—if only it could better secure what lay behind, and give a vantage ground for future operations whenever the time should come—this was the strictly practical object of Rome when she took up arms; this she kept in view when smarting under a defeat; and what is more remarkable, with this she rested content even when flushed with victory. In this way, always aiming only at what was feasible, making sure of every inch of her way, drawing her iron network of colonies and military roads over every district which she professed to claim, Rome found herself at length (B.C. 293) with not a single danger behind her, and with nothing in front save some luxurious Greek cities, and some insignificant tribes of Italian aborigines, to separate her from that which was at once the object of her highest hopes and of her most practical and stern resolves, the union of the whole of Italy beneath her sway.

We have said that there was but one obstacle to the

realization of the aim of Rome; but one other there shortly appeared, which, as it had been beyond the visible, so was it necessarily beyond the mental horizon of so matter-of-fact a body as the Roman Senate. The adventurous king of Epirus, whose erratic course it would have required a genius like his own to have anticipated, shot down like a meteor on the scene. Fired with the ambition of emulating his great relative Alexander, and of founding a vast Greek empire in the west on the ruins of Italy and Carthage, as Alexander had founded his on the ruins of Persia and of Egypt, he eagerly seized the opportunity afforded him by the appeal of the frivolous Tarentines, and offered to lead the Greek cities of Italy in their opposition to Rome.

War with Pyrrhus.

B. C. 280.

The struggle is rich, above most of those in which Rome engaged, in the play of individual character and in the traits of knightly chivalry and generosity, which lend to it a charm which is altogether its own. Even his sober-minded and severely practical enemies could scarcely come into contact with so high-bred and chivalrous a foe as Pyrrhus without catching some sparks of his courtesy and his enthusiasm; but the struggle is also memorable as the first occasion in which Greece and Rome met in the shock of battle. Here for the first time might be seen the Roman legion meeting the phalanx of Macedon; a national militia arrayed against highly trained and veteran mercenaries; individual military genius against collective mediocrity. For a moment fortune seemed to waver, or even to incline in favour of the adventurer; but she could not waver long. The victories of Heraclea and Asculum must have made the name of Pyrrhus a name to be spoken with bated breath even in the Roman

Its character.

Senate; and the lightning rapidity with which he swept Sicily from end to end, cooping the Mamertines in Messana on the extreme east, and the Phœnicians in Lilybæum in the extreme west, must have made his name a name of terror even among the burghers of Carthage. But the proud answer returned by the Roman Senate to the embassy of Pyrrhus after his first victory, that Rome never negotiated so long as an enemy was on Italian soil, must have at once opened the eyes of the Epirot king to the hopeless nature of the enterprise he had undertaken, and marked triumphantly the goal to which centuries of tempered aspiration and of impetuous resolve had raised the Latin city. To the Roman mind an ideal which could not be realized was no ideal at all, and the Romans had now realized their highest ideal to an extent which entitled them to take a wholly new point of departure.

Pyrrhus disappeared from the western world almost as rapidly as he had descended on it, crying with his last breath, half in pity, half in envy, "How fair a battle-field we are leaving to the Romans and Carthaginians!" He spoke too truly. The arena was already cleared of its lesser combatants, and for some few years there was, as it were, the hush of expectation, the audible silence of suspense, while mightier combatants were arming for the fray, and the great duel was preparing of which a hundred years would hardly see the termination.

B. C. 278.
Rome and Carthage face to face.

CHAPTER III.

FIRST PUNIC WAR.

(264–262 B.C.)

HARDLY had Pyrrhus turned his back for the last time on Italy when the first note of war between the Romans and the Carthaginians, who had so recently formed an alliance against him, was sounded. It came, as was to be expected, from that fair island which, by its position, seemed to belong half to Europe, half to Africa, and from that point in it which lay actually within sight of Rhegium, the town which was, as yet, the farthest outpost of the Roman alliance. For more than a century past Greeks and Carthaginians had been contending, with varying success, for the possession of the island. Few towns of any importance within its limits had escaped destruction, fewer still had escaped a siege, and many had been taken and retaken almost as many times as there had been campaigns. On the whole, in spite of the efforts of able leaders like Dionysius the Tyrant, Timoleon, and Agathocles, fortune had favored the Carthaginians; and the power of Syracuse, the head of the Greek states, was now confined to the south-eastern corner of the island.

Sicily a battle-field of Greek and Carthaginian.

But there was one town in the island, and that an all-important one from its geographical position, which had by a strange destiny ceased to be Greek without becoming Carthaginian, and, after outraging Greek and Carthaginian alike, and rousing their active hostility, had now, to make matters better, appealed for aid to a third power which was destined to prove mightier than either.

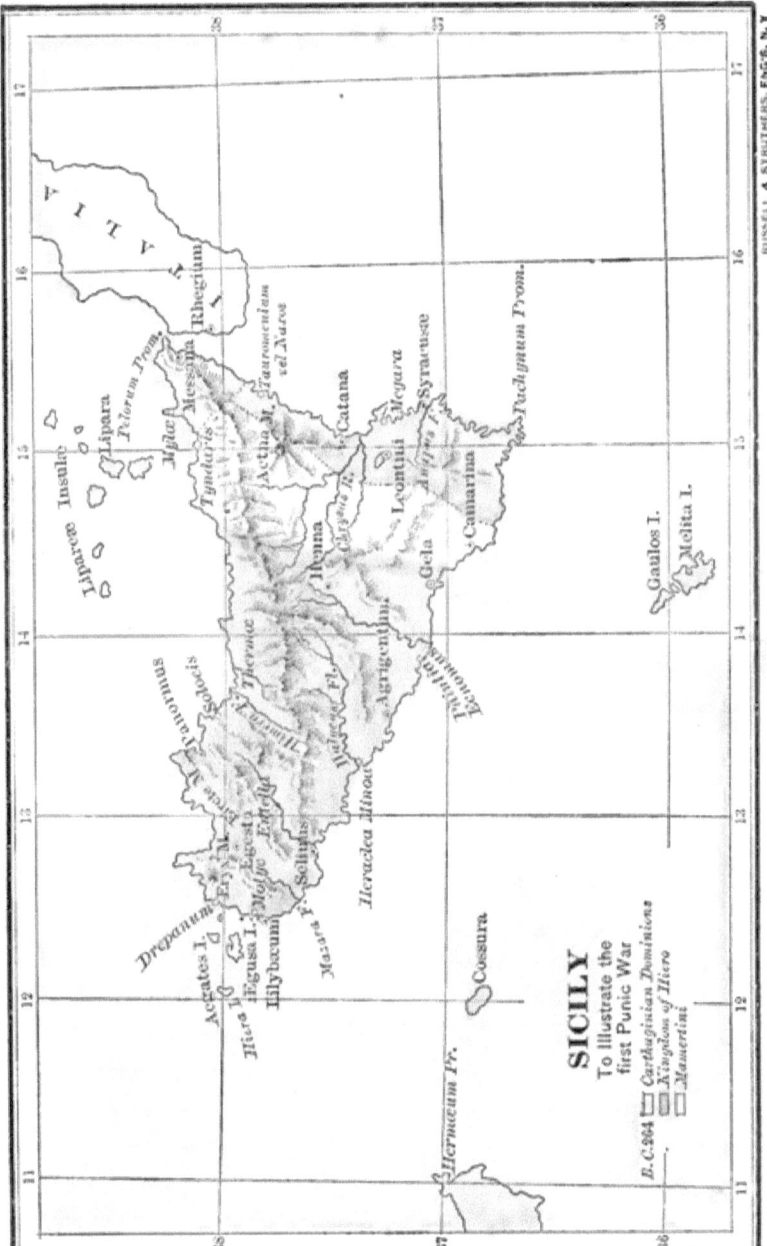

When Agathocles, tyrant of Syracuse, died, his mercenary troops were disbanded, and a body of them, on their way back to Campania, their native country, treacherously seized Messana, which had entertained them hospitably. *Mamertines at Messana B. C. 289.* They expelled or slew the male inhabitants, divided their wives and children, and, calling themselves the children of Mamers, or Mars, proceeded to justify their name by plundering or harrying all the surrounding country. Such outrages could not be overlooked by the Carthaginians. Still less could they pass unnoticed by the young king Hiero, who had lately obtained the vacant throne of Syracuse by the best of titles, the free choice alike of his comrades in arms and of his fellow-citizens; and he proceeded to lay siege to the town. The Mamertine councils were divided. It was clear that without allies they would not long hold out against the powerful foes whose deadly hostility they had provoked. One party among them was for surrendering the place to the Carthaginians to keep out the Syracusans; the other was for invoking the Romans to keep out both alike.

Never was a question fraught with more important issues, moral and political, brought before the Roman Senate; and never did they shirk their responsibility more shamefully. It is not perhaps so easy to see what was the right thing to do as it is to see that what the Roman Senate did was the very worst thing that they could do. *Moral questions involved in appeal of Mamertines.* Were they, on the one hand, to refuse to protect Italians who appealed to them avowedly as the head of the Italian confederation for aid against the Greeks and Carthaginians, and to look calmly on while the city of Messana fell into the hands of the Carthaginians to be used by them as a standing menace to their power and a vantage ground in the great conflict which could not now be far distant? Or were they, on the other hand, to lull their consciences to sleep, to turn round upon Hiero, their ally, who had recently lent them his aid in getting rid of the lawless banditti who had seized Rhegium as the Mamertines had seized Messana, and to take under their special protection a band of cutthroats on one side of the straits, while they had just scourged and beheaded every member of a similar, and perhaps a less guilty band, on the other? It was a question beset with difficulties. National honour and common gratitude pointed clearly in one direction; ambition and immediate interest pointed as clearly in another, and the Roman Senate took the most ignoble course of all open to it, that of shifting the responsibility from their own shoulders to that of the people assembled in their Comitia. The consuls Appius Claudius Caudex and M. Fulvius Flaccus were ambitious men, eager for war at any price. It was easy for them to raise a patriotic cry of Italians against foreigners, and to hold out visions of assignations of public land amongst the rich fields of Sicily to the multitude whose appetite for such booty had been recently whetted by the large distributions of land in Italy. The decision of the people was not doubtful; and the most momentous resolution ever arrived at by the Romans was taken without either the definite sanction or the explicit disapproval of the Senate (B. C. 264). It was possible for the Senate, perhaps, by such paltry conduct to deprive themselves of some of the credit which might ultimately be won by the war. It was not possible to relieve themselves of the shame of its commencement.

Nor was the step now taken less serious from a political than from a moral point of view, for, in truth, upon the passing of the narrow arm of sea which rages between Italy and Sicily hinged the future destinies of both countries; and not *Political questions.* of these alone, but of the ancient civilized world. Hitherto the policy of the Roman Senate had been definite and strictly practical, and had not carried them beyond the horizon of Italy proper. If they had owned ships of war at all, they had been of a small size and built upon an antique model. Now, for the first time, they were about to set foot beyond the seas, to embark upon a policy the course of which it would no longer rest with them to determine; to claim, without ships of their own, from the greatest of naval powers, a portion of the island which had for centuries been looked upon as her peculiar appanage. Some clear-sighted men there must have been among the Roman senators who recoiled from the results of what they had done, or rather from the results of what they had refrained, through moral cowardice, from doing; but their voices were not heard, and active operations began. War, indeed, against Carthage was not formally declared, for the diplomatists of either nation had yet to go through the solemn farce which usually precedes such a declaration by raking up forgotten grievances or inventing new ones to justify the resolution which had already been taken; but orders were given at once to relieve Messana.

The command was committed to Appius Claudius (B.C. 264), more easy work being found for his colleague, Flaccus, nearer home. The want of ships of war, and even of transports—for, by a strange short-sightedness, the Romans had *Romans cross to Sicily.* allowed such ships as they had to fall into decay at the very time when they most needed them—was met by borrowing them from the Greek cities of Italy, Tarentum, Locri, Velia, and Neapolis; but a more serious difficulty occurred when Claudius, the legate of the consuls and forerunner of the Roman army, appeared at Rhegium. Things had taken an unexpected turn at Messana. The party favourable to Carthage had got the upper hand, and the Carthaginian fleet was riding at anchor in the harbour, while a Carthaginian garrison was in possession of the citadel. Here was an awkward predicament for the Romans; but C. Claudius was, like most of his family, a man of energy and audacity. He crossed the straits at the peril of his life, invited the admiral, Hanno, to a conference, and then, in defiance of the law of nations and of honour, took him prisoner, and allowed him to purchase his liberty and life only by the surrender of the citadel. The Mamertines, who were equally ready to follow anyone who seemed able to promise them the lives which by their crimes they had so justly forfeited, were now besieged in Messana from the north side of the city by a second Hanno, whom the Carthaginians had sent out to replace the first, while Hiero attacked it from the south.

Such was the condition of affairs when Appius Claudius himself appeared with his army upon the scene. *First campaign.* How he managed to cross the straits with 20,000 men in the face of an enemy whose proud boast it was that without their leave no Roman could even bathe his hands in the sea, we do not know. But cross them he did, and by a double victory on two successive days he succeeded in raising the siege, and, after ravaging the country in every direction, pitched his camp under the walls of Syracuse and prepared to besiege Hiero in his own capital. Here he suffered far more from the malaria of the marshes of the

Anapus than from any active hostility of Hiero; and when the Romans thought fit to retreat towards Messana from so unhealthy a region, and were followed closely by the Syracusans, Hiero found that the troops of the rival armies were more disposed to meet in friendly gatherings at the outposts than in hostile array in the battle-field.

So ended the first campaign. With one small army the Romans had already attained the ostensible objects of the war. The Mamertines had been relieved, the protectorate of Rome over them asserted, much booty had been gained, the Carthaginians had been driven back towards the northwest, and the Syracusans towards the south-east, of the island. But Rome was not content to stop here. The horizon of the Senate had once more expanded with their achievements; and, no longer content with securing the corner of Sicily nearest to themselves, they had conceived the design of stripping Carthage and Syracuse alike of so much of their Sicilian possessions as would render them for ever innocuous neighbours. The second campaign was not less successful than the first. There was now no rumour of disturbance in the neighbourhood of Rome; and the two consuls, M. Octacilius and M. Valerius, were able to cross together into Sicily with their united armies amounting to 35,000 men. They met no serious resistance; fifty towns belonging to Hiero or the Carthaginians submitted to them; and Hiero himself, consulting, partly, no doubt, the wishes of his subjects, partly his own feelings of hatred towards the hereditary oppressors of his country, turned from the setting to the rising sun and made overtures of peace to Rome. The Romans were keenly alive to the advantages which an alliance with Syracuse would bring them

Second campaign.

while they were waging war in the interior of the island, and Hiero agreed to pay a war contribution of 200 talents and to surrender several of his towns. He became henceforward to the end of his long life and reign, to all appearance, the grateful, and certainly the faithful and the trusted ally of Rome. Under his wise and beneficent rule, Syracuse, though war was surging round her by land and sea, enjoyed a degree of prosperity and of internal quiet to which, it may perhaps be said, she had been a stranger for two centuries before, and which she has never enjoyed since.

But where were the Carthaginians all this time? Two campaigns had been fought and won, and they had nowhere yet shown themselves in force. They had allowed themselves, with hardly a struggle, to be swept from the larger half of the island. Would they allow themselves to be swept without resistance from the remainder? The truth is that they were neither inactive nor cowardly. They were simply, owing to the defects of their military system, unprepared; and they were all this time straining every nerve to raise a force in Africa, in Liguria, in Spain, and in Gaul, which they hoped might eventually be able to strike a vigorous blow and to retrieve their fortunes.

<small>Backwardness of Carthaginians.</small>

About half way between the promontories of Lilybæum and Pachynus, and drawn back a mile or so from the southern coast, was the important city of Agrigentum. It had once boasted a population of 200,000 souls—a fact to which the size and extent of its majestic ruins still bear witness—and though its ruthless destruction by the Carthaginians (B. C. 405), and the misgovernment of domestic tyrants had shorn it of much of its grandeur and prosperity, it had been

<small>Agrigentum.</small>

refounded by Timoleon, and was still at the time of the First Punic War the second Greek city in Sicily, and was able to give shelter to a garrison of 50,000 men. Here Hannibal, son of Gisco, concentrated the forces which had been gathered from such distant countries; here he determined to make a stand in the field, and behind its bulwarks, after collecting vast stores of provisions and of materials for war, he was prepared, if need be, to stand a siege. Hither also came all the forces which the Roman Senate thought necessary to deal with a foe who during two campaigns had seemed anxious only to keep himself out of sight—a small army, so it is said, of two legions only!

The consuls of the year, L. Postumius and Q. Mamilius (B. C. 262), pitched their camp eight stadia from the town, and imprudently sent out their troops in large numbers to forage in the surrounding country. Hannibal seized the opportunity, and only the heroism of some Roman pickets who, to allow time for the foragers to get back into the camp, died to a man, fighting bravely at their posts, saved the Romans from disaster. Both sides now displayed greater caution. The Carthaginians contented themselves with harassing the Romans with missiles from a distance, while the Romans broke up their army into two separate camps, connected by a double line of entrenchments— the one to protect them against the sallies of the besieged, the other to guard against possible dangers from the rear. The town of Erbessus, a few miles to the north, supplied them with abundant provisions, and seemed to remove famine, at all events, from the lists of contingencies to which they might be exposed. In this state of things five months passed away, and to all appearance the siege was no nearer a successful termination

Its siege.

than at the beginning; but provisions had begun to fail in the closely-packed quarters of the defenders, and in deference to the urgent solicitations of Hannibal, Hanno was sent to Sicily with a new army, and with orders, if possible, to compel the Romans to raise the siege. Making Heraclea his headquarters, Hanno managed to surprise Erbessus, and so cut off the supplies of the enemy. The Romans now found themselves in the position of besieged rather than besiegers, and pestilence as well as famine was at work in their lines.

Decisive operations could not now be long delayed. In a preliminary engagement the Roman horse experienced, for the first time, the superiority of the famous Numidian light cavalry; but in the battle which ensued, the motley Carthaginian infantry found that they were, as yet, no match for the soldiers of the legion. Fifty elephants—wild beasts Polybius, with an air of horror, still calls them—fought on the side of the Carthaginians, a number many times as great as that which a few years before, in the time of Pyrrhus, had carried dismay and confusion into the Roman ranks; but on this occasion, as often afterwards, elephants were found to be a two-edged weapon, which might be fatal to the hand that wielded it. Thirty of the fifty were killed, and eleven remained alive in the hands of the Romans, as vast moving trophies of the victory that had been won. Hanno saved a remnant of his army by his hasty flight to Heraclea, and Hannibal, whom the Romans looked upon as already within their grasp, sheltered by the darkness of a winter's night, and helped by the energy of despair, made a last effort to break through the lines of his victorious foe. The Romans, overcome with fatigue, or giving the reins to their joy, had relaxed their vigilance. With bags stuffed with

Its capture.

straw, Hannibal filled up the deep trenches, scaled the ramparts, and managed with the effective part of his army to pass through the Roman lines unobserved. In the morning the enemy, discovering what had happened, went through the form of pursuing the retreating Hannibal; but they were more eager to fall on the unhappy town which he had abandoned to their mercy. The inhabitants surrendered at discretion; but they had to undergo all the horrors of a place taken by storm. The town was given up to plunder, and 25,000 freemen were sold into slavery. Nothing throughout the whole of Sicily now remained in the hands of the Carthaginians save a few fortresses on its western coasts; and this was the precise moment at which, according to the explicit statement of Polybius, it first dawned upon the Romans that they had embarked upon a war the true and only object of which must be to eject the Carthaginians altogether from the island.

CHAPTER IV.

FIRST ROMAN FLEET. BATTLES OF MYLÆ AND ECNOMUS.

(262–256 B. C.)

IF the resolution now come to by Rome was to be carried out, it was clear that a complete change in the conduct of the war would be necessary. The Carthaginians had at length begun to put forth their real strength, and to assert the supremacy over the seas, which had, in fact, never ceased to belong to them. With a fleet of sixty ships they coasted round Sicily, and by sheer terror, without striking a blow, brought back to their allegiance many towns which had

Carthaginian naval supremacy.

gone over to Rome. The Romans might retain their grip on the interior of the island, but the coasts, it was clear, would belong to Carthage so long as she remained mistress of the seas. Nor was this all. By making frequent descents at distant points on the Italian coast, the Carthaginian fleet kept the inhabitants of the seaboard in a state of constant alarm, which it was quite beyond the power of any land forces raised by the Italians themselves to allay; for by the nature of the case the Carthaginians, choosing like the Northmen centuries afterwards, their own place and time, were able to destroy a town, or to harry a district, before alarm could be given to the nearest military station. It was apparent that the war might go on for ever, each of the combatants being able to annoy and injure, but not to paralyze or destroy the other, unless something should occur to change the conditions under which it was being carried on. The Carthaginians wanted only, what they had not yet succeeded in finding, a first-rate general, to enable them to make a descent in force in Italy, and so make Rome tremble for her own safety. The Romans wanted only an efficient fleet to enable them to meet Carthage on her own element, and then to transfer the contest to Africa. The all-important question was which would be found first. A life-and-death struggle generally finds out, and brings to the front, in spite of all artificial obstacles, a true military genius, even amongst a people whose collective genius is not military; but it has very rarely been known to change the whole character of a people at once, to transform land-lubbers into seamen, and what is more extraordinary still, to enable them to cope on equal terms with the greatest naval power of the time. The chances therefore were, so far, not in favour of Rome.

But we must beware of indulging in the exaggerations

in which it was natural enough for Polybius and other historians of the time to indulge, in their admiration of the energy of Rome. What the Romans did was wonderful enough without the addition of a single fictitious detail to make it more so. It may be true, as Polybius says, that at the outbreak of the war Rome had no decked ships, no ships of war, no, not even a lembus—a small ship's boat with a sharp prow—which they could call their own. But that the Romans were not so wholly ignorant of naval affairs as the ludicrous picture of a hundred batches of would-be sailors, training themselves to row on the sand, from scaffolds, would at first suggest, is clear from the fact that Rome had in the early days of the Republic fitted out ships with three banks of oars to keep in order piratical neighbours like the Antiates or the Etruscans; that there were magistrates, called *Duumviri navales*, who, from time to time, were appointed for the express purpose of repairing the fleet; and that the Carthaginians themselves had thought it worth their while repeatedly to form a commercial treaty with the Romans, restricting carefully their mutual rights and duties. Still the Romans had never been a really maritime or commercial people; they did not love the sea, much less had they been a naval power; and how were they to become so all at once?

The question was beset with difficulties. Triremes no doubt they might borrow from the Greek cities of Italy, as they had done once before; but these would no more face the bulky monsters, called quinqueremes, which now formed the Carthaginian ships of the line, than an English revenue cutter could board a frigate. The Romans must have felt all the needs, upon a vaster scale, which dawned upon a people as land-loving and as exclusive as themselves, when the conquest of Ezion Geber opened to the untravelled Israelites the navigation of the Red Sea, and the unknown possibilities of the East beyond it. But to the Hebrew subjects of King Solomon a way out of the difficulty was open which was not available to the Romans now. The gold of Solomon was able to procure Phœnician shipwrights who could construct, and Phœnician mariners who could navigate and steer, his vessels among the dangerous waters of the Red Sea and the Indian Ocean. The descendants of these selfsame Phœnicians, the heirs of their traditions and of a double portion of their maritime genius, were the deadly enemies of Rome; and the Roman landsmen must face the dangers of the sea, not with their aid, but against their most strenuous opposition. Again, the quinquereme was not merely twice as large as a trireme, but was of a different build and construction. It was necessary, therefore, to obtain either shipwrights or a model from some nation to which such moving castles had been long familiar. Here chance was on the side of the Romans. A Carthaginian quinquereme had run ashore on the coast of Bruttium two or three years before, and had fallen into the hands of the Romans. This served as the wished-for model; and it is asserted by more than one writer, that within sixty days a growing wood was felled and transformed into a fleet of a hundred ships of the line and twenty triremes. The next difficulty was to find men for the fleet, and when they had been found, to train them for their duties. How the large number of 30,000 rowers necessary to propel the ships, and of 12,000 marines necessary to fight on board of them, were raised, in so short a time, from a people that was not a seafaring people, we have no precise information ; but as soon as they had been got together, and while the building of the ships was still in progress, they went, if we may believe the well-known story, through a course of training for the most important of their functions, that of rowing in time at the voice of the *Keleustes*, by taking their seats on tiers of stages, and by making believe to go through the various evolutions which would be expected of them.

Probably never did a fleet set sail under greater difficulties of every kind than did this. The starting timbers of the unseasoned wood of which the ships were built, and the distressing maladies which would assuredly befall a herd of landsmen who had gone through only the mechanical preparation for the sea which we have described, might well have made men doubt whether either ships or crews would ever live to experience the shock of the Carthaginian battle. But we hear nothing of this. Perhaps after all, the ships were manned in part not by Romans, but by Greek and Etruscan mariners ; and we know only that hardly were the ships launched when they fearlessly set sail (B. C. 261). *[sidenote: The fleet sails.]*

But the skill in naval warfare which the Carthaginians had acquired in centuries could not be learnt by Rome in a day. There are many points connected with the equipment and management of an ancient trireme which have not been cleared up ; but it is certain that even for the simple manœuvres practised by the ancients—the *embole*, or charge on the side, and the *prosbole*, or charge beak to beak, the *periplus*, and the *diecplus*—there was an incalculable difference between trained and untrained rowers. It must also be borne in mind that the ancient rowers had often to contend in battle against wind and tide *[sidenote: Naval tactics of ancients.]*

as well as against the foe—for the sails and masts were always cleared away as a preparation for action—and if the sea was running high, the utmost nicety in steering and the most perfect time and skill in rowing would be essential to the success of even the simplest manœuvre. There was nothing but the voice of the *Keleustes* to keep the three tiers of rowers, ranged one above the other, with their oars of different weights and different lengths, in time, and that voice would necessarily be drowned by the least excitement or confusion amongst the crews. If such careful training was found to be essential for the management of the trireme, what must it not have been for the quinquereme, a ship nearly twice the size, with five banks of oars instead of three?

The immediate problem, therefore, for the Romans to solve was not how best to train their crews to charge with the beak—for no training would have fitted them for that task before the engagement which was imminent—but how best to parry the charge and then to convert the naval into a land battle, leaving as little opportunity as possible for subsequent manœuvring, and as much as possible for hand-to-hand conflict. The device which the Romans adopted to secure these ends was clumsy, but it was effectual. On the fore part of each vessel was erected an additional mast, and lashed to it by a powerful hinge was a species of drawbridge. On the end of this last and standing out from it at right angles was a sharp spike of the strongest iron, which, from its resemblance, when in this position, to the bill of the raven, gave the name of Corvus to the whole construction. When an enemy's vessel was seen approaching for the purpose either of charging directly beak to beak, or of striking obliquely the tiers of oars and so of incapacitating them for further use, the

The Corvus.

drawbridge by an ingenious contrivance could be swung round the mast towards the point where the danger threatened; and the moment the enemy came within reach, it could be let fall from its commanding height, and with its heavy weight upon the deck of the attacking ship. The iron beak would pierce through the planking of the deck and hold it fast in a death-grapple, and in a very few moments from the time the Corvus fell, the whole body of the Roman mariners would find themselves on board the enemy's deck. The sea fight would be practically over, and the land fight would begin, and the issue of this conflict between the " mere rabble of an African crew" and picked Roman legionaries, could not be for a moment doubtful.

Duillius, consul and admiral of the fleet, finding that the enemy were engaged in ravaging Mylæ, a peninsula and town on the north-west of the island, not far from Messana, sailed fearlessly towards them. The Carthaginians, when with 130 well-built and well-manned ships they saw the 100 ungainly Roman hulks, the timbers of which ought still to have been seasoning in the timber yard, and their landsmen sailors, drawn from they knew not where, must have felt something of the thrill of long-deferred delight which forced from Napoleon the exclamation, "At last I have them, those English, in my grasp," as, assuredly, they must have felt something of the keenness of his disappointment at the still more unlooked-for result. Not caring in their confidence and joy even to form in line of battle, they bore down at once upon the Romans as on an easy prey. When they drew near, they were for the moment taken aback by the strange appearance of vessels coming into battle with their masts left standing—masts, too, with such uncouth and

Battle of Mylæ.

extraordinary appendages attached to them. But their hesitation was only for a moment. Evidently these raw enemies of theirs did not even know how to clear their decks for action. With redoubled confidence thirty of the Carthaginian vessels charged beak to beak on as many of the Roman vessels, and each immediately found itself a prisoner, held fast by the grappling iron which had so excited their surprise and their contempt. Others of the Carthaginian ships, thinking to escape the fall of the drawbridge which had caught their comrades, charged sideways against other parts of the Roman ships; but round swung the fatal Raven, as though it were a thing of life, and descended upon them, pinning the vessels tight alongside of each other, and enabling the Roman legionaries to dispense with the bridge and to leap at once from every part of their vessel into that of the enemy. After fifty of their ships of war had been locked in this deadly embrace, the remainder, declining to fight at all with foes who were ill-bred enough to fight and conquer against all the rules of naval warfare, took to flight.

The Romans were overjoyed, as well they might be, at their success. It was their first naval battle, and their first great naval victory over the greatest naval power which the world had seen. Its importance was not to be measured by its immediate results, but rather by the omen it gave for the future. Honours, till then unexampled, were freely bestowed upon the plebeian Duillius. When he went out to supper it was to the sound of music; when he returned home it was with an escort of torch-bearers. A pillar was erected to his honour in the Forum, called the Columna Rostrata, for it was adorned with the brazen beaks of the vessels which his wise ignorance and his clumsy skill had enabled him to capture.

The great battle of Mylæ was fought in the year B. C. 260, and the Roman army improved the victory of their fleet by at once marching to Egesta, a town which claimed relationship to Rome by reason of their supposed common descent from Troy, and which was situated in a part of Sicily considerably beyond any in which we have as yet seen the Romans. The Roman fleet, too, now no longer confined its aims to the narrow Sicilian waters, but, striking boldly across the open sea, threatened the empire of Carthage in the rich Island of Sardinia also. In the savage mountains of the interior the natives still managed to maintain something of their independence and of their barbarism; but the coasts had been for centuries in the possession of the Carthaginians. Thither the unfortunate Hannibal, son of Gisco, had withdrawn shortly after his defeat at Mylæ, thinking doubtless that there, at least, he would be safe from Roman molestation; but even there the Romans, in the exultation of their first victory, pursued him. Penned within the harbour in which he had taken refuge, he lost several of his ships in an engagement, and on his escape to land was apprehended by his own men and crucified. They took the law into their own hands; but, doubtless, they only anticipated the sentence which would have been passed by the inexorable Hundred on an unlucky admiral who should have returned to Carthage after surviving so many and such unprecedented reverses. The Romans followed up their success by an attack on Olbia, the capital of the island. The expedition failed. But an attempt upon Aleria, formerly a Phocean colony, and now the capital of Corsica, was more successful. Corsica had probably never belonged outright to Carthage; but it had, at least, acknowledged her maritime supremacy, and the second treaty between Rome and Carthage seems to have recognized it as a kind of neutral territory between the two. The epitaph of L. Cornelius Scipio, which is still preserved, tells us how he took Corsica and Aleria, and how on his return to Rome he dedicated a well-deserved temple to the tempest which had almost overwhelmed him in the Corsican waters.

But the absence of the Roman fleet in Corsica and Sardinia proved a serious, if only a temporary, drawback to the progress of the Roman arms in Sicily. Rome could not yet afford so to dissipate her energy, and Hamilcar, commander-in-chief at Panormus, now gave evidence of a vigour and capacity such as had hitherto not been witnessed among either of the contending parties. Hearing that the Romans and their allies, on their return from Egesta, were at discord amongst themselves, he surprised and cut to pieces 4,000 of the enemy in their camp near Himera. He destroyed the town of Eryx and transferred its inhabitants in a body to the neighbouring fortress of Drepanum; and it was doubtless the bold front he showed which, in the following year, compelled the Romans to retire from before Panormus, after merely convincing themselves of the strength of its fortifications. Meanwhile both sides were straining every nerve to raise such a navy as should be able by sheer strength to bear down all opposition to it—the Romans with the avowed intention of fighting their way into Africa, and so compelling Carthage to submit to the terms of peace which they might be willing to offer her; the Carthaginians with the hope of recovering the empire of the seas which had now been half torn from her, and of excluding the Romans, if not from the whole of her dependencies, at all events from her home domain in Africa.

<small>Energy of both sides.</small>

The material results in the way of shipping obtained by either side were not disproportionate to the efforts that had been made. Probably never, either before or after, did such vast naval armaments put to sea. The most important naval combats of ancient and of modern times—the battle of Artemisium, Salamis, and Naulochus, of Lepanto, Trafalgar, and Navarino—sink into insignificance, as far as mere numbers go, when compared with that of Ecnomus. Other battles, doubtless, enlist the sympathies more fully on one side or the other, or interest more keenly those who care for war merely as war. The stake fought for at Salamis was an infinitely higher stake, and was fraught with vastly more momentous issues for the whole human race; for it was the cause of Greek freedom and civilization against Asiatic slavery and barbarism. At Trafalgar the darling scheme of the heartless oppressor of all Europe was for ever frustrated by the crowning naval victory of a war which, the worst calumniators of England must admit, was not a selfish war. In all these points—in the motives of the combatants, in its purely military or scientific interest, and in its results—the battle of Ecnomus is not specially remarkable. It is imposible to give our undivided sympathies to either side. It was a battle, in the main, of brute force and not of consummate skill; it was not decisive even of the results of the war of which it formed so bulky a part. Still less can it attract those who look upon all wars except those waged in self-defence or for purely moral ends—all wars, that is, except those waged ultimately in the interests of peace—with horror and condemnation. Yet men are men, and even the Carthaginian mercenaries, though their employers did not think so, were worth something more than the pay they earned by their services; and size is size, and

will always, apart from everything else, and whether it
ought to or not, attract to itself the attention of mankind.
And from the point of view of mere size—the number,
that is, of its ships and the crews who fought in them—
the battle of Ecnomus is certainly entitled to a conspicuous place in history. The vicissitudes of the battle are
somewhat complicated; but it is necessary for one who
would understand aright the First Punic War to dwell
awhile upon a conflict which is so eminently characteristic of it.

The Romans set sail from Messana (B.C. 256) with
330 ships, while the Carthaginians mustered the still
more portentous number of 350 ships in their
famous port of Lilybæum; so that, if we are to
accept the deliberate calculation of Polybius,
who assigns 300 rowers and 120 mariners to each ship of
war, nearly 300,000 men must have met in the battle
which ensued. The Carthaginians, who knew too well
what an invasion of Africa meant, and who felt that the
ravages of the Roman army would not be the worst of
evils that it would involve, moved slowly forward to
Heraclea Minoa, determined to crush the invaders before
they could leave the Sicilian coast.

Battle of Ecnomus.

The Romans, having taken on board their legions at
Phintias, divided their immense fleet into four squadrons.
The two first squadrons formed two sides of
an equilateral triangle, while the third, having behind them the transports laden with
cavalry, formed its base. To the rear of these again,
and forming at once a rear guard and a reserve, came
the fourth squadron, which Polybius calls, from the important function allotted to it, the Triarii. At the apex
of the triangle, their prows standing out to sea, and pointing the rest of the fleet the way to Africa, sailed abreast

Order of battle.

Plan of Ecnomus.

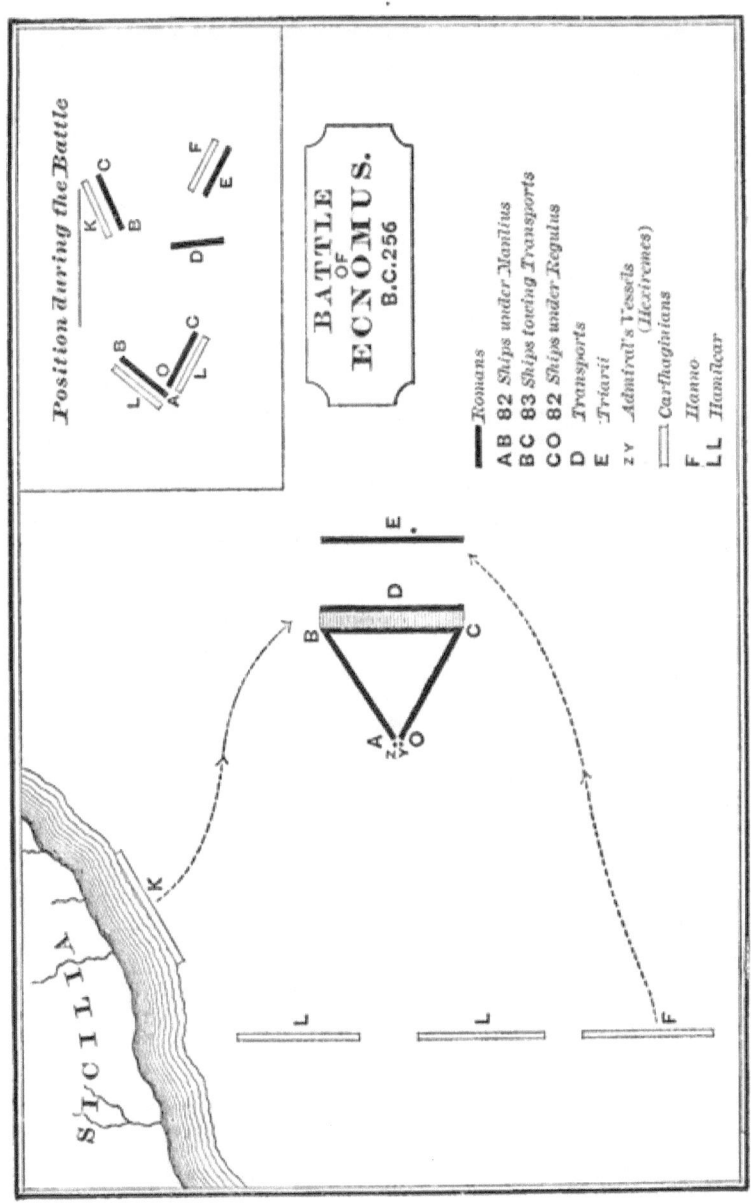

the two monster hexiremes—ships as large probably as our ships of the line—of the consuls and admirals in one, M. Atilius Regulus and L. Manlius. The whole Roman fleet together thus formed the figure called in nautical manœuvring an *embolon*, or wedge, a figure said by Polybius to be suited to energetic action and very difficult to break through. On the other hand, it postulated a skill in seamanship, and a confidence in their own powers both of attack and of defence, very different from that which marked the Roman fleet at their victory at Mylæ, only three years before. The Carthaginians, reminded by their admirals—Hanno, who had in vain attempted to raise the siege of Agrigentum, and Hamilcar, who had lately fought, not without credit to himself, at Tyndaris—of the momentous issues that were at stake, and asked to choose whether they would henceforward fight for the possession of Sicily or in defence of their own hearths and homes, moved westward along the shore in good spirits and order. They hove in sight of the enemy, as it would seem, to the west of the promontory of Ecnomus, and, observing the four-fold division of the Roman armaments, they divided their own fleet into a similar number of squadrons.

The Carthaginian admirals, in order to detach the first two squadrons of the Roman fleet from the third, which was retarded by the transports, arranged that the part of their line which should be first attacked by the thin end of the Roman wedge should give way before it and feign a flight. The stratagem was partially successful, for the flying Carthaginian ships, wheeling round suddenly, closed in upon the sides of the Roman triangle, which had pursued them too far; and by their superior rapidity and skill seriously threatened its safety. But the knowledge that they were

Victory of Romans.

fighting under the immediate eye of the consuls, and the confidence inspired in them by the possession of the Raven, enabled the Romans to hold their own, till Hamilcar, in sheer exhaustion, was compelled to save himself by flight. Meanwhile a fierce double combat had been raging elsewhere. Hanno, who was on the Carthaginian right, had forborne to take any part in the first onset, but, keeping out to sea, as soon as the three first Roman squadrons had got well past him, had fallen upon the rear guard. "*Ventum erat ad Triarios*," and, for a time, it seemed as if even the Triarii would give way. The Carthaginian left, which had hitherto hugged the shore in a long line at right angles to the rest of the fleet, as soon as they had got well behind the Roman position, attacked the third squadron, which was impeded by the transports. These, however, slipped the ropes, and did battle with their assailants. There were thus three distinct sea-fights, simultaneous and well maintained. Hamilcar, as has been said, was the first to give way, and his fight practically decided the battle. Hanno followed his example, and Manlius just then coming up, both consuls bore down together on the left wing of the enemy, which, had they only been less afraid of the boarding-bridges, must ere this have been victorious. A few only of the Carthaginian ships escaped. The Roman victory was complete, and there was now nothing left to bar the conquerors from Africa.

CHAPTER V.

INVASION OF AFRICA. REGULUS AND XANTHIPPUS.

(256–250 B.C.)

THE resolution of the Roman Senate had been long since taken. But it is hardly to be wondered at that when the hour had come for carrying it out, the hearts of some among the Roman soldiers should have been filled with misgivings, and that these should have found expression in the mutinous language of a tribune. Xenophon has told us how anxiously Cyrus the Younger concealed from the Ten Thousand Greeks the real nature of the perilous adventure he had undertaken; and how, before he revealed to them the fatal secret, he took care so far to commit them to the enterprise that a retreat would be then not less dangerous than an advance. The Romans were now entering on a phase of the great contest which to them must have seemed hardly less perilous than the Anabasis to the Greeks. They had to cross a sea which to them was as unknown and, under existing circumstances, as fraught with the possibilities of mischief as the trackless deserts of Mesopotamia. They were to enter a new continent, peopled not by the wild ass and the antelope and the scudding ostrich which had amused the Ten Thousand Greeks, but, as popular imagination would have it, and as a grave historian had related, " by lions and by dog-headed monsters, and by creatures with no heads and with eyes in their breasts." However, threats of a more summary kind used by Regulus overpowered these forebodings of distant disaster and crushed the rising mutiny, and the Roman fleet, after it had been

Invasion of Africa.

revictualled and repaired, stood right across the Mediterranean to the nearest point of Africa, a distance of only ninety miles.

The Hermean Promontory is the north-eastern horn of the Bay of Carthage. Here the Romans waited awhile to muster their forces. It was the precise point beyond which—as treaty after treaty, made with the jealous commercial state, had stipulated—no Roman ship should dare to pass, whether to trade, to plunder, or to colonize; and it must have been with feelings, not of satisfaction or of curiosity alone, that, after a short pause, the Roman fleet began to penetrate deeper into the mysteries of that great Carthaginian preserve by coasting along till they reached a town which, from the shield-shaped eminence on which it stood, they called Clypea, as the Greeks had already named it Aspis. They set foot without opposition on African soil, and when the town refused to surrender they besieged and took it. Meanwhile the Carthaginians had been forewarned of the coming danger. Hanno, after his defeat at Ecnomus, had made straight across for Carthage, and, though he must have risked his life in so doing, had bidden the citizens prepare for the worst. But to be forewarned was with the Carthaginians, at this period of their history, not necessarily to be forearmed; their best armies were absent in Sicily; their navy was demoralized and half destroyed, and the native Libyans were in a state of chronic disaffection. Had the Romans marched at once upon the capital—without an adequate army or a competent general as it then was—it is just possible that it might have fallen. But this was not to be. The rich territory which lay between Clypea and Carthage was too tempting and too easy a prey for the needy Roman soldiery. It had now

Prosperity and short-sightedness of Carthage.

quite recovered from the devastations of Agathocles, and the Romans, strangers as yet, happily for themselves, to luxury, contemplated with amazement and delight the pleasant gardens and the opulent palaces of the merchant princes of Carthage, which had sated the greed of the mercenaries of Agathocles fifty years before. Nor did their hands spare what their eyes admired. The palaces were ransacked of their valuables, and then ruthlessly set on fire; the cattle were driven in vast herds towards the Roman camp; and 20,000 of the inhabitants of the surrounding country found themselves collected in the Roman ships to be sold into slavery. Nor had the Carthaginians, in the interval which had elapsed since the invasion of Agathocles, grown less fatally distrustful of their own subjects. They still forbade the subject cities to surround themselves with walls, not because, like the Spartans, they thought a living rampart of men was a better protection than any masonry, but because they had good reason to suspect that such defence might be turned against themselves. Accordingly, Regulus passed with facility from village to village, or from town to town, till, as the Romans boasted, he had nearly doubled the number of 200 townships which Agathocles had conquered before him.

But just now came from Rome the astounding order, which may well have aroused the misgivings even of the triumphant Roman army, that one of the two consuls was to return home at once with his troops and his ships, leaving the other in Africa with what Polybius calls—one would think with a touch of irony—a "sufficient force" to bring the war to a conclusion. It was not so much that the Roman Senate actually underestimated the difficulty of conquering Carthage, as that it did not occur to a body

Recall of Manlius.

of so conservative a frame of mind, that, now that the
scale of their warfare had been so enlarged, it might be
advisable to make a corresponding alteration in all the
conditions under which they carried it on. The principle that every soldier is, above all and before all things,
a citizen, and that he ought not to forego any of his civil
rights or duties for a longer time than is absolutely necessary, is in itself a noble principle, and one which
modern states, with their overgrown and appalling
standing armies, would do well to remember. But the
rule that an army should always return to Rome, either
to go into winter quarters or to be disbanded, was a
practical application of the principle which, though it
had its advantages, must have been inconvenient even
in the early struggles of the Roman republic; while the
maxim of state policy that the commander-in-chief,
whatever his talents and whatever the complication of
his military plans, should, as soon as a particular day of
the year came round, be superseded by a civil magistrate, whatever his military incapacity, was a maxim
which, though it may have acted well enough in a border
warfare against a discontented Latin or Etruscan town,
had broken down completely in the Samnite wars, and
would be absolutely fatal in the far more gigantic struggle against Carthage.

But the Roman Senate, whatever its practical ability
and courage in carrying out the current business of the
state, was not more foresighted than other
deliberative assemblies, and needed the bit- *Victory of Regulus.*
ter teaching of experience to bring home to
them what seems to us so obvious a truth. Its orders
were obeyed without a murmur, and Manlius set off for
Rome, with his prisoners, his army, and his fleet, leaving Regulus behind him, the heir to that strange inher-

itance of a reputation for military rashness and disaster on the one hand, and for disinterested patriotism on the other, which, immortalized as it has been by Horace, has gone the round of the world, and will doubtless survive the most convincing demonstration of its groundlessness by pitiless critics. The army with which he was expected, as it would seem, to complete the conquest of Africa amounted only to 15,000 infantry and 500 cavalry. He immediately threatened Adis, a town of some importance; and to raise its siege the Carthaginians occupied a hilly district where they could make but little use of the arm in which they were really strong, their elephants and cavalry. The Romans were not slow to perceive this mistake, and, in spite of the strenuous resistance of some of the mercenaries, assaulted and carried the position, while the Carthaginian cavalry and elephants extricated themselves, as best they could, from the broken ground, and as soon as they reached the plain saved themselves by flight. The Romans now fell to devastating the country with redoubled energy and with even less of caution than before. Tunis, an important town in sight of the capital, fell into their hands, and Regulus encamped on the banks of the Bagradas in the heart of what was then the most fertile country in the world.

The prospects of the Carthaginians looked desperate indeed. Their only available army had been defeated, and what the Romans had spared in their devastations, the Numidians, a people always on the move and always eager for plunder, carried off. If the Romans had chastised the country districts with whips, the Numidians, maddened with oppression as well as thirsting for booty, now chastised them with scorpions. All the inhabitants who

Desperate plight of Carthaginians.

could flee took refuge in the capital, and the vast increase of population was already threatening the city with the famine and the pestilence which are usually the last outcome and not the forerunners of a siege.

Regulus seeing their miserable plight, and anxious lest his successor, who, according to Roman custom, might be soon expected, should reap the glory of the war which he had so far conducted prosperously, offered to negotiate for peace. *Terms of peace rejected.* The proposal was joyfully accepted; but Regulus, intoxicated with success, offered the Carthaginians terms which could scarcely have been harder if the Romans had been within their walls. The conquered people were to acknowledge the supremacy of Rome, to form an offensive and defensive alliance with her, to give up all their ships of war but one, to cede, not Sicily only—for that the Carthaginians, acknowledging the fortune of war, would have been glad to do—but Corsica and Sardinia and the Lipari Islands also, to surrender the Roman deserters, to ransom their own prisoners, to pay all that it had cost the Romans to bring them to their knees, and a heavy tribute besides! Terms intolerable in themselves were made still more intolerable by the insolent bearing of the Plebeian consul towards those whom he looked upon as prostrate before him. He had already written to Rome that he had "sealed up the gates of Carthage with terror," and now he told the ambassadors roughly that "men who were good for anything should either conquer or submit to their betters." The Romans, when after the battle of the Ægatian Isles they had to recoup themselves, as best they could, for fifteen more years of tedious warfare, for the loss of four fleets, and for the humiliation which befell this very Regulus so soon afterwards in Africa, did not propose such ruinous conditions as these; and Scipio himself, after Zama, if only because so many of the tiger's teeth had been already drawn, did not think it necessary to clip its claws as well. It argues an insensate ignorance on the part of the Romans of what was truly great in their antagonists, if they thought that they would accept such terms. The spirit of the ambassadors rose with their adversity. They refused even to discuss the conditions offered them, and the Carthaginian Senate determined to die, fighting bravely with arms in their hands, rather than sign voluntarily their own death-warrant. Be the story of the subsequent heroism and self-sacrifice of Regulus ever so true, a serious abatement must be made in estimating his qualities both of head and heart, for the insolence and infatuation which he displayed on this critical occasion.

The moment at which the Carthaginians were obliged to give up all hopes of peace was also, luckily for them, the precise moment at which a recruiting officer happened to return from Greece with a band of soldiers of fortune whom he had induced to place their swords at the disposal of the rich republic. Among these was Xanthippus, a Lacedæmonian of inferior grade, but one who had been well schooled in war by the admirable training which the Spartan discipline still gave, and by the troublous times in which the whole of Greece was involved. Observing the excellence of the Carthaginian cavalry and the number of the Carthaginian elephants, and hearing also the story of the recent defeat, he remarked casually, as the story goes, to his friends, that the Carthaginians had been conquered not so much by the enemy as by themselves, or by the blunders of their generals. The words were caught up

Xanthippus.

and ran from mouth to mouth in the eager and anxious city. Before long they reached the ears of the government, probably of the dreaded Hundred themselves. The Hundred, seldom backward, if our accounts are trustworthy, to listen to anything to the prejudice of the instruments they employed, summoned Xanthippus before them. He justified what he had said by argument, and pledged his word that if only the Carthaginians would keep to the plains and utilize that in which their real strength lay, they would be victorious. It is little creditable to the insight either of the Carthaginian government or the generals that they should have required a Greek soldier of fortune to apprise them of the mistake they had made; but there seems to be no reason to doubt the plain statement of Polybius.

The command, but not, as yet, the sole command, was entrusted to Xanthippus. His confidence was contagious, and there ran through the city the joyful news that now the hour had come and the man. Confidence grew into enthusiasm when men saw the way in which Xanthippus handled his troops, and contrasted it with the sorry performances of the other generals. A cry was raised for instant battle; for all were convinced that no evil could befall them under such a leader as Xanthippus. A council of war was held, but the popular enthusiasm carried everything before it; and the other generals, pocketing their pride, or sharing, as it would seem, in the general enthusiasm, handed over the undivided responsibility to Xanthippus.

Is made sole commander.

The Carthaginian army, reinforced by the addition of the recruits from Greece, numbered 12,000 infantry, with 4,000 cavalry, and a formidable array of 100 elephants. Regulus, surprised at the novel sight of a Carthaginian army encamping on the plains, hesitated a moment, as though there was something more in this change of tactics than met the eye, and pitched his own camp at a distance of a mile from them. But finding that the Carthaginians meant to fight, and flushed with his hitherto unbroken success, he drew up his army in order of battle. His small body of cavalry he placed, as usual, on the wings ; but his infantry he massed much more closely together and in much deeper formations than was common among the Romans, thinking that they could thus be better able to resist the onset of the elephants. At last Xanthippus ordered the elephants, to charge, while the cavalry were to attack and then to close in on the wings of the enemy. The Roman horse, outnumbered in the proportion of four to one, took to flight without striking a blow, and the elephants rushing wildly into the foremost ranks of the Roman infantry, laid them low in every direction, and trampled them to death by scores. The main body, however, stood firm, and when the elephants turned aside towards the flanks, it found itself face to face with the Carthaginian centre, which had not yet drawn the sword. Attacked in front by the infantry, on the flanks, which the flight of their own cavalry had left unprotected, by the Numidian cavalry and on the rear by the elephants, the majority of the Roman legionaries stood their ground nobly, as they did under similar circumstances at the Trebia forty years later, and died where they were standing. A few took to flight ; but the flight of foot soldiers, from Numidian cavalry over level ground only meant a slight prolongation of the miserable struggle for life. Regulus himself, at the head of six hundred men, surrendered to the conquerors, and of the whole army 2,000 only, who had at the first onset defeated the mercenaries, and after pursuing them to their camp had taken no other part in the battle, escaped to Clypea with the news of the disaster.

Clypea was the only spot in the whole of the country which the Romans had so easily overrun that they could now call their own. The Carthaginians first spoiled the slain, and then leading the Roman consul himself and the other survivors in chains, returned in triumph to the capital. Results of victory. It was the first pitched battle which they had fairly won; but that one battle had reversed the whole fortune of the war. The Roman army had been all but annihilated, and its miserable remnant was besieged upon the spot where they had first landed. The inhabitants of the country districts could now return to their homes and rebuild their shattered homesteads; and the richness of the incomparable soil, with its abundant irrigation, would soon efface all traces of the invaders. The citizens themselves once again breathed freely, for they were delivered from the prospect of an immediate siege, the last horrors of which, in the shape of sickness and starvation, they had already begun to taste. What wonder, as Polybius says, if, in the exuberance of their joy, all ranks alike gave themselves up to feasting and thanksgivings to their gods?

But what kind of thanksgiving did the Carthaginian deities delight to receive and the Carthaginian worshipper bring himself to give? We know from Diodorus that when Agathocles was threatening Carthage fifty years before, 200 children of the noblest Carthaginian families had been offered alive to appease the angry Moloch, and 300 men had willingly devoted themselves for the same purpose, if haply they so might save the city from the impending siege. Nor can we doubt that the greater agony through which the Carthaginians had now passed, and the still more unlooked-for triumph by which they had issued from it, were marked by the same horrible offerings on a more imposing scale. There stood the huge brazen god with arms outstretched to receive his offerings, as though a father to clasp his children to his breast. But the arms sloped treacherously down towards the ground, and the victim placed upon them rolled off into a seething cauldron of fire below, his cries drowned, as in the vale of Hinnom, by the rolling of drums and the blare of trumpets. This was the end, no doubt, of some of the noblest among the Roman captives. For Moloch was a jealous god. No alien children, bought with money and reared up for human sacrifice, would he accept. He allowed no substitutes, nor would he take from his worshipper that which cost him nothing or cost him money only. An only child, a first-born child, a child remarkable for its beauty, its wealth, or its noble birth, this was the offering which touched the fire-god's heart; and the parents, who had sacrificed their own children to avert the siege, would now, not unnaturally, come forward to give the noblest among the Roman captives as thank-offerings to the god who had heard their prayer and, as they believed, delivered them from their distress.

The Romans, when they heard of the disaster which had befallen Regulus, fitted out a large fleet for the rescue of the survivors (B. C. 255); while the Carthaginians, rightly judging that the resolution of Rome would not be broken by any one calamity, however great, also set to work to build a new fleet which should protect them from a second invasion. But in vain did they endeavour to reduce Clypea before the Romans could reach it. The desperate cour-

Efforts of Romans.

age of the small garrison repelled all assaults, and enabled it to hold out till the ensuing summer, when the Roman fleet arrived. A naval battle took place off the Hermæan promontory. The Romans gained the day, and took on board, at their leisure, the defenders of Clypea who had so well earned their lives.

They had well earned their lives, but they were not long to enjoy them; they turned their backs with joy upon Africa, but they were not to see Italy. The armament had reached Camarina in safety, and was about to round Pachynus, and to sail home through the Straits of Messana, when a terrific storm, such as is common in those parts and at that time of the year, broke upon them. Some of the Roman ships foundered in the open sea; more were dashed to pieces against the sharp rocks and numerous promontories of that iron-bound coast, and the shore was strewed for miles with wrecks and corpses. Out of 340 ships it was said that only eight escaped; and what must have given an additional sting to the calamity was the consciousness that it might have been avoided. The pilots, probably the only persons on board who had had real experience of the sea, or who knew what ugly weather was, had warned the admirals of the dangerous storms to which the south of Sicily was exposed after the rising of the tempestuous Orion. Along the northern shore they would be in calm water. But the maritime experience acquired in five years wherein nothing had gone wrong with them had taught the Romans, as they fondly thought, that there was nothing in the terrors of the sea with which Roman courage could not cope; and the admirals were deaf to the voice of the weather-wise pilots, who shook their heads at dangers which could neither be seen nor handled. Moreover, they wished to

Destruction of Roman fleet.

make the most of their recent victory, and by its prestige to bring over to themselves a few small towns on the south coast of Sicily which still wavered in their allegiance. The prize was small, as Polybius significantly remarks, and the stake large; but they staked, and lost it.

Elated as they were by the rapid departure of the Roman fleet from Africa, the spirit of the Carthaginians must have risen higher still when they heard of its sudden and complete destruction.

<small>Fresh efforts on both sides.</small>

Like Athens or like Venice, Carthage might well call herself by the proud title of "Bride of the Sea," and her citizens, like the Vikings of after times, might well boast that they were "friends of the sea and enemies of all that sailed upon it." The war might now be once more transferred to Sicily, and thither Hannibal was sent with all the available land forces, with 140 elephants, and with a fleet which was to co-operate with the army. He made straight for Lilybæum, and taking the field, prepared to ravage the open country. With unconquerable resolution, however, the Romans determined to fit out a new fleet to replace the one that had been destroyed; and the miracle of speed which we have noticed before is said to have been repeated again. Within three months 220 vessels were built from the keel, and were ready for action.

The two consuls, A. Atilius and Cn. Cornelius Scipio Asina, who had been released from his captivity, picking up on their way the few vessels which had escaped to Messana from the general wreck, made for Panormus (B. C. 254), and in the hour of their humiliation hazarded an attack upon its strong fortifications, which they had shrunk from even after their victory at Mylæ; and, what is more

<small>Romans take Panormus.</small>

surprising, they took it with ease. A tower which commanded the fortifications towards the sea was first destroyed. This disaster put the new city into the hands of the Romans, and the old at once surrendered. Never was a war more fertile in vicissitudes and surprises than had been the first nine years of this. Here were the Romans stronger and more energetic after a defeat than after a victory; taking by a sudden onslaught an almost virgin fortress, which had never yet been taken but by Pyrrhus; baffling all the calculations of a not inexperienced foe, and then sailing back to Rome as though nothing extraordinary had happened, leaving only a small garrison in what had been the Carthaginian capital of the island, the head-quarters of its armies and its fleets.

In the following year (B. C. 253), the Romans tempted fortune again by reconnoitring the African coast. They landed here and there, and ravaged the surrounding country, but with no result proportionate to the danger they ran; and they ended, owing to their want of maritime experience, by falling into the Syrtis, whose name expresses the power with which an unlucky vessel coming within its reach is sucked into its deadly embraces. The vessels ran aground, and were rescued only by a sudden rise of the sea, which the crews helped by throwing overboard their valuables. The moment they were extricated from their danger, like animals that have been in the toils, they made their way back to Panormus, only too thankful if they could escape the pursuit of the enemy. But the worst was still to come. In crossing from Panormus to Italy they were overtaken, off the promontory of Palinurus, by another storm, which, as it must have seemed, could not now let even the seas to the north of

Sicily alone if Romans were to be found in it. Never since the tempest had raged day after day on the southern coast of Magnesia, and strewn the coasts of Thessaly and Euboea with the wrecks of the vast Persian fleet, had the god of the sea shown himself so decided a partizan in a naval contest, or demanded so costly a series of sacrifices. The Roman spirit at length began to show some symptoms of giving way. At all events the Senate determined not again at present to tempt the sea, but to depend upon their land forces; and for the next two years the war was carried on under conditions not very dissimilar to those under which it had been begun.

The Carthaginians were now once more able to carry the war into Sicily, and the large army which they sent under Hasdrubal to Lilybæum had that within it which seemed able, for the time at least, to demoralize, nay, even to paralyze, their foes. The havoc wrought by the elephants amongst the troops of Regulus in the battle near Carthage had been duly reported to the Roman armies in Sicily, and it had lost nothing in the transmission. To be knocked down, and then trampled to pieces by a furious beast against which neither fraud nor force could avail aught, would be terrible enough to any well-regulated mind; but the fear which it seems to have inspired completely unnerved the Romans. It was not death itself—for that they would have faced gladly in a hundred fair battle-fields or forlorn hopes; it was the instrument and the manner of death that they feared. They refused to face the elephants, much as the bravest troops now-a-days might refuse to measure their collective strength against the brute power of a steam-engine, or as men armed with muzzle-loaders might demur, however great their

Carthaginians threaten Panormus.

valour, to stand up against the cold and cruel mechanism of a mitrailleuse. Once again did the two armies face one another at a few furlongs distance, in the territory of Selinus, and once again did they part company without coming to blows. It takes two to make a quarrel, and the Romans clung steadfastly to the hills where their experience in Africa had taught them that the one hundred and forty elephants would be useless, and where the Carthaginians therefore could not attack them with any hope of success. There were symptoms, too, of serious disaffection and discontent among the Roman officers, and once again it was clear to the Roman Senate that the sea itself would be less terrible than such an indefinite and purposeless prolongation of the war. They accordingly reconsidered their resolution, and began to build a third fleet.

Hasdrubal meanwhile, encouraged by what he thought the cowardice of the Romans, issued from Selinus, and proceeded to carry off the rich harvests, just then ripe, from under the eyes of the Roman army at Panormus. Cæcilius Metellus was in command there, a man of prudence and self-restraint, but able to strike a vigorous blow when there was occasion for it. When Hasdrubal and his elephants had crossed the river near the city—a step for which he had been anxiously waiting—he sent forth his light troops in such numbers as to induce the Carthaginians to draw up in line of battle. In front of the city wall ran a broad and deep ditch, within which the light troops were warned to take shelter, if, after they had provoked an attack from Hasdrubal, they should find themselves hard pressed. Here they would find fresh weapons awaiting them, thrown down by the townsmen from the walls above, and, safe under their protection, would be able

B.C. 251. Battle of Panormus.

to shower missiles upon the advancing elephants. The order of Metellus was carried out to the letter, and the result answered his expectations. The elephant-drivers —Indians, Polybius here and elsewhere calls them— eager to assert their independence of Hasdrubal, or to win special credit for themselves, advanced to close quarters before the word of command was given. The light troops gave way, and, leaping down into the ditch, received the unwieldy monsters, which came blundering on to its very edge, with showers of darts and burning arrows. Unable to vent their rage on their assailants in the ditch, the elephants rushed wildly back on the Carthaginian army, and wrought amongst them the havoc which the Romans had feared for themselves. Now was the moment for Metellus. Unobserved by the enemy, he had massed the main body of his army close behind the gate of the town. He sallied out in force, charged the enemy, who were already in confusion, on the flank, and, routing them completely, drove them headlong back towards Selinus. It was the greatest pitched battle of the war, and restored confidence to the Romans at the time when they needed it most sorely.

But we must dwell a moment on the fate of the elephants who had played so important a part in the battle itself, and whose terrors exercised so critical and so characteristic an influence on this part of the First Punic War. Ten of the elephants had been taken prisoners during the battle, with their drivers. The drivers of the remainder had been either thrown to the ground by the elephants themselves or killed by the weapons of the Romans, and the creatures were still, after the battle, rushing wildly about, no Roman daring to lay hands upon them. The promise of their lives to the captured drivers induced some

Fate of the elephants.

among them to exercise their moral control when physical force was out of the question, and in time the panic-stricken monsters, 120 in number, were reduced to order. It was determined to send them to Rome to grace the well-deserved triumph of Metellus; but it was no easy matter to convey them across the stormy Straits of Messana. Huge rafts were lashed together, earth and herbage were scattered over the planks, and high bulwarks carried round the whole; and the animals allowed themselves to be ferried quietly across the straits under a total misconception as to the operation which they were undergoing. They marched in stately procession up the Sacred Way and were drawn thence, like so many captured kings or generals before and after them, to the place of execution, the Roman Circus. There, after being baited with "arms of courtesy," to familiarize the people and the soldiers that were to be, with their formidable appearance, they received the *coup de grâce* with *armes à outrance;* and the fatal appetite for blood which was then just beginning to show itself among the Roman populace must have been sated to the full by so gigantic and horrible a sacrifice. The noble family of the Metelli always cherished, as well they might, the memory of the great battle of Panormus among their most precious heirlooms, and coins of theirs are still extant representing the formidable beast which their ancestor had, by his victory at this critical point of the war, robbed of half its terrors.

It was, probably, about this time that an embassy appeared at Rome from Carthage to negotiate, if possible, a peace, but anyhow an exchange of prisoners. It was accompanied by Regulus, who had been languishing for five years in a Carthaginian prison, and who came upon his parole to

<small>Story of embassy of Regulus.</small>

return to Carthage if his mission should prove unsuccessful. Everyone knows the beautiful touches with which the story of what follows has been filled in by the genius of Horace and of other late poets and orators; how Regulus refused to enter the city as a citizen, or the Senate house as a senator, since he had lost his right to both on the day when he became a captive; how, when at length he brought himself to speak before the Senate, he spoke in terms such as no Roman had ever heard before. "Let those who had surrendered when they ought to have died, die in the land which had witnessed their disgrace; let not the Senate establish a precedent fraught with disaster to ages yet unborn, or buy with their gold what ought only to be won back by arms. He was old, and in the short time of life that still remained to him could do no good service to his country, while the generals who would be exchanged for him were still hale and vigorous;" how, when he saw the Senate still wavering between pity for him and their sense of duty to their country, he nailed them to their purpose by telling them he had taken a slow poison which was even then coursing through his veins; and how, last of all, he strode off, with his eyes indeed fixed upon the ground, lest he should look upon his sorrowing wife and children, but with a step as light and a heart as free as though he were going for a holiday to his country estate. It is an ideal picture of a brave man bearing up under a great misfortune, and striving, as best he could, to wipe out disgrace; and as an ideal picture we are content to let it pass.

Story of his death. But it is otherwise with the sequel to the story, with that which not only idealizes the Roman character, but sets it off by blackening that of its rivals, as if it was the Carthaginians who enjoyed a monopoly of cruelty, and as if the Romans themselves had always behaved with ordinary humanity to a conquered foe, a foe like C. Pontius for instance, far more generous and high-spirited than Regulus himself. This we are bound to scrutinize carefully and to mete out stern justice to those who seem to deserve it. We could hardly wonder if, under the circumstances, Regulus had been put to death as soon as he was taken prisoner by a nation which must have been stung to the quick by his insolent bearing in the hour of his success, and which showed so little mercy to its own defeated generals; but it is so far from being true that Regulus was put to death with horrible tortures by the Carthaginians that there is reason to believe that he died a natural death, and that the story of the tortures was invented to cover those which had been really inflicted on two noble Carthaginian prisoners by a Roman matron. No writer before the time of Cato knows anything of the cruel death of Regulus, and when once the legend had been set going, we find that there are almost as many different versions as there are authors who refer to it. Moreover, the silence of Polybius, the most trustworthy of historians, who relates the exploits of Regulus in detail, and whose chief fault it is that he is too didactic—seldom adorning a tale, but always ready to point a moral—is in itself sufficient to outweigh the vague rhetoric and the impassioned poetry of the late Republic.

On the other hand, as has been already hinted, we have the authority of a fragment of Diodorus Siculus for a story, which, when we remember his anti-Carthaginian bias, we can scarcely suppose that he invented, of the shocking cruelties inflicted on Bostar and Hamilcar, two Carthaginians given over by the Roman Senate to the wife of Regulus, *Examination of story.*

as hostages for the safety of her husband. Regulus died —so clearly implies Diodorus—a natural death; but his widow thinking, in her vexation, that there had been neglect or cruelty on the part of the Carthaginians, ordered her sons to fasten the two captives into a cask of the smallest possible dimensions, and kept them there five days and nights without food or water, till Bostar, happily for himself, died of the torture and the starvation. In that same cask she kept the living and the dead for five more days, by a cruel kindness supplying Hamilcar with just so much food as might serve to keep life in him and enable him to realize the horrors of the situation. At last the advanced putrefaction of the body roused the pity of even the servants of the Atilii. They brought the matter before the tribunes of the people, and Hamilcar came forth from his living death and was protected from further violence by the more merciful people. To palliate the story of the foul cruelty of the widow of Regulus, for which the Romans at large were certainly not responsible, was invented, as seems likely, the story of the cruel death of Regulus himself.

CHAPTER VI.

HAMILCAR BARCA AND THE SIEGE OF LILYBÆUM.

(B. C. 250–241.)

THE victory which the Romans had won before Panormus nerved them to make a strenuous effort for the expulsion of their enemies from Sicily. The Carthaginians were now hemmed up in the north-western corner of the island; and of all their former possessions, the three for-

Carthaginian fortresses in Sicily.

tresses of Lilybæum, Eryx, and Drepanum alone remained to them. If the first of these could by any means be taken, the other two would not offer any prolonged resistance. The war might then, once again, be transferred to Africa, and the Romans, whose proud boast it was that they first learned from their enemies and then surpassed them, would be able to prove to the Carthaginians that this war was no exception to the rule. Fourteen years had passed since the war had broken out, and both sides were fully alive to the vital importance of the crisis at which it had arrived.

With the siege of Lilybæum, B. C. 250, opens the last scene of the First Punic War. It is the last scene, but a long and tedious one. The siege is one of the longest known in history. Strictly historical as it is, it equals in length the mythical siege of Troy, and the semi-mythical siege of Veii. The Romans distinguished themselves in it by their heroic perseverance, and by little else; but it was that kind of heroic perseverance which lay at the root of most of what they achieved, and is not, after all, so far removed from genius. The Carthaginian defence was marked by all the versatility and inventiveness, the prudence and the daring which characterize the Phœnician race; above all it was marked by the appearance on the scene of at least one real military genius, the great Hamilcar Barca. *Siege of Lilybæum.*

Lilybæum was built upon the promontory which formed the extreme western point of Sicily. It was the point nearest to Africa and directly fronted the Hermæan promontory. It was therefore, so long as it remained in the hands of the Carthaginians, the most important support to their power in Sicily. It would be a standing menace even to *Its position and importance.*

their home rule in Africa as soon as it should pass into the hands of their enemies. It possessed a fine harbour, to the capabilities of which the name given to it by the Arabs in mediæval times of Marsa Allah, or the Harbour of God, still bears witness (Marsala). But the entrance to it was rendered difficult by the constant winds that blew off the headland, and by the treacherous sandbanks and sunken reefs which lay off the shores; and these, if they were dangerous to the inhabitants who knew them well, would be doubly dangerous to an enemy who did not. Pyrrhus, a few years before, had overrun all the rest of Sicily with ease; but the impetuosity of his assault had been beaten back by the solid walls of Lilybæum. Would the Romans succeed where Pyrrhus had failed? They saw that a place so situated and so defended could only be attacked with any hope of success by a strong army and a strong fleet at once, and they supplied them ungrudgingly.

Two consular armies, consisting of five legions and two hundred vessels, appeared before the place. The first attack was directed against the wall which stretched from sea to sea right across the peninsula on which the city was built, and the immediate success obtained by the Romans was such as appeared to promise an early termination of the siege. By regular approaches the Romans worked their way up to the city wall, undermined some of its towers, and when these had fallen, brought up their battering-rams to threaten the whole line of defence. But Himilco, the commander of the garrison, was a man of energy and of fertility of resource. By building a second wall behind the first, he made the weakening of the first to be of small importance. He met the mining operations of the enemy by countermines, and he

Opening of siege.

quelled, by his address and personal influence over the better disposed of the mercenaries, a formidable conspiracy which had broken out among them to betray the town to the Romans.

Meanwhile the Carthaginians, knowing the weakness of their naval force off Lilybæum, and fully conscious that the place could not hold out unless relieved from home, made vigorous efforts to throw succour into it. Hannibal, son of Hamilcar, was despatched with all haste to Sicily, with fifty ships and 10,000 troops. He moored his fleet among the Ægatian Isles opposite to Lilybæum, waiting for the moment when he should be able to face, with some slight chance of success, the double dangers of the Roman squadron, and the rocks and reefs that girt in the harbour. A favouring, although a violent, wind sprang up. He spread every inch of his canvas, and massing his troops on deck to be ready for an engagement, with that happy rashness which is the truest prudence, he made his way in safety through the narrow entrance, while the Roman guardships remained at anchor close by, the sailors stupidly looking on, aghast at his rashness, and expecting to see him dashed to pieces upon the rocks. The sea walls of the city were thronged with the eager inhabitants, hoping, as it seemed, against hope, that some few of the ships might, by a lucky chance, pass safely through; and amid their loud cheers Hannibal rode into the harbour under full sail, without losing a single vessel, and deposited in safety his 10,000 troops and his stores of provisions.

Efforts to relieve it.

His example was contagious. A Rhodian mercenary, of the same name, volunteered with a single vessel to do as he had done. Again and again he ran the blockade, and found his way out in safety, as though he bore a charmed life, through the midst of the Roman vessels which were drawn up at the entrance of the harbour for the very purpose of preventing his escape. Doubtless he held the clue to the dangerous navigation of the straits, which, now that the buoys were removed, no enemy could discover. Each venturesome visit breathed fresh courage into the garrison, and spread fresh despondency in the blockading fleet, while it enabled the Rhodian to communicate to the Carthaginian government the wants and wishes of their beleaguered subjects. The Romans tried to block up the entrance to the harbour by sinking ships fil ed with stones in its narrowest part; but the depth of the sea and the violence of the current, helped by opportune tempests, carried them away and opened the passage again. It seemed that the sea was never going to desert its favourites, when, in an unlucky moment, a Carthaginian quadrireme ran ashore upon a part of the mole which the Romans had just sunk, and fell into their hands. They immediately manned it with their own men, and lay in wait for the return of the Rhodian. He had run the blockade once too often; and in trying to force his way out he was followed by a vessel whose speed and build convinced him that she must be of Carthaginian workmanship, though the rowers who propelled her were clearly Romans. Finding that he could not escape by flight, he turned boldly round and charged the enemy. But a trireme had no chance against a quadrireme. It was taken prisoner, and the adventurous Rhodian's vessel henceforward formed part of the blockading squadron of the very fortress which it had done so much to relieve.

Hannibal the Rhodian.

The condition of the Roman army was not an enviable one. A plague had broken out in their camp, occasioned partly by the unhealthy climate, partly by the want of bread—a want which all the efforts of their zealous ally, Hiero of Syracuse, could not meet. The Romans were ordinarily vegetarians, and the abundant supply of meat which they had till very recently received from the Sicilian flocks and herds had not mended matters. And now to complete the tale of their misfortunes, P. Claudius was sent out to take the command (B. C. 249), a man who proved to be as incompetent as he was arrogant, and who mistook, if our accounts do not do him injustice, severity for discipline, violence for strength, and childish weakness for manly courage. Despising alike the consuls who had preceded him and the officers who served under him, he first renewed the attempt to block up the mouth of the harbour, as though a Claudius must succeed where others had failed; and when the waves showed that they had no more respect for patrician than for plebeian blood, he determined, as though the siege of Lilybæum was not enough to occupy his energies, to attack Drepanum, fifteen miles away, in hopes of taking Adherbal and his fleet there by surprise! His generals remonstrated, and the sacred chickens—so the augurs reported—refused to eat. "If they will not eat, they shall drink," said he, and ordered them to be flung into the sea. It is possible that this story may have been invented to account for the calamity that followed; but the words attributed to Publius have a genuine Claudian ring about them. "Neither gods nor men should stay a Claudius from his purpose!" The generals were browbeaten into compliance. Ten thousand troops had just arrived from Rome. Claudius put the best of them on board his vessels to serve as marines, and there was no lack of volunteers for the enterprise, not probably because

Arrival and character of Claudius.

they trusted the abilities of the consul, but because anything seemed better than a blockade which was no blockade at all.

The fleet set out at midnight, and by daybreak its foremost ship had reached the entrance of the harbour of Drepanum. The surprise was complete. Adherbal, knowing how hard pressed the Romans were at Lilybæum, ignorant that they had been reinforced, and ignorant also of the character of the new consul, had never dreamed that they would molest him at Drepanum. He who would attempt it must be either a fool or a military genius, and Rome, in this war at all events, had not been fertile of either. A respectable mediocrity had hitherto been the order of the day alike among the Romans and the Carthaginians. But Adherbal was not disconcerted. Determined not to be besieged, like Himilco at Lilybæum, he set his rowers to their work, and summoning by the sound of the trumpet the mercenaries from the city to the beach, he addressed them in a few stirring words, and then, distributing them over his ships, he led the way in his own ship out of one side of the sickle-shaped harbour of Drepanum, while Claudius was still hovering near the entrance of the other. Surprised at this, and fearing in his turn to be enclosed between a hostile navy and a hostile town, Claudius turned round, hoping to make his way out of the harbour by the way he had entered it. But the signal could not reach the whole of the long column round the headland at once, and it was with difficulty that the consul got all his ships out of the trap into which he had drawn them, and arranged them in line of battle close along the coast, their prows pointing towards the fleet of Adherbal, which was already in line, and ready, with superior forces, to

Battle of Drepanum.

bear down upon them. In the battle which ensued we hear nothing of the Ravens of Duillius. When the ships did close with one another there was hard and free fighting, for the decks carried the pick of either army; but in every other respect—the build, the number, and the speed of their ships, the experience of their rowers, and the space for manœuvring—the advantage was with the Carthaginians. The Roman ships, when hard pressed, could not retire behind the line, for there was no room left between it and the shore; and for the same reason they could not give help to one another in their distress. The consul, as he was the first to get into the mess, was also the first to get out of it. He took to flight, and his example was followed by the thirty ships nearest to him. It was well, perhaps, that he did so; for the whole of the remainder, ninety-three in number, fell into the hands of the Carthaginians, who, it is said, did not lose a single vessel.

Whether Publius cared aught for the lives he had thus thrown away we are not told; but probably his sister, some years afterwards, expressed pretty accurately the family feeling for the loss of the mere rabble of the fleet. She was taking part as a Vestal Virgin in a procession, and when the crowd pressed upon her more closely than she liked, she was heard to exclaim that she wished her brother were alive to get rid of some more of them at sea. Loud must have been the curses of the Roman army at Lilybæum when the consul brought back the news of his own defeat and flight; and deep, certainly, was the resentment of the Roman Senate at his reckless incapacity. He was recalled; and, being ordered to nominate a Dictator in his stead, he named, with true Claudian effrontery, a freedman of his family, M. Claudius Glycia; but he was shortly after put on his trial, and met with the punishment which he deserved.

The blockade of Lilybæum, such as it was, was for the time practically at an end, and the Romans were more anxious to keep the troops who were already there from starving than to supplement their number or to make the blockade effective.

<small>Destruction of third Roman fleet.</small>

A fleet of 800 merchant vessels, laden with supplies of every kind, and convoyed by 120 ships of war, was despatched from Rome, and reached Syracuse in safety. Anxious to take on board the provisions offered him by the ever-zealous Hiero, the consul, L. Junius Pullus, lingered awhile at Syracuse with half his fleet, while he sent forward the other half towards its destination. But the Carthaginians were on the look-out for them. Adherbal, admiral at Drepanum, was determined to push his victory to the utmost. After sending as trophies to Carthage the ships which he had taken, he despatched his vice-admiral Carthalo first to Lilybæum, to attack the remainder of the Roman fleet which had taken refuge there, and thence to Heraclea, to await the arrival of the provision ships. The advanced portion of the Roman convoy, hearing of the approach of Carthalo, and unable to offer battle or to take to flight, ran into the nearest roadstead on that inhospitable coast, and protected themselves, as best they could, by the military engines planted on the cliffs above. Carthalo, not caring to run unnecessary risk, and sure now of his game, kept watch at the mouth of a river hard by till they should be obliged to move. Meanwhile the other portion of the Roman fleet had left Syracuse, had rounded Pachynus, and was sailing quietly along the coast in ignorance of the close proximity of their own and of the enemies' ships. To prevent the junction of the two fleets Carthalo advanced to meet them, and they too, knowing their weakness, made for the nearest shore, a spot which, unfortunately for them, had neither harbour nor roadstead, and was exposed to every wind that blew. Carthalo, sure of his game, now lay-to in the offing, half way between them, pinning with his small fleet the two much larger ones to the shore; but the weather-wise Carthaginian pilots saw the signs of a coming storm, and warned the admiral, while there was yet time, to make for shelter. He sailed round Pachynus eastward and was in calm water, leaving the storm to take care of the Romans; and the storm did take care of them. Some of the crews, indeed, escaped to land, but the 800 ships were broken into fragments, " not a plank of them remaining," says Polybius, " which could be used again," and for miles along the coast the hungry foam was discoloured by the corn intended for the famishing Roman army before Lilybæum.

When this sad news reached Rome—the destruction of a third fleet by the waves and the undisputed mastery of the sea won back by the Carthaginians in the fifteenth year of the war (B.C. 249)— there were symptoms of despondency even in the Roman Senate; but the consul Junius was among those who had escaped from the wreck, and he made his way to Lilybæum, burning by some signal achievement to wipe out the blame which he felt might be thrown upon him. Nor was he disappointed. A few miles to the north of Drepanum, between it and Panormus, and standing back a little from the coast, rises a mountain then called Eryx, and now known by the name of St. Giuliano. It stands by itself and, rising to a height of some 2,000 feet in solitary grandeur, is so imposing an object that ancient geographers and historians mention it in the same breath as Ætna, which is really four times its height. Right on its summit stood a temple of immemorial antiquity, dedicated to Venus, and celebrated for the wealth which it had amassed and had managed to retain amidst the vicissitudes of all the conflicts that had raged around it. It had been taken and retaken many times in the long contest between Dionysius of Syracuse and Carthage, and more recently it had fallen before the assault of Pyrrhus; but, revered alike by Sicilians and Phœnicians, by Greeks and Romans, it had escaped plunder even at the hands of the adventurous prince who did not spare the wealthy sanctuary of Proserpine at Locri. Half-way up the mountain was a city which was not so proof against all the storms that blew as was the temple on its top, for it had been partially destroyed by the Carthaginians in this war, and its inhabitants transferred to Drepanum; but heaps of its buildings must have still remained, and it was evidently still an important position for defence. Of this natural stronghold—mountain, fallen city and temple, one of the only three strongholds that still remained to the Carthaginians in Sicily, the consul Junius managed to get possession by a sudden attack, and held it firmly against any similar surprise from the enemy in the closely adjoining Drepanum.

Such was the general condition of affairs (B. C. 247) when the great Hamilcar, "the man whom Melcarth protects," appeared upon the scene. Hamilcar Barca was the head of the great family named after him the Barcine—the word Barca is the same as the Hebrew Barak—and well did Hamilcar justify the name which succeeding ages have always coupled with his and his alone of his family, by the "lightning" rapidity with which, in this the sixteenth year of the war, he would now sweep the Italian coast

Hamilcar Barca.

with his privateers, now swoop down and carry off a Roman outpost, and anon would seize a stronghold, which the terror of his name alone rendered impregnable, under the very eyes of an opposing army. Equally great as an admiral and a general, after ravaging the Roman coasts from Locri to Cumæ, he landed suddenly in the neighborhood of Panormus and seized the commanding elevation called Ercte (now Monte Pellegrino). This hill, like Eryx, rises to a height of about 2,000 feet, but, unlike it, on two of its sides rises sheer from the sea; a third side rises equally perpendicular from the plain, while on the fourth alone, which directly faces Panormus, at the distance of a mile and a half, is the plateau at all accessible. This stronghold Hamilcar seized, and this he held for three years in sight of the Roman garrison at Panormus, and in the near view of a fortified camp placed almost at its base, in spite of all the efforts of the Romans to dislodge him, and, when he left it, he left it only of his own free will to occupy a similar, though a less advantageous, position elsewhere.

The place was admirably adapted for his purpose. At its base was a little cove into which his light ships might run laden with the spoils of Italian or Sicilian towns, accessible from the high ground occupied by his troops, but not accessible from any place on shore. There was an abundant spring of water on the very summit, and above the precipitous cliffs that underpinned the mountain was a broad plateau which in that delicious climate Hamilcar found that, even at such an elevation, he could cultivate with success. A rounded top which crowned the whole as a post of observation commanding the country round, and, in case of need, would serve as an acropolis where no one of the defenders need die unavenged.

But neither the success of the consul Junius at Eryx, nor the presence of a master spirit among the enemies—which the Romans could not fail to see—could now rouse the Senate to take the active measures which the times required. The drain upon the resources of the State had been too enormous. The muster-roll of the citizens had fallen in the last five years from 297,000 to 251,000—a sixth part of the whole. The *As*, the unit of value among the Romans, which had originally weighed twelve ounces of copper, had now fallen, as Pliny tells us, to two ounces, to one-sixth, that is, of its former value. The State was bankrupt, and the Senate could neither make up their minds to withdraw altogether from the war, nor yet to prosecute it with the necessary vigour. They still made believe to continue the blockade of Lilybæum; but the seas were open to the Carthaginians, and every one knew that as long as the seas were open to them they might laugh at all the efforts of the Roman armies.

Nor were the Carthaginians on their part more self-sacrificing or more far-sighted. Finding that the Romans had retired from the sea they cut down their navy by a wretched economy to the narrowest possible dimensions, and were quite content if only they could supply with food their heroic garrisons at Lilybæum and at Drepanum, not to make an effort to reconquer any of the places which had so recently belonged to them. Having lighted at last upon an able general, they would not, indeed, interfere with his making the best use he could of the small band of mercenaries whom they had given him at so much a head, and, so far as they were concerned, he might utilize his few ships to collect supplies; but not to them must he look henceforward for more ships or men.

The war, or his part of the war at all events, must henceforward support itself. If Hamilcar, they argued, was successful in his venturous enterprises, so much the better for them; if unsuccessful, he and not they lost.

Hence the five or six long and listless years of war which followed the appointment of Hamilcar; discreditable enough to the governments of the contending states, but redounding to the honour of that one heroic soul who, learning from the past the lesson which no Carthaginian general had yet been able to learn, applied it to the exigencies of the moment with a patience, a perseverance, and an energy which seemed more than human; and conscious all the time, as it would seem, that his efforts were, for the present at least, foredoomed to failure, was yet content to sacrifice himself if only he might prepare the way for vengeance in the remoter future. What mattered it if Sicily was lost? A greater Sicily might be found beyond the seas in Spain; a new world might be called into existence to redress the balance of the old. In that great coming struggle Africa should turn back the tide of aggression upon Europe, and Rome, not Carthage, should tremble for her safety. Hamilcar Barca was not far wrong. The genius of the son carried out what the father had planned and had prepared. The army of Hannibal, welded by the spark of his genius out of the most unpromising materials into one homogeneous and indissoluble whole, was the legitimate counterpart of the small band of mercenaries trained so painfully by Hamilcar. The ultimate result of Hamilcar's patient struggles on Mount Ercte was the victorious march of Hannibal on Rome.

To explain a little. Hamilcar saw that the real defect under which the Carthaginians had laboured all along

Greatness of Hamilcar.

had been the want of a trustworthy infantry. Their cavalry was excellent; their elephants more than once had borne down all before them; their ships had been beaten, not by skill, but by brute force. But as long as they were without a body of infantry who, man for man, could stand up against the Roman legionaries, so long it was impossible that they could beat their enemies. The mercenaries who formed the bulk of the Carthaginian armies had sold their services to Carthage for gold; what wonder if they transferred their services at the critical moment to those who would appraise them more highly? What wonder that Lilybæum had been all but betrayed, and that the temple of Eryx itself was on the point of being seized by Gallic deserters from the Carthaginian army? To the task of remedying these defects Hamilcar addressed himself with a patience and a self-restraint which is the more surprising the more conscious he must have been of his own superlative talents for aggressive war upon a mighty scale. By enforcing strict discipline at any price; by never fighting a battle, and therefore never risking a defeat; by maintaining a daily and hourly warfare with the Roman outposts, he gradually trained his troops to face the terrors of the Roman presence, as the Romans on their part had at last trained themselves to face the terrors of the elephants. Knowing that he could expect no efficient aid from Carthage, he determined, if possible, to save her in spite of herself. To attach the mercenaries to Carthage by ties of gratitude or respect or patriotism was impossible; but it might not be impossible to attach them to himself by that close tie which always binds soldiers to a general whom they can alike fear and trust and love, and then to utilize that attachment not for his own but for his country's good.

His plans.

How nobly Hamilcar carried out his resolve every action of his life proves. Day after day he would sally from his mountain fastness, like a lion from its den, on the fair plains of Sicily. Unob- *His achievements.* served or unattacked, he would pass by the Roman camp placed at the foot of the mountain, and return with the supplies necessary to keep his small force from starving. Once we hear of him even at Catana, on the east coast of the island. His galleys, in the same way, would harry or alarm the coast of Italy even as far as Cumæ. Never was a more harassing warfare waged, and yet there is little to record. Polybius remarks, that it is as impossible for the historian to do more than state these general facts, as it is for the spectator at a prize-fight either to see or to describe the blows rained by practised pugilists on one another when the contest is nearing its end. They know, perhaps, the strength and the skill of the combatants; they hear the heavy thud, and they see the lightning lunge; they note the result, but they cannot accurately observe or recount the process. So was it with Hamilcar; and yet it must be remembered that the struggle was hardly at present a life-and-death struggle, for the Romans seem never to have tried seriously to beard the lion in his den, and Hamilcar, with his handful of troops, can hardly have hoped to raise the siege of Lilybæum. At most he might distract the attention of the Romans and impede their progress.

So things might have gone on forever, when Hamilcar (B. C. 244) surprised even the Romans—though by this time they could hardly have been surprised at anything Hamilcar did—by voluntarily *He seizes Eryx.* abandoning the stronghold endeared to him by three years of hair-breadth escapes and romantic adventures, and attacking Mount Eryx, a stronghold which lay nearer indeed to the beleaguered Carthaginian cities of Drepanum and Lilybæum, but in all other respects was less advantageous, and at that very time was held in force by the Romans. He managed to dislodge the garrison from the ruined city half way up the mountain; but he failed in all his efforts to take the temple on the summit, occupied as it then was by a band of Gallic deserters, who had been taken into their pay by the Romans, and who, since they carried their lives in their hands, were prepared to sell them as dearly as possible. Here, then, once more, was Hamilcar on an isolated hill, two miles from the coast, and therefore beyond the reach of immediate succours from his galleys, with a band of desperate enemies above him, and a Roman army encamped below! Well might it seem that a single strenuous and united effort on the part of the Romans might bring Hamilcar to his knees, or that at all events he might be starved into a surrender. But this was not to be. For two more years did Hamilcar hold out in this most impossible of situations, fighting, says Polybius, like a royal eagle, which, grappling with another eagle as noble as himself, stops only to take breath from sheer exhaustion, or to gather fresh strength for the next attack. The war was fought out elsewhere, and its issue was decided by men of other mould and making than the royal soul of Hamilcar.

It must have long since been apparent to the Roman Senate that unless they could fit out a fleet more effective than any that had preceded it, Drepanum and Lilybæum might hold out forever, and that while they held out, their own hold on the rest of Sicily must be precarious. They had built four fleets since the war began, and all had been utterly

Supreme effort of Romans.

destroyed; with what conscience could they now propose to throw more public money into the gulf, and to commit themselves to the mercies of the hostile and insatiable sea? Even if they should decree a property tax, it was doubtful—such was the general distress—whether it could be levied. But where public enterprise failed, it should be recorded to the eternal credit of the Romans that private citizens were forthcoming who volunteered, either singly or in combination, to furnish ships of war to make up another fleet. If the venture should prove successful, the State might repay them, should it like to do so, at its own time. If it failed, as every fleet had failed before, they would have done nothing more than their duty, and duty must be its own reward. A good model was found in the Rhodian's vessel which had been captured off Lilybæum; and, as if to complete the dramatic history of this unlucky craft, the very trireme which had performed such prodigies of speed and daring for the Carthaginians in the siege of Lilybæum was now to reproduce itself in the shape of two hundred Roman vessels, which should raise the siege of that very town, and bring the war to its conclusion.

The consul, C. Lutatius Catulus, took the command of this pre-eminently patriotic armament early in the year B.C. 242; and once again Roman ships of war were to be seen riding in the harbours of Drepanum and Lilybæum. Hamilcar could now no longer receive supplies by sea, and unless he could break out in force, his surrender was, as it seemed, only a question of time; but the Carthaginians, hearing of the danger, and finding to their surprise that a Roman navy was again in Sicilian waters, made for the first time a serious effort to support him. For four long years Hamilcar had borne the

Supreme effort of Carthaginians.

brunt of the conflict, without receiving supplies of men or money from home, and, now that they were about to lose him, the Carthaginians awoke to a consciousness of his true value. But a fleet could not be built in a day, even by the Carthaginians; and by the time the transports—for they were transports rather than ships of war—reached Sicily, Catulus had, by dint of constant training, transformed his landsmen into tolerably experienced sailors.

In March of the following year (B. C. 241), Hanno, the Carthaginian admiral, made for Hiera, one of the Ægatian Isles, in hopes of being able from thence to communicate with Mount Eryx. His plan was to land his heavy cargo of corn there, to take on board instead the pick of Hamilcar's men, and above all the great Hamilcar himself, and then, and not till then, to fight a decisive action. Catulus had already selected the best from among the Roman troops before Lilybæum to serve the same purpose on board his ships; and he now made for Ægusa, the principal of the Ægatian Isles, with the intention of cutting off Hanno from the shore, and bringing on a general action. On the morning of his intended attack a strong wind sprang up from the west, the very thing which the Carthaginians needed to carry them rapidly into Drepanum. To intercept them the Romans would have to contend against wind and tide as well, and from this even the bravest mariners might shrink. Catulus, or rather the Prætor Q. Valerius—for Catulus was laid up by a wound—knew the odds against him, and hesitated for a moment to face the risk; but reflecting that if he did not strike a blow, the enemy would be able to take Hamilcar on board, and that Hamilcar was more formidable than any storm, he determined to close with the lesser of two dangers. Down came the Carthaginian

Battle of Ægatian Islands.

ships, heavy with their cargo of corn, but flying before the wind with all their sails spread, and the rowers using their oars as well. When they saw the Romans venturing out on such a sea to intercept them, they struck sails and prepared for action. But the battle was over almost as soon as it began. After the first shock, the well-made, slightly-built Roman ships, with their practised crews and their veteran soldiers, obtained an easy victory over the awkward and heavily-laden Carthaginian vessels, with their inexperienced rowers and their raw recruits. Fifty of the Carthaginian ships were sunk and seventy taken, the remainder escaping with the help of an opportune wind to Hiera.

This great victory, the victory of the Ægatian Isles, ended the war. Both sides had played their last card, and the Carthaginians had lost. Their spirit was not altogether broken; but it was impossible to fit out a new fleet in time to relieve Hamilcar, and they wisely resolved, by utilizing his great name and the indefinite possibilities of his future when driven to stand at bay, to obtain more favourable terms than would otherwise have been offered them. We could hardly wonder if Hamilcar had declined the thankless duty, and had left the task of surrendering Sicily to those who far more than himself were responsible for it. But no thought of self seems ever to have entered his great soul. For his faithful band of followers and their honour he was jealous; but of his own feelings of outraged pride and righteous indignation we hear nothing. He rejected with scorn the ungenerous proposal of Catulus that his troops should give up their arms and pass under the yoke; and it was arranged that when peace should have been concluded, they should depart with all the honours of war.

Magnanimity of Hamilcar.

H

The terms of peace were then agreed upon by Catulus and Hamilcar, subject to the subsequent ratification by the Roman people. The Carthaginians were to surrender Sicily to the Romans, and to bind themselves not to wage war on Hiero or his allies; they were to restore the prisoners they had taken without ransom, and to pay within the next twenty years a war indemnity of 2,200 talents. The Roman people were not satisfied with these conditions; but the plenipotentiaries who were sent out to the spot contented themselves with raising the indemnity by half as much again, while they halved the time in which it was to be paid. The easy terms thus granted—so far easier than those demanded by Regulus fifteen years before in the hey-day of his success—are to be explained partly, no doubt, by the exhaustion of the Romans themselves, but partly also by the dread they felt as to what Hamilcar might still dare, if driven to desperation. As such it is the noblest homage paid by the conquerors to the military genius of the "unconquered general of the conquered nation." Two individuals, and two only in the whole course of Roman history, seem by the mere fact of their existence to have inspired real terror into the Roman heart. The one was Hamilcar Barca, the other his, perhaps, still greater son.

So ended the First Punic War; the longest war, says Polybius, the most continuous, and the greatest which the world had then seen; and it may be questioned, even now, whether there has ever been a war in which the losses were so frightful, and the immediate gain to either party so small. The Romans had indeed gained Sicily; but Sicily with the exception of the dominions of Hiero, which were still to belong to him and not to the Romans, was then drained of everything which made it worth having. Its territories had been ravaged, its population swept away, its towns destroyed one after the other. Greek as well as Phœnician enterprise and civilization had been almost blotted out. The island has never entirely recovered its prosperity. Its soil is still in great part uncultivated, its population is one of the most degraded in Europe. To set against this equivocal gain, the Romans had lost 700 ships of the line, containing not less than 70,000 men, and army after army had fallen victims to starvation, to pestilence or the sword. The Carthaginians, on their part, had lost 500 ships of war, but the crews which manned them, and the soldiers who formed the staple of their armies, were such as, in their callous indifference, they could bear to part with ; for more were to be had for money from their still vast recruiting ground. The richness of their soil, and the abundance of their irrigation had already repaired the injury done by Regulus. They had been driven indeed from Sicily ; but had not the Phœnicians been driven before, in like manner, from Crete, from Cyprus, and from Asia Minor ? What mattered it if, with the enterprise and buoyancy of their race, they could still found new colonies, and build up a new empire in countries whither the Romans had never penetrated, and of which they had hardly yet heard the names ?

Everything portended an early renewal of the conflict on a more gigantic scale. Rome by crossing the narrow straits of Messana had entered on her career, for good or evil, of universal conquest and aggression. Carthage was still mistress of the western half of the Mediterranean, and had no intention of voluntarily retiring from it. More than this : Hamilcar Barca was still alive—Hamilcar Barca, with his patience and his genius, with his burning patriotism and his thirst for revenge; above all, with his infant son.

CHAPTER VII.

HAMILCAR BARCA AND THE MERCENARY WAR.

(B.C. 241–238.)

THE twenty-two years which separated the First from the Second Punic War were not years of rest to either Rome or Carthage. The Carthaginians had barely concluded peace when they found that they had to face dangers far more terrible, and foes far more implacable than any they had met with in the twenty-three years' war from which they had just emerged. The Romans, on their part, busied themselves in organizing their newly conquered province; in appropriating to themselves, with shameless meanness and injustice, the island of Sardinia, the oldest foreign possession of the Carthaginians, and that which, next after Sicily, had been the object of her most jealous precautions; in suppressing Illyrian piracy and extending their northern frontier from the Apennines to the Alps. Let us bridge over the interval between the war of Hamilcar and the war of Hannibal, not by describing these events in detail; but by touching on them just so far as they bring into clear light the dealings of either nation with their dependencies, or as they directly influenced the mightier struggle which was looming in the distance.

Events between first and second Punic wars.

The great Hamilcar, during his three years of warfare at Mount Ercte, had managed to make the war support itself; but during the last two years at Eryx, when he was cut off from the sea, and was hard pressed by enemies alike on the peaks above and in the plains below him, he had found it difficult enough to procure the bare necessaries of life for his troops, and he had been able to pay them by promises, and by promises only. That he was able to keep his band of fickle barbarian followers in so dangerous a position for a couple of years without remunerating them for their services, and yet without any symptom of mutiny or insubordination on their part, is not the least striking testimony to his commanding personal qualities. When the war was finished he handed them over, with spirits still unbroken, to Gescon, the Carthaginian commander at Lilybæum, and to Gescon fell the disagreeable duty of transporting them to Africa, and of informing the home government of their obligations towards them. But the party then in power at Carthage were at once short-sighted and unscrupulous. They neither paid the mercenaries their arrears of pay, nor told them boldly that they could not do so.

Things soon assumed a threatening aspect. The mutineers to the number of 20,000 marched for Carthage and pitched their camp near Tunis; and the government, thoroughly frightened, began to cringe when they could no longer threaten, and sent out provisions to be sold at a nominal price in the hostile camp. This only made the mutineers despise them the more. New promises and new concessions were met by new and more exorbitant demands. The mutiny had come to a head. It had found leaders in Spendius, a runaway Campanian slave, in Matho, an African, who had served with distinction in Sicily, and in Autaritus, a Gaul. Gescon, who, in a fit of impatience at the insolence of their demands, had let slip the wish that the malcontents would lay their demands before Spendius and not before him, was taken at his word. He was thrown into chains; the money he had brought with him was seized, and the war began. Messengers were at once despatched by Spendius and Matho to the peoples of Africa summoning them to liberty; the joyful news spread from village to village, and was enthusiastically responded to by the natives.

Men flowed in so plentifully that the rebel generals were able at once to begin the siege of Utica and Hippo Zarytus, the two places which, alone of the surrounding African and Phœnician cities, had hitherto signalized themselves by their attachment to the oppressor. Money was so abundant that Spendius was able not only at once to discharge all the arrears of pay to his troops, but also to meet all the immediate expenses of the war. The Carthaginian government had never yet been in such sore distress. In a moment they had been cut off from the rich districts which supplied them with food, which filled their treasury with money, and their armies with their best troops. They had no ships, for their last fleet had just been destroyed in Sicily, and they had no independent allies, for it was the fate of Carthage—the fate, it must be added, she too well deserved—never to possess any. It was useless to treat for peace with men who were loaded with the accumulated wrongs of centuries, and were burning for revenge. The natives remembered the crucifixion of 3,000 of their countrymen, the finale of their partial and unsuccessful attempt at revolt during the invasion of Regulus a few years before; and they were determined that this revolt should be neither partial nor unsuccess-

Rising of natives.

ful. Bitterly must the Carthaginians have rued their cruelty when they reaped its natural consequences, when they found that the proverb "as many slaves, so many enemies," was in their case no figure of rhetoric, but the stern and simple truth.

Among the magistrates who had acquired the special confidence of the governing clique at Carthage by the amount of money which they had squeezed out of the subject communities, no one was more conspicuous than Hanno, and he it was whom they now selected for the chief command in the Libyan war, a sad omen of the character which it was likely to assume. Hanno was the personal enemy of Hamilcar, and was as incapable as he was self-confident. If he won a partial success he failed to follow it up, and after having won, as he thought, a complete victory, he allowed his camp to be surprised and taken. The government in its distress was obliged to apply to Hamilcar, the man whom they had treated so ill in Sicily, and whom they had treated worse still in the persons of his trusted veterans when the war was over. But Hamilcar, still placing his country before all else, consented to serve the government which had betrayed him. He induced or compelled the easy-going citizens to enlist, and having got together a force of seventy elephants and 10,000 men, he managed to slip through the armies, which, stationed as they were, one at Utica and the other at Tunis, had almost cut Carthage off from Africa; and then, by his strict discipline, by his energy, and by his influence with the Numidian chiefs, he defeated the enemy in a pitched battle and, over-running the country, recovered several towns which had revolted, and saved others which were being besieged. Deserters, some of them, doubtless, veterans of his own, came over to his side; and Spendius

Hanno and Hamilcar.

and Matho, fearing wholesale desertions, determined to cut down their bridges and burn their boats, by involving the whole force in an act of atrocity which not even Hamilcar could forgive.

Panic is always cruel, and the panic of barbarians, if less culpable, is far more uncontrollable than the panic of civilized men. By a well-laid plan Spendius and Matho contrived to create such a panic.

The truce-less war.

Those who counselled moderation were greeted with the cry of "Treason, treason!" or "Smite him, smite him!" and when in this way a reign of terror had been established, the Irreconcilables carried everything their own way. Gescon, "the soldier's friend," lay ready to their hand. He and his company of 700 men were led out to execution, and, having been cruelly mutilated, were thrown, still living, into a ditch to perish, and from that day forward the war deserved the name by which it is known in history, the "war without truce," or the "Inexpiable War."

Upon its horrors we need not here dwell. Suffice it to say that Hamilcar was driven to make reprisals for the barbarities of the Libyans by throwing his prisoners to be trampled to death by the elephants, and the war was henceforward in the literal sense of the word, internecine The Carthaginian government managed, even in this supreme hour to thwart Hamilcar by allowing his inveterate enemy Hanno, discredited as he was, to share the command with him. Nor was it till after the quarrels which ensued had led to many reverses; till the news arrived of the total destruction of their own ships in a storm, of the revolt of Hippo and of Utica, the towns which alone had been faithful to Carthage in the invasions of Agathocles and Regulus; above all, till the news had come

Its horror and end.

of the insurrection of the mercenaries in Sardinia, and the probable loss of that fair island, that the Carthaginians allowed the voice of the army to be heard, and committed to Hamilcar once again the sole command. Hamilcar soon penned the Libyans in their fortified camp near Tunis, and so effectually cut them off from all supplies that they were driven to eat first their prisoners and then their slaves; and it was not till they had begun to look wistfully upon one another that some of the chiefs, with Spendius at their head, came forth to ask for the parley which they had themselves forbidden. Hamilcar demanded that ten of the mercenaries, to be named by himself, should be given up, while the rest of the army should be allowed to depart unarmed with one garment each. This having been agreed upon, Hamilcar immediately named Spendius and his fellow legates, and threw them into chains. The rebel army, thinking, as well they might, that Hamilcar had been guilty of sharp practice, flew to arms. They were still 40,000 in number, but they were without leaders, and they were exterminated almost to a man. Matho still held out at Tunis, and when Spendius was crucified by Hamilcar in front of its walls, Matho, by a sudden sally on the other side of the town, took a Carthaginan general prisoner, and shortly afterwards crucified him with fifty others on the very spot which had witnessed the last agonies of Spendius. A horrible interchange of barbarities! The army of Matho was soon afterwards cut to pieces. The rebel chief himself was taken prisoner, and, after being led in triumph through the streets of the capital, was put to death with terrible tortures (B.C. 241-238). So ended the Truceless War, after a duration of three years and four months, with the total extermination of those who had made it truceless; "a war," says Polybius, and he says truly, "by far the most cruel and inhuman of which we had ever heard."

CHAPTER VIII.

HAMILCAR BARCA IN AFRICA AND SPAIN.

(B. C. 258-219.)

DURING the desperate struggle for life on the part of the Carthaginians which has just been related, the Romans had, on the whole, behaved with moderation, or even with generosity, to their conquered foe. Had it pleased them to make one more effort and once again to risk a Roman army upon African soil, when they were invited to do so by the revolted Uticans and by the mercenaries themselves, there can be little doubt that Carthage would have fallen, and that there would have been no Second and no Third Punic War to relate; and had they dreamed of what lay deep hidden in Hamilcar's breast, or of the vast military genius which was being reared amidst those stormy scenes in his infant son, no exertion would have appeared too great to make, and no danger too desperate to dare, even to the cautious Roman Senate.

Rome during Mercenary War.

But when the genius of Hamilcar had saved Carthage and an expedition was being fitted out by the government to recover Sardinia which had revolted, the Romans, professing to believe that the armament was intended to act against themselves, and hatching up various fictitious grievances, threatened the Carthaginians with instant war if they dared to molest those who had thrown themselves on their protection. It was an act of unblushing and yet, at the same time, hypocritical effrontery on the part of the

Seizes Corsica and Sardinia.

Romans, hardly less base, and certainly more inexcusable, than had been their support of the Mamertines. But the Carthaginians had no choice but to submit to the right of the strongest, and they gave up not Sardinia only, but such parts of Corsica as they had ever claimed, and were compelled also to atone for their warlike intentions by paying an indemnity of 1,200 talents to the outraged and peace-loving Romans. Hamilcar once more showed his greatness by submitting to the inevitable; but the iron must have entered into his soul more deeply than ever, and he must have bound himself by still more binding oaths, if such could be found, to drink the cup of vengeance to the dregs when the time should come, or to perish in the attempt.

It might have been thought that the incapacity of the governing classes at Carthage and the double disasters which they had brought upon the country would have so seriously discredited them that Hamilcar Barca and his Patriotic Party would for a time, at all events, have been supreme in the State; but so far was this from being the case that, while Hamilcar was returning redhanded from the desperate victory which had saved the State, the party of Hanno was strong enough and impudent enough to place the deliverer upon his trial. He had been—they did not scruple to assert—the cause of the Mercenary War, for he had made promises of pay to his troops which he had not been able to perform! But it was beyond the power or the impudence even of the Carthaginian Peace Party to find him guilty, and the indictment seems to have fallen by its own weight or its own absurdity. There had been sharp conflicts for some time past between the War and the Peace Party, between the reformers and the reactionaries, at Carthage; and the events of the last few years had made the distinction between them sharper still. Around Hanno—called, one would think in irony, Hanno the great—gathered all that was ease-loving, all that was short-sighted, all that was selfish in the great republic. The commercial, the capitalist, the aristocratical interests seem, on the whole, to have followed his lead. Around Hamilcar Barca, on the other hand, gathered all that was generous and far-sighted; all, in fact, who were not content to live in peace, knowing that after them would come the deluge. Jewish kings, and those by no means the worst of their race, were often consoled when they heard on their repentance that the evil should come not in their own but in their sons' days. Not so was Hamilcar Barca and not such were his followers. But he was the head of a minority only, and finding that it was impossible to bring the majority over to his way of thinking, or to reform them by pressure from without, he determined to accept, or, it may be, to demand, a post in which he could serve his country more effectually. He obtained from the fears, the hatred, or the hopes of those opposed to him, the command of the army, an appointment which, for different reasons, must have been equally acceptable to his friends and his enemies. He first stamped out the embers of the Libyan revolt which were still smouldering in the country to the west of Carthage, and then, accompanied by the fleet, made his way slowly along the Mauritanian coast towards the immediate goal of his long-cherished schemes. When he reached the Pillars of Hercules (B. C. 237), on his own undivided responsibility, he crossed the straits and set foot in another country and another continent.

It was a bold step, but it was a wise one. If Carthage was to be saved at all from the ruin which Hamilcar and all keen-sighted men saw impending over it, it must be by Hamilcar and Hamilcar's army. But where in Africa could he raise an army? and how, when it was raised, could he have fed it there? The merchant princes of the city who, under the pressure of necessity, had enrolled themselves in his ranks to defend their all, had returned to their businesses or their pleasures as soon as the immediate danger was over. His own veterans, and thousands of other Libyans who under his training might have become as valuable as they, had been, by the most tragic of necessities exterminated by Hamilcar himself in the late war; and he could hardly hope just then to enlist others who could serve him as their predecessors might have done. A few of his Sicilian officers indeed, still followed the banner of their chief, and a few devoted friends and members of his family were left behind at Carthage, and these last, if they held no office in the State, showed that they could do more. If they were not allowed to govern, their ability and their patriotism yet gave them the divine right to rule. Of this nothing could deprive them ; and, like the Medici at Florence, or the Dukes of Orange in the Netherlands, this half-outlawed Barcine family actually received foreign embassies and concluded foreign treaties, as an independent body, co-ordinate with the Senate itself! But officers alone cannot make an army, and the Barcine family, powerful as it was, could not induce the money-loving Carthaginian merchants to untie their purse-strings in support of the distant and chimerical projects of Hamilcar. Nothing could be done at Carthage without money; and it was necesary for Hamilcar, if he would hold his own, not only to pay his troops but to remit large sums to Carthage in order to keep his supporters there together and to maintain his influence.

Hamilcar crosses to Spain.

Now it must have seemed to the eager eye of the Carthaginian patriot as though Spain had been created for the very purpose of supplying all these various and conflicting wants. It was from Spain, if from anywhere, and by Hamilcar, if by anyone, that Carthage might be saved. The previous history of the Spanish peninsula, and its immemorial connection with the Phœnicians, the fathers of the Carthaginian race, were all in favor of his projects. It was from Tarshish, or Tartessus, the district abutting on the very straits which he had to cross, that, as far back as the time of Solomon, had come the strange animals and the rich minerals which were landed in the harbours of Phœnicia proper, and which had so enlarged the ideas and transformed the instincts of the untravelled and exclusive Israelites. In more recent times Gades (Gaddir), on almost the same spot, itself a Phœnician colony, and boasting of a splendid temple to Melcarth, the patron god of both Tyre and Carthage, had served as an emporium for the products alike of the Scilly Isles and the Niger. For centuries Phœnicians had thus found in Spain what, centuries after, Spain herself was destined to find in Mexico and Peru; and it was principally to maintain her connection with this Eldorado that that long line of factories, known in later time as the *Metagonitæ Urbes*, had been planted at equal distances on the most suitable points of the barren Mauritanian coast. It was no slight advantage, too, for Hamilcar's purposes, that the connection of Spain with Carthage had hitherto been commercial only and not imperial; otherwise the deadly hatred which accompanied the spread of the Carthaginian rule in Africa must have sprung up in Spain as well, and Hamilcar would have had as much to do in pulling down as in building up, and his great constructive genius would not have had free play.

It was into such a land of promise that Hamilcar now passed. Its gold and silver mines, worked henceforward by Phœnician enterprise and skill, yielded many times as much as they had ever yielded before. With part of the produce Hamilcar paid the Spaniards themselves who had flocked to his standard; but, as with his Libyan followers at Ercte and at Eryx, it was the spell of his personal influence, far more than the gold he was now able to promise, and to give them, which kept them ever afterwards indissolubly attached to him. Part he remitted annually to Carthage, as the price he paid to her for being allowed to carry out his schemes for her safety and her empire. His soldiers, his generals, his own son-in-law, Hasdrubal, intermarried with the natives and made their interests one with their own. For nine long years — years to which Polybius, unfortunately, has devoted scarcely as many lines—Hamilcar worked steadily on, with his eyes, indeed, fixed upon the distant goal, but using no unworthy means in order to reach it; and when the end was almost in view, when it seemed that he might himself carry out his magnificent schemes, he died a soldier's death, fighting sword in hand, and left to the "lion's brood," as he loved to call—and well might he call—his sons, the rich but the dangerous heritage of his genius, his valour, and his undying hatred to Rome. We know all too little of Hamilcar's heroic struggles in Sicily, of his death-grapple with the revolted Libyans, and of the achievements of the last nine years of his life, alike in peace and war, in Spain. Did we know more, the world would, in all probability, admit that, in capacity if not in performance, in desert if not in fortune, he was the equal of his wonderful son. But we know at least enough to justify the judgment passed half a century later by one who was, assuredly, no friend to Carthage, and yet who, in spite of his narrow Roman prejudices, and his " *Delenda est Carthago*," judging solely by the traces he saw in Spain of what the great man had done pronounced emphatically that there was " no king like Hamilcar."

Hamilcar died in battle in the year B. C. 228. His son, Hannibal, was then not quite nineteen years of age, and was too young at once to succeed his father; but the command did not pass out of the family. It devolved on Hasdrubal, the son-in-law and faithful companion of Hamilcar, one who was endowed with something of his military talents and with no small part of his influence over men. The empire which Hamilcar had founded in Spain Hasdrubal organized and enlarged. Above all, he gave it a capital in New Carthage, a town which, from its admirable situation on the south-east coast, from its convenient harbour, and from its proximity to some rich silver mines which were just then discovered, seemed destined to be all that its proud name implied, and to spread the Phœnician arts and empire in Europe and the ocean beyond, even as the old Carthage had spread them over the Mediterranean and in Africa. Tribe after tribe of Iberians solicited the honour of enrolling themselves as subjects of a power which knew how to develop their resources in the interest of the natives as much as in its own; which found them work to do and paid them well for doing it; and when Hasdrubal, B. C. 221, in the eighth year of his command, fell by the hand of a Celtic assassin, he had extended, in the main by peaceful means, the rule of the Barricades from the Bætis to the Tagus.

[margin: Hasdrubal in Spain.]

Hannibal was now in his twenty-sixth year. The soldiers unanimously proclaimed him commander-in-chief, and their choice was ratified by the Carthaginian government. He was still young for the herculean task which lay before him; but he was strong in the blood of Hamilcar which was flowing in his veins, strong in the training which he had received, strong above all in the consciousness of his religious mission; none the less so that the secret of it remained locked in his own breast till all chance of fulfilling it in its entirety had passed away forever. It was not till he was an old man, living in exile at the court of King Antiochus, but, even so, an object of suspicion and of terror alike to the Syrian King and to the Roman Senate, that he told the simple story of that which, far more than military ambition, more even than the love of country and the consciousness of his supreme ability, had been the ruling motive of his life. In his ninth year, so he told Antiochus, when his father, Hamilcar, was about to set out for his command in Spain, and was sacrificing to the supreme god of his country, he bade the attendants withdraw, and asked the little Hannibal if he would like to go with him to the wars. The boy eagerly assented. "Lay your hand then," said Hamilcar, "on the sacrifice and swear eternal enmity to the Romans." Hannibal swore, and well did he keep his oath. It suits the purposes of Livy to say that Hannibal was a man "of worse than Punic faith, with no reverence for what was true or sacred, serving no god and keeping no oath." The accusation is untrue in every point; but even Livy must have himself admitted that to this oath, at least, he was true, that this God at least he reverenced, and that this religious mission he kept before his mind and carried out to the best of his superlative ability, from that day even to the day of his death. From the age of nine to eighteen he had watched in silence the patient

development of his father's far-sighted designs. From
eighteen to twenty-five his had been in the main, the
hand to strike and the will to carry out, while Hasdrubal's had been the mind to plan and the right to command; and now in his twenty-sixth year he was called
upon to stand alone, to enter upon his great inheritance
of obligation, and by his patience and his impetuosity,
by his powers of persuasion and of command, by his
energy, and his inventiveness, by his arts and by his arms
to redeem his early pledge.

But why had the Romans been looking calmly on
while the Barcine family were winning back for themselves, and for the State at large in Spain,
all, and more than all, that they had lost in
Sicily? They had to face a formidable
enemy nearer Rome. The whole of the region to the
north of the Apennines and the Rubicon still belonged
to the Gauls, and one of their tribes, the Boii, who dwelt
between the Apennines and the Po, frightened at the
work of the popular champion Flaminius—the division
of the lands which had once belonged to their Senonian
brethren amongst the poorer citizens of Rome—and
fearing that their own turn would come next, determined
to anticipate the evil day. A movement amongst the
Gauls was known by a name of terror (*tumultus*) even
in the later days of the Republic, and at this time the
memories of the Allia and of the burning of Rome were
too fresh to allow the Roman Senate to take any half-
measures. A Gallic man and woman were buried alive
by order of the Senate in the Ox market, in hopes of
thus fulfilling the dread oracle which promised a share
of Roman soil to the Gauls. A *levée en masse* of the
military resources of the confederation was decreed;
and those actually under arms in various parts of the

Gallic war in Italy.

Roman dominions are said by Polybius to have reached the astonishing number of 170,000 men. "Against such a nation under arms," as Polybius significantly adds, Hannibal was on the point of marching with 20,000 men!

But the terrors of the Gauls were destined, on this occasion (B. C. 225), soon to pass away. The Transalpine barbarians, who fought, many of them, stark naked, with two javelins (*gæsa*) in their hands, or with swords that bent at the first blow, fell an easy prey to the skilful dispositions of the Roman armies. Surrounded by the two consuls near Telamon in Etruria, they were almost exterminated, and the Roman Capitol was filled with the standards and the golden necklaces and the bracelets which were the trophies of the victory. The Romans followed up their success with vigour, and transferred the war into the enemy's country. The Boians suffered the fate which they had anticipated and which they had in vain tried to avert, and the name of Italy might be now extended, on the east of the peninsula at all events, to the line of the Po. In the following year, C. Flaminius, a man whose name has been already mentioned, and of whom we shall hear again at a critical point in the Second Punic War, led a Roman army, for the first time in their history, across that river and, attacking the Insubrians, took their capital city, Mediolanum (Milan); while Marcellus, the consul of the year B. C. 223, was able to dedicate, in the temple of Jupiter Feretrius, the *spolia opima* which he had taken in single combat from the Gallic chieftain. The Romans riveted their grasp on their new conquests by founding, *more suo*, two new colonies, Placentia and Cremona, on either side of the Po, and by completing that imperishable monument of their organizing and constructive genius, the Flaminia

Via, the great military road of Northern Italy, from Rome to Ariminum. Nor were these precautions taken a moment too soon; for before the Romans had established themselves firmly on the line of the Po, Hannibal was on the Ebro; and to the surprise of the Roman Senate, and the terror of not a few among the Roman citizens, it was now apparent for the first time that the approaching contest might possibly be waged, not in Africa for the possession of Carthage, but in Italy for the possession of Rome.

But we must now return to Hannibal. During the first two years of his command (B.C. 221–219) the young general had crossed the Tagus, and had reduced the whole of Spain to the south of the Ebro to submission. But there was one exception. The town of Saguntum, a Greek colony— so the inhabitants boasted—from Zacynthus, and near the site of the modern Murviedro (Muriveteres), though far to the south of the Ebro, the stipulated boundary line between the two powers, had formed an alliance with Rome; and Hasdrubal, nay Hannibal himself, had up to this time forborne to attack it. Hannibal knew that he could choose his own time for picking a quarrel, and now the ground seemed clear before him. To the Roman ambassadors who came to warn him not to attack any ally of theirs, he gave an evasive answer, and referred them to the Carthaginian Senate, while he prosecuted the preparations for the siege with redoubled vigour. For eight months the Saguntines held out, and when they could hold out no longer, the chiefs kindled a fire in the market-place, and threw into it first their valuables, and then themselves. Hannibal, who had been wounded in the course of the siege, divided a part of the booty amongst his troops; a part he dispatched

Hannibal besieges Saguntum.

to Carthage, in hopes of committing those who received it beyond the hope of recall to his great enterprise. He then retreated into winter quarters at New Carthage, and, dismissing his Spanish troops to the enjoyments of their homes for the winter, bade them return to the camp at the approach of spring, prepared for whatever it might bring forth.

The Romans had by their dilatoriness allowed Saguntum to fall; but they were now not slow in demanding satisfaction for it. An embassy was sent direct to Carthage demanding the surrender of Hannibal, the author of the outrage, on pain of instant war. The Romans fondly hoped that the Carthaginian peace party would seize the opportunity of compassing their chief end at the easy price of the surrender of so troublesome a servant, or master, as was Hannibal. But the gold of Hannibal had done its work, and was more potent than Hanno's honeyed tongue. The peace party dared hardly to mutter their half-hearted counsels; and when Q. Fabius, the chief of the embassy, held up his toga, saying, "I carry here peace and war; choose ye which ye will have;"—"Give us whichever you please," replied the Carthaginians. "War, then," said Fabius; and the decision was greeted as is usual in times of such excitement, by the shortsighted acclamations of the masses. They feel the enthusiasm of the moment; they do not realize its tremendous responsibility. They see with their mind's eye the pomp and pride and circumstance of war; they do not see its horrors and devastations. They hear the din of preparation; they are deaf, till it is too late, to the cry of agony or to the wail of the bereaved; else war would never, as experience proves it so often is, be welcomed as a boon; it would be submitted to only as the most dire necessity.

War declared.

The die was now cast, and the arena was cleared for the foremost man of his race and his time, perhaps the mightiest military genius of any race and of any time— one with whom, in this particular, it were scant justice to compare either Alexander, or Cæsar, or Marlborough, and who, immeasurably above him as he is in all moral qualities, may, on the score of military greatness, be named without injustice in the same breath with Napoleon, and Napoleon alone.

CHAPTER IX.

SECOND PUNIC WAR.

(B. C. 218–201.)

PASSAGE OF THE RHONE AND THE ALPS.

B. C. 218.

THERE was still a brief interval of preparation before the rival nations could meet in battle array, and Hannibal utilized it to the utmost. He took measures for the safety of Spain during his absence by garrisoning it with 15,000 trusty Lybians, while Lybia he garrisoned with as many trusty Spaniards, thus making, in a certain sense, each country a security for the good behaviour of the other. The supreme command in Spain he committed to his younger brother, Hasdrubal, and during the winter friendly messages passed and repassed between New Carthage and the chieftains of Transalpine and Cisalpine Gaul. It is said that negotiations were carried on even with Antigonus, king of Macedonia, to arrange for a combined attack on Italy from east and west at once.

Preparations of Hannibal.

But was Italy to be reached by land or sea? The

Phœnicians had not yet lost their maritime skill; the sea was their home, and, had the Carthaginians so willed it, a fleet might have been collected in the harbour of New Carthage which probably could have bidden defiance to any that the Romans could have raised against it. Why, then, did Hannibal, the greatest product of the Phœnician race, perhaps of all the Semitic races—and certainly the noblest embodiment of the national spirit and will of Carthage—prefer a land journey which involved the crossing of broad and rapid rivers, of lofty and unknown mountain chains, amidst races proverbial for their fickleness and faithlessness; a journey which would take months instead of days, and which, if it failed at all, must fail altogether? Was it that the Carthaginian government was backward or unable to supply the ships? or was it that Hannibal miscalculated the distance and under-estimated the dangers of the route which he chose? Perhaps both in part. It is no slur upon the military qualities of the great Carthaginian to suppose that he did not fully realize the difficulties of the task he was undertaking, a task which no description given by interested and friendly mountaineers could have brought adequately home to him. But what, no doubt, especially determined him to make the attempt was the alliance which he had already concluded with the formidable tribes of Gaul itself and of Northern Italy. Swooping down from the Alps on the rich fields of Italy, his numbers swelled by the reinforcements he would have gathered in his course from Farther Gaul, he would, by a first success, rally all their brethren in Hither Gaul to his standard. The basis of his operations for the Italian war would then be no longer Spain or Gaul, but Italy itself; and it would be strange indeed if the Samnites and the Etrus-

He determines to go by land.

cans, the Umbrians and the Lucanians, whom Rome had so recently and so hardly conquered, did not flock to his standard as he swept victoriously on towards the South to wreak condign vengeance on the common oppressor of them all. Such were the hopes, not altogether ill-founded, with which Hannibal undertook the gigantic enterprise which astonished and still astonishes the world.

The army with which he set out from New Carthage early in the summer of B.C. 218, consisted of 90,000 foot, of 12,000 horse, and of thirty-seven elephants; a force far smaller than that which the Carthaginians had often employed before in their petty conflicts with the Sicilian Greeks. He crossed the Ebro, and, not without heavy loss to himself, subdued the hostile Spanish tribes beyond that river who, so far as a treaty could make them so, were already the allies of Rome and, as the Romans believed, a firm bulwark against Carthaginian encroachments. Leaving Hanno with 10,000 foot and 10,000 horse to hold the country which he had conquered, he actually sent back to their homes 10,000 more of his already much-thinned army, men whom, like Gideon at the Well of Trembling, he saw to be faint-hearted and therefore cared not to retain in his service. Then, confident in those that remained, and in the future, he crossed the Pyrenees and, without opposition from the Gallic tribes, reached the Rhone in safety.

Size of his army.

The Romans, as behind hand in their arms as in their diplomacy, still, it would seem, believed that the contest which was beginning would be fought out at a distance from their own shores. Scipio, as had been arranged, started from Pisa and, coasting leisurely along to Marsalia (Marseilles) learned to his extreme surprise that Hannibal

Hannibal's passage of the Rhone.

had already crossed the Ebro and the Pyrenees, and was in full march through Gaul.

Well knowing that a prolonged delay might render the Alps impassable for that year, and, if for that year, perhaps forever, Hannibal, when he found that the Gauls were disposed to dispute his passage, had sent Hanno with a considerable force two short days' march up the river to a point whence he could cross unopposed. After a brief pause to refresh his men, Hanno moved down the left of the stream and kindled the beacon fires for which Hannibal was anxiously waiting. He had already laden with his light-armed horsemen the boats which he had hired from the natives, while the canoes which he had extemporized were filled with the most active of his infantry, and he now gave the order to put across. The signal was obeyed with alacrity; and the horses swam the stream, attached by ropes to the boats which carried their riders. Down poured the barbarians in disorder from their fortified camp, fully confident that they could bar the passage; but the flaming camp behind them, and the fierce onset of Hanno's force upon their rear, showed them that they had been outgeneralled, and they fled in confusion, leaving Hannibal to transport the rest of his army in peace. The army rested that night on the Italian side of the river, and on the following day the most unwieldy, and not the least sagacious part of his force, the thirty-seven elephants, were cajoled, as at Messana, in the First Punic War, after the battle of Panormus, into entrusting themselves to a raft. Some, in their blind panic, leapt into the mid river, drowning their drivers; but raising instinctively their trunks above their heads, they reached the opposite bank in safety.

But the real difficulties of the undertaking were only

now beginning. How little accurate knowledge of the localities through which he had to pass Hannibal can have gained even by the most careful inquiries, is evident from the obscurity which has always hung over his march itself. That march riveted the attention of the world; it was described by eye-witnesses, and one great historian, at least, who lived within fifty years of the events he was recording, took the trouble to go over the ground and verify for himself the reports which had reached him. Yet many of its details and even its general direction are still matters of dispute. The fact is that the ancients, even the most observant of them, had no eye for the minute observation of nature, and no wish to describe its phenomena in detail. Accordingly there is hardly a pass in the whole Western Alps which has not been made—as though they were cities contending for the honour of a Homer's birth—to lay claim, with some show of reason, to be the scene of Hannibal's march. Yet broad geographical facts, and the few data of time and place given by Polybius, enable us, in the light of recent researches, to restrict the choice to two, if not to one, of the total number. These passes are the Little Mont Cenis, to the north of the Cottian, and the Little St. Bernard to the north of the Graian Alps. Mont Cenis appears to have been unknown to the ancients as a practicable passage; moreover it would have brought Hannibal down among hostile Ligurian tribes. The Little St. Bernard, on the other hand, was not only the easiest of approach and one of the lowest available passes, being only 7,000 feet high, but once and again in history, it had already poured down the Celts of the north upon the plains of Italy. It was in fact the highway between Transalpine and Cisalpine Gaul. Where

Passage of the Alps selected.

Celtic tribes had passed before, the expected ally and deliverer of the Celts might well pass now, and with this hypothesis nearly all the facts given by Polybius will be found to agree. On the Italian side of the pass lay the Salassians, the hereditary friends of the Insubrians, who would give their messengers, as they passed to and fro, a safe-conduct, and would secure to Hannibal himself the rest and refreshment which after his own passage he would so sorely need.

He had crossed the Rhone at a spot "nearly four days' journey from the sea," probably the reach above Roquemaure. He marched thence, we are told, four days up the river to the spot where the Isère joins the Rhone, the apex of the triangle, afterwards called the "Island of the Allobroges." It was then, as now, populous and well-cultivated, and Hannibal, it would seem, preferred to continue his march northward through its champaign country rather than to take the shorter route eastward by following at once the mountain valley of the Isère. There would be enough of mountain climbing later on. Accordingly he followed the course of "the river" northward, as far probably as Vienne; then, turning eastward, he took the part of one of two rival brothers whom he found contending for the throne, and so obtained from him supplies of food and clothing and trusty guides. Then, once more striking the Rhone where it leaves the frontiers of Savoy, he reached the first outwork of the Alps, probably the Mont du Chat, a chain 4,000 feet high.

Hannibal had taken ten days to cross the Island of the Allobroges, and had hitherto met with no difficulty or mishap of any kind; but here, where the great physical difficulties began, the first symptoms of open hostility appeared also. The native guides had returned to their master, and amidst the precipitous ravines the Numidian cavalry were no longer formidable. The one track over the mountains, the Chevelu Pass, was occupied by the mountaineers in force; but Hannibal, learning that it was their practice to return to their homes for the night, lighted his camp fires, as usual, at nightfall, and, leaving the bulk of his army behind, climbed the steep in the darkness with the most active of his troops, and occupied the position which had been just vacated by the natives. Slowly and toilfully on the following day his army wound up the pass, aware that Hannibal was waiting to receive them at its head, but exposed to loss and to annoyance at every step from the attacks of the enemy who moved along the heights above. The path was rough and narrow, and the horses and the sumpter animals, unused to such ground and scared by the confusion, lost their footing, and either rolled headlong down the precipices themselves or, jostling against their fellows in the agony of their wounds, rolled them down with the baggage which they carried. To an army crossing a lofty mountain, baggage and provisions are a matter of life and death, and Hannibal risked his own life and those of his few brave followers to save the rest. Charging along the heights, he put the enemy to flight, and the immediate peril was surmounted.

The first ascent.

For the next three days Hannibal followed the Tarentaise, or the rich valley of the Isère, which he had struck on his descent from the pass, and there was now no symptom of hostility or opposition. On the fourth day, the people whose homesteads he was passing, presented themselves to him, bearing garlands and branches of trees, the signs

The main ascent.

of goodwill, and proffering provisions, nay, even hostages, as pledges of their sincerity. But the wary Carthaginian was not to be deceived by a foe who offered him gifts. He received them kindly, accepted their provisions and their hostages, but pursued his march as one prepared for treachery. The cavalry and beasts of burden led the way, and at some distance behind came Hannibal himself with his infantry. They were now entering the defile which leads up to the main mountain wall of the Alps, the one barrier which still separated Hannibal from the land of his hopes, and the cliffs rose more precipitously above, and the torrent (the Réclus) foamed more angrily below, as they neared the spot where both would be left behind.

Hardly were the infantry well entangled in the defile, when the stones which came thundering down from the heights above showed that the barbarians had at length thrown off the mask. The destruction of the whole army seemed imminent; but Hannibal drew up, or rather drew back, his part of it to an escarpment of white rock, which rose in a strong position facing the entrance of the gorge, far enough back, it would seem, to be out of the reach of the descending stones, but not so far as that he could not keep the attention of the enemy concentrated on himself. The cavalry at the head of the column pressed on almost unmolested till they emerged into more open and therefore safer ground. The white gypsum rock—*la roche blanche*—as it is called by the natives, still stands conspicuous in front of the grey limestone mountain which towers above it; and here, if at no earlier point in the route, the traveller may well feel that he is treading the very ground which Hannibal trod, and looking upon the solemn assemblage of peaks and pinnacles, of mountain

The white rock.

torrent and of mountain valley, on which his eager eye must have rested in this supreme moment of anxiety and peril. Here Hannibal stood to arms, with half his forces, the whole night through; and the following morning everything like organized resistance had disappeared from the cliffs which flanked the pass. And on the ninth day the whole cavalcade reached the summit in safety.

It was only nine days since Hannibal had begun the first ascent of the Alps; but they were days of hard work and danger, and he now rested for a time to recruit his troops, and to allow stragglers to rejoin him. But no stragglers came. Those who had dropped behind from exhaustion or from their wounds, on such a route, were not likely to be heard of more. Only some beasts of burden which had lagged behind, or had slipped down the rocks, had in the struggle for bare life managed to regain their feet, and, following instinctively in the footprints of the army, now came straggling in one after the other, half dead from starvation and fatigue. It was a sorry spot on which to recruit. It was late in October; the snows were gathering thick on the peaks above the Col; and the troops who had been drawn from burning Africa or from sunny Spain shivered in the mountain air, which is keen and frosty even in the height of summer. Rest only gave them time to recollect the difficulties through which they had so hardly passed, and to picture, perhaps to magnify, perils which were still to come.

The summit.

Symptoms of despondency appeared; but Hannibal, seizing the opportunity, called his troops together and addressed them in a few stirring words. There was one topic of consolation, and only one. Below their feet lay one of the Italian valleys, and winding far away among its narrow lawns and humble homesteads could be seen the silver

Hannibal's speech.

thread of one of the feeders of the Baltea torrent which leaped forth from where they stood. It seemed in the clear atmosphere, which Alpine climbers know so well, that they had but to take a step or two down, and to be in possession. "The people who dwell along that river," cried Hannibal in the inspiration of the moment, "are your sworn friends. Ye are standing already, as ye see, on the Acropolis of Italy; yonder"—and he pointed to the spot in the far horizon where, with his mind's eye, he could see the goal of all his hopes, and the object of his inextinguishable and majestic hate—" yonder lies Rome." The spirits of his men rose at his words, and on the morrow the descent began.

After a toilsome climb, the first steps of a descent are always pleasantly deceptive, and there was now no sign of an enemy, unless indeed a few skulking marauders might be so called. But the descent was not less dangerous, and perhaps still more destructive, than the ascent. *Dangers of the descent.* The Alps rise more sheer from the plain on the Italian than on the French side, and the slope is almost everywhere steeper. The snow too began to fall, hiding dangers which would otherwise have stared them in the face. A false step on such a gradient would have been fatal anyhow, and the curtain of snow made false steps to be both numerous and inevitable. The army had to cross what seems to have been, in the greater cold which was then prevalent throughout Europe, a glacier or an ice-slope covered with a thin coating of newly-fallen snow. This was soon trampled into a solid sheet of ice, on which the men kept sliding and rolling down, while the beasts of burden, breaking through the bridges of frozen snow which concealed crevasses beneath, stuck fast and were frozen to death. At last, the head of the column reached a projecting crag round which neither man nor beast could creep. An avalanche or a landslip had carried away some three hundred yards of the track, and even the eye of Hannibal failed to discover a practicable route elsewhere. Destruction stared the army in the face; but Hannibal drew them off to a kind of hog's back, from which the snow had been just shovelled, and, pitching his camp there, directed his men with such engineering skill, and with such implements as they could muster, to repair the broken passage. Never was an Alpine road made under greater difficulties; but the men worked for their lives, and by the following day the horses were able to creep round the dangerous spot, and to descend till they found a scanty herbage. The elephants, owing to their uncouth appearance, had hitherto enjoyed immunity from the attacks of the natives; but they too now had their share of suffering. It was three whole days before the roadway was sufficiently wide and strong for them to pass. On the high Alps on which they then were, neither tree nor pasture could be found, and from regions of Arctic rigour these inhabitants of the torrid zone made their way down, half dead with cold and hunger. After the great danger had been surmounted, the descent became more practicable. The eyes of the perishing soldiers were soon gladdened with the sight of umbrageous trees, of upland lawns, and even of human habitations, and three days saw them safe in the valley of Aosta below.

The passage—1,200 stadia of mountain climbing—had been accomplished; but was it worth the price which had been paid for it? Of the army which had crossed the Pyrenees scarcely half had lived to cross the Alps. Without provisions, without a commissariat, without even an assured base of

<small>The passage accomplished.</small>

operations, or the certainty of reinforcements, Hannibal was about to enter on a war which stands forth without a parallel in ancient history. With 20,000 foot and 6,000 horse he was about to attack a power which had only lately put into the field to serve against the Gauls an army of 170,000 men. And in what condition was this handful, this forlorn hope, of soldiers? The cold and hunger, and exposure and fatigue, of fifteen days of mountaineering had done their work with them. "They had been reduced to the condition of beasts," says the accurate and unimaginative Greek historian; "they looked not like men but like their phantoms or their shadows," said the Roman general who was about to meet them in the field, and, as he thought, like shadows to sweep them away. Under any general but Hannibal, and, it may also be added, with any enemy who were not so dilatory as the Romans, the remnant of the Carthaginian army would have conquered the Alps only to perish in the plains of the Po. That Hannibal crossed the Alps is a marvel; but that with troops so weakened he was able after a few days' delay to chastise the hostile barbarians, to take from them their city of Turin, to force some of them to join his army, and then to face all the power of Rome, is a greater marvel still.

It is difficult throughout this period of the war, and, indeed, throughout the whole of it, to withdraw the attention even for a moment from its presiding genius. With sound judgment did the Romans, who calumniated his character and tried sometimes to make light even of his abilities, call the war which was now beginning, not the Second Punic War, but the War of Hannibal. His form it was which haunted their imagination and their memories; his name was for centuries the terror of old and of young alike. Nearly two hundred years later the frivolous and the pleasure-loving Horace pays Hannibal the homage of a mention which is always serious and often awe-stricken. Once in his Odes he is "the perfidious," but three times over he is "the dread Hannibal;" and rising, with a thrill of horror, into epic dignity, he compares the march of the Carthaginian through Italy to the careering of the east wind over those Sicilian waters which had engulfed so many Roman fleets, or to that most terrible and magnificent of sights, the rush of the flames through a blazing forest of pines.

CHAPTER X.

BATTLES OF TREBIA AND TRASIMENE.

(B. C. 218-217.)

IT is time now to ask what the Romans were doing to meet the storm. Publius Scipio, after his encounter with the enemy's cavalry on the Rhone, had marched up the river to the camp which Hannibal had just left, and discovering that he was already off for Italy had flattered his soldiers and, perhaps, himself, by representing his march as a flight. He showed, however, that he was himself alive to the gravity of the occasion by returning at once to Italy, while he sent his brother Cneius with the bulk of his army on to Spain. As for the Senate, the last message that had reached them from that country had told them of the taking of Saguntum, and they had accordingly despatched troops who were to stop Hannibal at the Ebro. The news they now received was to the effect that Hannibal had crossed, not the Ebro only, but the Pyrenees, the Rhone,

Measures of Roman Senate.

and the Alps, and he might be expected at any moment across the Po. They now awoke—they could not help waking—to the character of the war. Orders were sent to Sempronius to return at once from Sicily for the protection of Italy. He obeyed with a heavy heart, and sending his troops some by land and some by sea, bade them rejoin him at Ariminum, an important town on the Adriatic, situated just where the great Flaminian road ends and the plain of the Po begins.

But meanwhile Scipio and Hannibal had come into collision, and the first Roman blood in the great duel had been shed. From the valley of the Dora Baltea Hannibal had advanced towards the Po; but by turning aside westward to chastise the Taurini, he had given Scipio time to cross that river near Placentia, and to throw a bridge over the Ticinus, a stream which, issuing from the Lake Verbanus (Maggiore), flows southwards into the Po near Pavia. Not far from this stream the armies, or rather a part of them, met in battle. Both generals had led out their cavalry in person to make a reconnaissance in force. Scipio, to compensate, as he hoped, for his inferiority in that arm, had also taken some light infantry with him; but these proved one of the causes of his defeat. Fearing to be trampled under foot by the cavalry, they retired behind their supports. The Gallic horse, who formed his centre, gallantly withstood the charge of the bridled Spanish cavalry of Hannibal. But the bridleless Numidian cavalry, on which he most relied, and which he had placed upon his wings, outflanking the enemy, and riding round towards their rear, first fell on the retreating infantry, and dealt them the very death which they had tried to avoid; then, charging in their peculiar fashion, sometimes in twos and threes, sometimes in a compact

Battle of Ticinus.

mass, they fell on the Roman centre. This decided the conflict. Scipio received a dangerous wound, and was only, as it is said, rescued by his son, a youth of seventeen, who risked his own to save his father's life, and lived to conquer Hannibal at Zama, to finish the war, and to win the proud name of Africanus.

The retreat of the Romans, though a hasty retreat, was not a rout; but it was ominous of what was to follow.

Hannibal's advance. It proved the superiority of the Numidian cavalry to any which the Romans could bring against them; and, seeing that the plains of Lombardy would always give them the advantage, Scipio determined to place the Po between himself and the enemy. He crossed in safety; but a party of 600 men, who were left behind to cover the retreat and to cut down the bridge, fell into Hannibal's hands. Unable to cross the river there, Hannibal marched up its right bank till he found a convenient place. He there threw a bridge of boats across, and then marching down on the left side of the Po crossed, as it would seem, the Trebia, and pitched his camp six miles to the south of Placentia, under the strong walls of which Scipio's army lay entrenched.

The whole country to the north of the Po, with the exception of the recently planted colony of Cremona,

Hannibal selects his ground for another battle. was now lost to the Romans. Already, before the battle of the Ticinus, the Ligurians and the Gallic tribes along the upper Po had joined Hannibal; and now embassies flowed in from almost all the remaining tribes of Cisalpine Gaul, offering their alliance. Scipio was now alarmed for his safety; better, he thought, the exposed hill-sides than the fortified camp before Placentia, if only he could quit himself of these Gauls, so formidable as enemies, so doubly formidable as allies. Accordingly he

broke up his camp by night, put, as it would seem, the
Trebia between himself and Hannibal, and, marching
southward, took posession of some high ground formed
by a spur of the Northern Apennines. It was a perilous
operation, for his line of retreat took him near to Hannibal, who discovered the movement before it was completed; and had not the Numidian horsemen sent in
pursuit turned aside to plunder the deserted camp, it
might have fared ill with the whole Roman army. But
the hills to the west of the Trebia, on which Scipio's
camp now lay, protected him at all events from the
dreaded cavalry, and he could afford to wait patiently
for the arrival of Sempronius from Sicily. Why Hannibal did not seize what seems to have been a golden
opportunity, and, thrusting himself between the two
armies, crush Sempronius as he crossed the level country, so favourable for cavalry, between Ariminum and
the Trebia, must remain a mystery. But the junction
was effected without any opposition from him, and he
now found himself confronted by two consular armies of
40,000 men. Scipio, impeded by his wound, and appre-
hensive of the result, as one who had already felt the
weight of Hannibal's arm, was for delay. Sempronius,
on the contrary, was eager to fight, for if Rome could
not be defended by two consular armies, it might well
seem that she could not be defended at all. A petty
success won by his cavalry over some squadrons of
Numidian horse, who were harrying the country, made
him doubly confident. Hannibal knew his man, and
knew also that the consular elections at Rome were not
far off. If a battle was not fought in the next few days,
it would be fought not by Sempronius, but by his successor. Accordingly he laid all his plans for the battle
which he knew he could at any moment force on.

In the plain of the Trebia, and on the eastern side of it where Hannibal still lay, was a water-course over- grown with bulrushes and brambles, and deep enough with its steep banks to hide even cavalry. It was the very place for an ambuscade, for no one would expect an ambush in a country which seemed to the ordinary glance so level and unbroken. Hannibal saw his chance, and here, during the night, he placed his brother Mago, with two thousand horse and foot whom he had picked out for the purpose. Mago was young and adventurous, and sprang at the task assigned him. At dawn of day Hannibal sent his Numidian horse across the river, with orders to ride up to the enemy's camp and draw them out. Sempronius was ready to be caught; and the Numidian horse falling back, as they had been instructed, across the river, drew the Roman horse and foot, flushed with their apparent success, after them.

Plan of battle.

It was mid-winter. Heavy rain had fallen on the previous night, and the swollen waters of the Trebia rose to the breasts of the soldiers as they made their way across. When they reached the opposite bank they found themselves face to face with Hannibal's army. Sleet was falling fast, and the wind blew icily cold over the plains which lay between the eternal snows of the Alps and those which had lately fallen on the Apennines. In the hurry of the call to arms the Romans had taken no breakfast; and now, faint with hunger and numbed with the cold, they stood on the river's bank with the day's work still all before them. Hannibal, on the contrary, had ordered his men to take their breakfasts by their firesides, and then, buckling on their armour and saddling their horses, to remain in the shelter of their tents till the sig-

Battle of the Trebia.

Plan of Trebia.

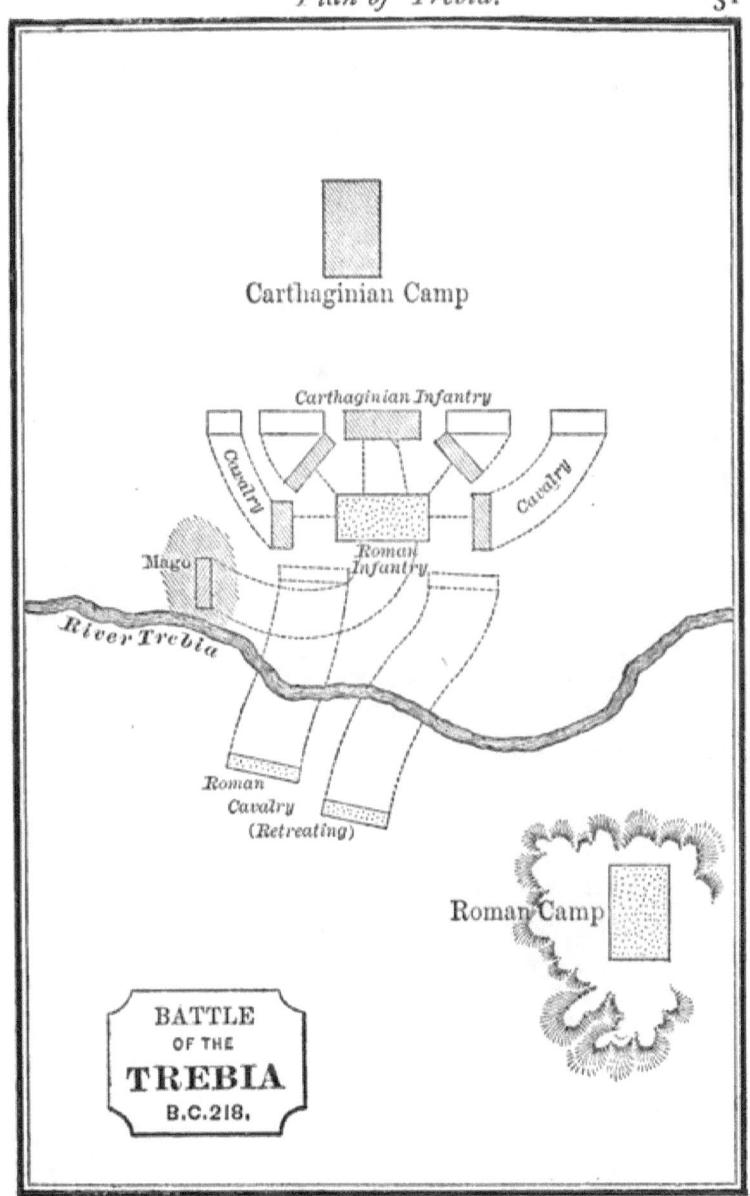

nal should be given. Hastily throwing forward his light-armed troops and sharpshooters, to occupy the attention of the enemy, he now drew up his main line of battle immediately behind them; his Gallic, Spanish, and African troops in the centre, and his cavalry and elephants on the wings. The light-armed troops, having played with the Romans for a time, fell back between the intervals of the maniples behind, and the 4,000 Roman cavalry, finding themselves suddenly exposed to the attacks of more than double their number, broke and fled, leaving the dreaded Numidians to attack the infantry on their now unprotected flanks. Many of the Roman infantry stood their ground nobly, and for a short time kept the conflict doubtful; but then Mago, starting up from his ambuscade, fell upon their rear. Surrounded as they were on every side, one body of 10,000 men yet fought their way, with the courage of despair, through the Carthaginian ranks in front, and managed by a circuitous route to make their way to Placentia; but the rout of the remainder was complete. In vain they tried to reach the river which they had crossed so imprudently in the morning, for they were ridden down as they fled by the Numidian cavalry, who seemed to be everywhere amongst them, or were trampled to death by the elephants. A mere remnant escaped across the river, and were saved from further pursuit by the violence of the storm.

Well might Hannibal rejoice at the victory which he had won. He had beaten two Roman armies; the difficulties and the dangers and the disasters of his march from Spain had been crowned by a triumphant success; and it was doubtful whether any force remained to bar his march upon Rome. In vain did Sempronius try to disguise the magnitude of

Results of battle.

the disaster which had overtaken him. He had fought a battle, so he sent word to Rome, and it was only the storm which had prevented him from winning a decisive victory. How came it then, people asked—and well they might ask—that Hannibal was in possession of the field of battle, that the Gauls had joined him to a man, that the Roman camp had been broken up, and that the Roman armies—all that remained of them—were cowering in the fortified camp before Placentia or behind the walls of Cremona, while Hannibal's cavalry were scouring the fair plains of Lombardy? The truth was too clear; but the spirit of the Roman Senate showed no signs of breaking. They prepared even now to take the offensive. Armaments were despatched to the remotest corners of their dominions,—to Tarentum, for instance, to Sicily and to Sardinia; a new navy was fitted out, the consular elections held, and four more legions levied; "for," says Polybius emphatically, "the Romans are never so terrible as when real terrors gird them in on every side."

At the first approach of spring Hannibal attempted to cross the Apennines; but a storm more terrible even than those of the Alps drove him back to his winter quarters. When the spring began in earnest, Hannibal made a second, and this time a successful, attempt to cross the mountains, which lay immediately to the south of his position. *Passage of the Apennines.* Two routes alone seem to have been deemed practicable by the newly elected consuls for his advance into Central Italy. The one was by the Central Apennines in the direction of Fæsulæ; the other along the coast of the Adriatic. Cn. Servilius lay at Ariminum, prepared to block the one against his passage; Flaminius at Arretium, in the heart of Etruria, to block the other. But Hannibal did not confine himself to any authorized routes, nor did he care to strike only when he could do so by the recognized laws of war. His genius could dispense with both. Accordingly he crossed the Apennines where they approach the western coast of Italy, near the head waters of the Marca, and reached, without serious difficulty, the plains of the Arno near Lucca.

The region which lies between Lucca and Fæsulæ is intersected by lakes, and the melting of the snow on the hills had then caused the Arno to overflow its banks, making the whole one vast morass.

Passage of the marshes.

How would his army stand this renewal of horrors in the very land of promise? Of the fidelity and courage of his Libyan and Spanish veterans Hannibal was well assured, but as regards the Gauls, his newly formed allies, it was far otherwise. He placed them, therefore, in the middle of his line of march, that they might be encouraged by the troops who led the van, or be driven back to their duty, if they tried to turn homeward, by Mago and his cavalry who were to bring up the rear. For four days and three nights the army went toiling on through the water or the mud, unable to find a dry spot on which they could either sit down or sleep. The Gauls, driven forward by Mago's cavalry over ground which was all the more difficult to pass from the trampling it had already undergone, and unused to fatigue, stumbled amidst the deep morasses, and fell to rise no more. Disease attacked the horses and carried away their hoofs. Hannibal himself, tortured with ophthalmia, rode on the one elephant which had survived the last year's campaign, and escaped only with the loss of an eye.

At last the invading army reached the high ground of Fæsulæ, and there Hannibal learned, one would think with surprise, that the consuls were still at their respective sta-

Character of Flaminius.

tions some fifty miles apart, and with the Apennines between them. Servilius, it would seem, was still expecting the attack of Hannibal on his front at Ariminum when the Carthaginians had already crossed the mountains and had shown themselves in his rear at Fæsulæ. The other consul, Flaminius, was at Arretium, to the south of the central chain of the Apennines, and, lying as he did between Hannibal and the probable line of his advance on Rome, was likely to bear the brunt of his assault. Flaminius was a marked man in more ways than one. Of a plebeian family, he had long since incurred the deadly hatred of the patricians by preferring the interests of the citizens at large to those of their order; a senator, he was hated by the Senate because he had supported a law which forbade senators to amass large sums by trading with merchant vessels. Sixteen years before, as tribune of the people, he had carried, in spite of the interested opposition of the aristocracy, a law for the division of the conquered Gallic territory in Umbria amongst the poorer citizens. Such a man the Senate might fear as well as hate, and envy as well as fear. But no efforts and no malice of theirs could blot out those splendid monuments of his recent censorship, the Circus and the great military road which, to this day, bear his name. And now, in the year 217—a year so big with the destinies of Rome—the popular favour secured for him, in spite of all the old opposition, a second consulship. If the wave of destruction which was breaking over Italy was to be driven back at all, his, the people were determined, should be the hand to do it.

The winter at Rome had passed amidst gloom and doubt; the augurs and the priests alone had a good time of it, and their hands were

Hostility of patricians to Flaminius.

full enough. The general anxiety gave birth to portents, and was, in its turn, increased by them. When Flaminius was elected consul, the omens increased in number and in horror. In the vegetable market an infant six months old shouted "Triumph!" In the cattle market an ox rushed up the stairs of a house to the third story and threw itself out of the window; fiery ships were seen in the heavens; and from all parts of Italy stories of terrible appearances came dropping in, which lost nothing as they passed from mouth to mouth. Once previously the Senate had attempted to annul the appointment of their enemy to the mastership of the horse, because a mouse had been heard to squeak during the election; and now, when the very atmosphere seemed charged with portents, when showers of stones were falling, bucklers gleaming in the heavens, the statues of the god of war perspiring, and strange and unheard of creatures coming to the birth, it needed no prophetic insight to foresee that the proper obstacle would be forthcoming on the day of Flaminius' entry on his office, and that if religious awe could avail aught, the consul-elect would never become consul in reality. Impatient of such chicaneries, Flaminius took the law into his own hands, and, making light of the sacred rites which he would have to perform on his entry into office, went off to the camp at Ariminum before the Ides of March came. Legates were sent to recall him, but he heeded them not. Evil omens, so the Senate said, pursued him even now. When he offered his first sacrifice as consul the victim escaped from the altar and sprinkled the bystanders with its blood. When he had fallen back to Arretium, and the time came for him to break up his camp there, and to follow Hannibal on his march to Rome, as he was in duty bound to do, even then the malice of the Senate, or the folly of the annalists, represents the gods as still taking part against him. It was clear that the man whom the gods intended to destroy they first drove mad. Flaminius ordered the standard-bearer to advance; but the standard, it was said, stuck fast in the ground. He mounted his horse, and it straightway threw him. The annalists forgot, or they did not know, that the greater the terrors which the science of the augurs put in his way, the greater was the credit due to him for despising them when duty called. It is difficult to say how far this army of angry portents may have paralyzed the Roman legionaries when they found themselves surrounded in the defiles of Lake Trasimene. It is not difficult to see that, if it did so, it was the aristocracy, and not the legionaries, who were to blame; for it was the aristocracy who, for their own selfish ends, had long been working on popular superstition to crush the true friend of the people.

Hannibal had advanced from Fæsulæ, laying waste with fire and sword the rich plains of Etruria. The plunder, and the slaughter, and the smoke of burning homesteads, with which he attempted to draw the consul from the shelter of his camp to risk a battle, might have roused a man who was less hot-headed than his enemies represent Flaminius to have been. But it was not till Hannibal had marched leisurely by his camp, and went devastating on towards Rome, that Flaminius left his position and followed him. It was not, as Polybius imagined, mortified pride at the fancied slight which Hannibal had shown him; still less was it, as the annalists tell us, and as the circle of the Scipios perhaps believed, the selfish desire to win the credit of a victory, before his colleague could come up, which made Flaminius follow so closely on Hannibal's steps. Hannibal knew better than the detractors of Flaminius what Flaminius was bound to do. He knew that he could do nothing else but follow him closely, and he laid his plans and chose his ground with his own consummate skill. He had violated all the rules of war by leaving a hostile force of 60,000 men in his rear and upon his line of communications. It remained for him now to justify his temerity by success, and the greatest sticklers for the rules of war will admit that he did it with a vengeance.

Hannibal had reached the shores of Lake Trasimene. Near its northern margin ran the high road from Cortona to Perugia, and above the road rose a line of undulating hills which at two points, the one near the tower now called Borghetto, and the other near the small town of Passignano, approach the lake so closely as to cut off what lies between them from the outer world. Between these two points the hills retreat from the lake in the form of a semicircle, leaving between themselves and it a plain which seems broad by contrast to its narrow entrance and outlet. Along these retreating hills Hannibal placed the main part of his army, and the plain which they enfold was the scene of the terrible catastrophe which followed. On the spur near Passignano and the hills behind it he stationed, in a conspicuous position, his Gallic cavalry and his veteran Libyans and Spaniards. Near Borghetto, and on either side of the road which descends into the plain, but carefully concealed from those who might pass along it by some broken ground, were his Gallic infantry and his Numidian cavalry. On the hills to the north of the plain, or rather behind their crests, were placed the light-armed troops and the Balearic slingers. Flaminius reached the hills which shut in the lake late in the evening, too late,

Lake Trasimene.

Battle of Trasimene.

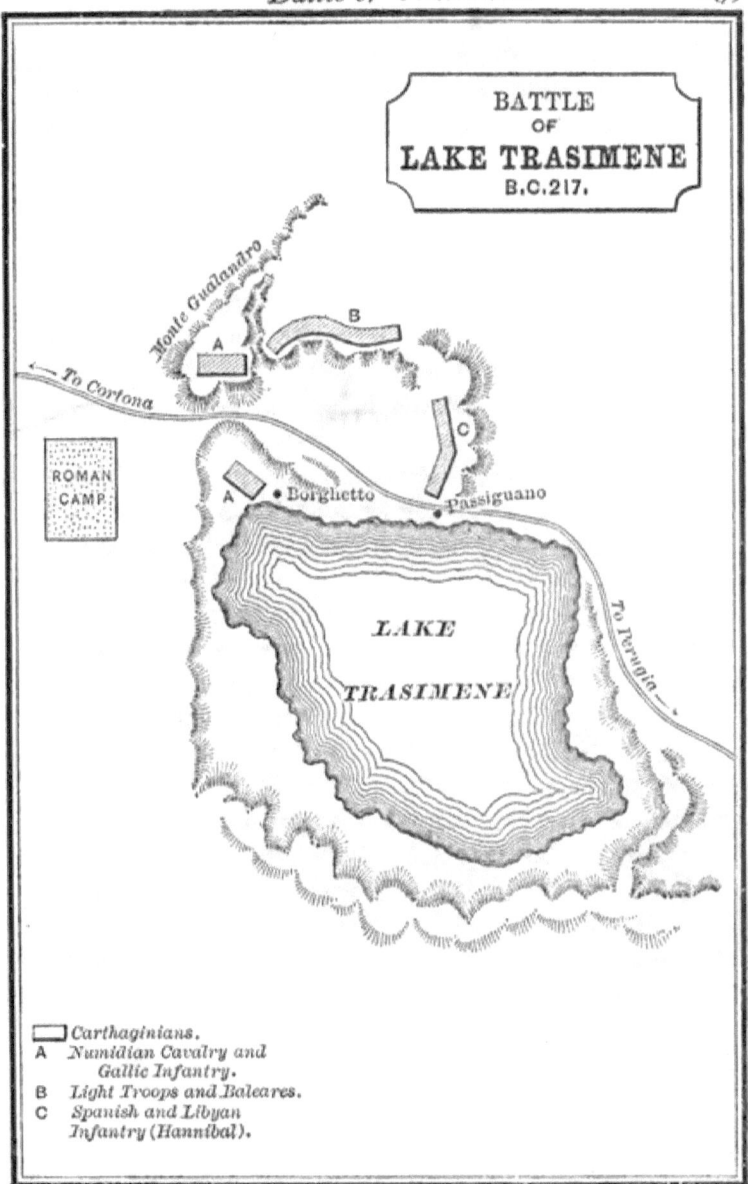

it would seem, to attempt to pass them then; but next morning, before it was broad daylight, and without sending scouts forward to see that the further end of the pass was clear, he continued the pursuit.

It was a fatal mistake. In heavy marching order, and without a thought of danger, the Roman army entered the valley of death and moved along the road that skirted the margin of the lake.

<small>Battle of Lake Trasimene.</small>

A thick curtain of mist hung over the lowlands which the army was crossing, and hid from view the base of the adjoining hills, while their tops were catching the first rays of the rising sun. With grim delight, and in a fever of expectation, must the soldiers of Hannibal, as they saw above the mist the whole crest of the hills and each glen and hollow which lay between their folds crowded with their brothers in arms, have listened to the tramp of the 30,000 men whom they could hear but could not see, as they passed along a few hundred yards below, each step making the destruction of the whole more sure. As soon as the rear of the Roman army had got well within the passage, Hannibal gave the signal. The Gauls and the Numidian cavalry hastened down and closed up the entrance, while the passage out was already blocked by the Gallic cavalry and the veterans. And now from all sides, from above and from below, from the front and from the rear, the battle-cry arose, and the enemy were upon the Romans. It was a carnage, and a carnage only. There was no time or space to form in order of battle; orders could neither be given nor heard; the men had hardly time to adjust their armour or to draw their swords. The majority stood where they were, and were cut down. Six thousand who led the van fought their way, sword in hand, in a compact mass, through the troops that blocked the outlet, and reached a hillock, where they halted. The mist still hung heavy on the ground below, and half ignorant of what was going on behind them, they waited in dread suspense, unable to help their comrades, yet unable also to tear themselves away from the scene of the conflict. It was their turn now to hear and not to see. At last, as the sun rose higher in the heavens, the mist lifted and revealed the extent of the butchery below. For three hours the slaughter had gone on, and 15,000 Roman corpses covered the ground, or were floating on the waters. Some in their terror had tried to swim across the lake, but were drowned by their heavy armour; others who had waded into the water might be seen standing in it up to their necks, and begging for their lives, till the cavalry rode in and struck off their heads. Of the conquering army barely 1,500 had fallen, and these were chiefly Gauls, the troops whom Hannibal could best afford to lose.

The Roman army was annihilated. To make the disaster more complete, the six thousand infantry who had so gallantly fought their way out of the pass were overtaken on the following day by Maherbal and forced to surrender; while four thousand cavalry, who had been sent forward by Servilius as his forerunners to co-operate with Flaminius, fell also into Hannibal's hands. Flaminius himself, after in vain trying to play the general's part amidst the blind panic and confusion, had died a soldier's death, fighting bravely. A Gallic Insubrian recognizing him, cried aloud, "Yonder is the consul who has slain our legions and ravaged our territory," and rushing at him, ran him through with his spear. In vain did Hannibal search for his body to give him the honourable funeral which he never refused to a worthy foe. Flaminius

Death of Flaminius.

may not have been a great general, he may have been impetuous and headstrong, and he certainly made one fatal mistake ; but amidst the calumnies heaped on him by the Senate, and the gloom which always gathers round defeat, we can safely say that he was the worthiest and least self-seeking Roman of his time.

CHAPTER XI.

HANNIBAL OVERRUNS CENTRAL ITALY.

(B.C. 217–216.)

AT Rome no effort was made to disguise the extent of the calamity which had overtaken the State. The attempt had been made after the Trebia, and had not succeeded then ; still less could it succeed now. The only man who might have had anything to gain by hiding the naked truth lay unrecognized amidst the heaps of slain in the fatal valley. It was the interest of the survivors to blacken his memory, not to strew flowers upon his grave; and they succeeded in the attempt. Roman senators even then consoled themselves for the defeat by the reflection that it was the presumptuous folly of their private foe which was responsible for it; and Roman orators and historians, for centuries afterwards, pointed their morals or adorned their tales by a reference to the well-deserved fate of the man who had withstood the patrician order and had despised the gods. When the first vague rumour of the disaster reached the city, an anxious crowd gathered in the Forum. Towards sunset the prætor mounted the rostrum, and simply said, "We have been defeated in a great battle." The scene of

News of Trasimene reaches Rome.

consternation which ensued brought home to the few survivors who had managed to reach the city, more vividly than the scene of slaughter itself, the full reality of what had happened. The Senate alone preserved its dignity and its self-restraint. Thinking not of the past, but of the present and the immediate future, they sat, day after day, from sunrise to sunset, concerting measures for the defence of the city. To remedy the evils of a divided command, they determined to revive the office of Dictator, an office unused for thirty-nine years past, and therefore nearly unknown to that generation. Their choice fell on the most prudent and respected, if not the ablest, of the patricians, Quintus Fabius Maximus, Marcus Minucius being selected as his master of the horse. The Dictator first made his peace by vows and offerings with the angry gods, and then took more practical steps for the defence. By his order the walls were repaired and manned, the bridges over the rivers were broken down, the country through which Hannibal's advance was likely to take place was turned into a desert, and everything prepared to withstand an immediate attack.

Why did not Hannibal at once advance on Rome, as the most cool-headed of his opponents expected that he would? The answer is the same that must be given on a yet more critical occasion in the following year. He knew, what the Romans themselves hardly yet fully knew, that every Roman citizen could, when occasion required, become a soldier; he knew also that amid a hostile population— for no Italian town had as yet come over to him—his attack, however impetuous, must break upon the walls of the city. If he delayed a little longer, and allowed his victories to produce their natural result, he would be borne

News of victory sent to Carthage.

back, he hoped, upon a wave of Italian national enthusiasm, and, bearing the banner of Italian independence, would strike down at his leisure the common oppressor. Accordingly, when the cup which he had so eagerly desired to drain seemed to be at his lips, he wisely dashed it from them. Crossing the Tiber, with stern resolve he crossed also the Flaminian Road, which must have seemed to his victorious army as if it were there for the express purpose of inviting an immediate march on the capital; and, hazarding an attack upon the adjoining Latin colony of Spoletium, he proved to demonstration the soundness of the judgment he had formed as to the courage of the Italians behind stone walls, and the impossibility, with so small a force as his own, of coping adequately with it. After traversing Umbria, he crossed the Apennines a second time, and at last laden with the plunder of Central Italy, he entered the territory of Picenum. Here the Carthaginians caught sight, for the first time since many months, of their native element, the sea; and Hannibal dispatched his first messenger with tidings of what he had done, to the Carthaginian Senate. Never probably, before or since, did a general send despatches to his government weighted with such brilliant achievements. From New Carthage to the Adriatic, what a catalogue of dangers met and overcome, and what crowning victories! The Ebro, the Rhone, and the Po; the Pyrenees, the Alps, and the Apennines; the Ticinus, the Trebia, and the Trasimene! Well can we believe, what we are expressly told, that such news disarmed all opposition to the lion's brood at Carthage, and closed the mouths of even the peace party. In the enthusiasm of the moment all parties determined to send reinforcements (why had they not taken steps to do so before?) alike to Hasdrubal in Spain and to Hannibal in Italy.

Meanwhile the Phœnician hero rested his troops, fatigued with all that they had undergone, in the plains of Picenum. They lived on the fat of the land, and the Numidian horses, diseased as they were from their bad or their scanty food, soon recovered their condition when they were groomed day by day with the old wine of Italian vintages. Here, too, Hannibal took the opportunity—a hazardous one even for him in the midst of a campaign—of arming his Libyan and, perhaps, some of his Spanish troops in the Roman fashion. The victor of the Trasimene could be in no want of Roman suits of armour. When the troops had been sufficiently recruited, and were again eager to advance, he marched at his leisure through the territories of the Marrucini and Frentani, the Marsi and Peligni, ravaging them as he went, and at length pitched his tent near Argyrippa, or Arpi, in Apulia.

Hannibal in Picenum.

Fabius, on his part, after levying four new legions led them off in pursuit of Hannibal. He came up with him at Arpi, and Hannibal immediately offered the battle which it might be presumed that a pursuing army, under a successor of Flaminius, would at once accept. But Fabius had made up his mind to a policy; a policy inevitable if Rome was to be saved, but requiring no ordinary firmness and courage to carry out. The policy was to commit nothing to fortune, to follow Hannibal wherever he went, dogging his footsteps constantly, but never risking a battle, and never, so far as human foresight could prevent it, giving the enemy a chance of taking him at a disadvantage. In vain did Hannibal order the richest country to be devastated before the Dictator's eyes; in vain did he shift his camp from place to place, in hopes that his

Policy of Fabius.

rapidity might wrest from the old man what insults and annoyances could not. Never close to Hannibal, but never far behind him, with admirable resolution, and with still more admirable self-restraint, did Fabius follow his foe from place to place, always clinging to the hills, occasionally cutting off stragglers, or intercepting the booty which the flying Numidian squadrons had captured, but giving no chance of a general engagement.

It was not in flesh and blood—certainly not in the flesh and blood of the hot-headed master of the horse—to submit patiently to this for ever. The name of "Lingerer" (Cunctator)—given to Fabius, at first as a mark of approval by those who blamed Flaminius for his rashness—became for the time a term of bitterest reproach. The lingerer was called a do-nothing, and his caution was put down to cowardice or even to treachery. "Hannibal's lackey," so the soldiers, aptly enough from their point of view, nick-named their general, would go anywhere if his master gave him the lead; without it he would go nowhere. But the old Dictator was as proof against the murmurings of his soldiers and mutinous speeches of his own master of the horse, Minucius, as he was against all the devices of Hannibal. At last, wearied out by his delay, Hannibal determined that Fabius, if he would not tire himself out by hard fighting, should at least do so by hard marching; and leaving Apulia behind, where he had already taken the strongly fortified town of Venusia, he marched into Samnium, the most inaccessible and mountainous part of Italy, ravaged the territory of Beneventum, in its very centre, took Telesia by assault, and then passed straight on out of Samnium into Campania.

Hannibal's march into Campania.

The plains of Campania were certainly the most fertile and beautiful plains in ancient Italy; the Italians thought them the most beautiful and fertile in the world. "Campania the blessed, where all human delights meet and vie with each other," says Pliny of it. One of two things was evident. In defence of all this wealth and beauty, either Fabius must at length risk a battle, or it would be clear to all Italians that the whole of Italy was at Hannibal's mercy, and its towns would, if from the instinct of self-preservation alone, at length join the conquering side. Fabius had followed Hannibal more quickly than was his wont, and his troops were in high spirits, for they thought that their general was at length in earnest, and would strike a blow rather than leave Campania to fall into the enemy's hands. But they were disappointed. They reached the ridge of the Calliculan hill which overlooked the plain, and then they sat down to enjoy, or to endure, as best they could, the now well-known sight of devastated fields and burning homesteads. Their discontent broke out with two-fold force, and it was evident from the reception which they gave to a mutinous speech of Minucius, that the soldiers thought the master of the horse would make a better commander than the Dictator; an opinion in which it was also evident that the master of the horse himself fully coincided. Aware that the discontent of the army had spread to Rome, and even to the aristocracy whose representative he was, Fabius yet held on steadfastly to his purpose. He knew that Northern Campania, with all its riches, could not support the Carthaginian army through the winter, and that Hannibal must attempt to retreat by the pass through which he had advanced. He therefore flattered himself that he had caught his enemy as in a trap, and placing 4,000 men at the head of the pass by which Hannibal must needs retreat, drew up his main army on the hills near its entrance.

marginal note: Continued inaction of Fabius.

Laden with booty, the spoils of Campania, Hannibal halted just below him, while Fabius made all his dispositions to repel the attempt to force a passage which would, doubtless, be made on the following day. But Hannibal had no intention of fighting at a disadvantage, or indeed of forcing the pass at all. He intended to march quietly through it. Accordingly, he selected from the vast herds of oxen which he was driving towards his winter quarters, two thousand of the strongest, and bidding his sutlers cut as many faggots of dry brushwood, and fasten them to their horns, he ordered that when the night was well advanced, the faggots should be kindled, and the oxen, with their horns ablaze, be driven up the hills which hung over the pass. Maddened with fear and pain, the affrighted beasts ran wildly up the steep sides of the valley, and Fabius himself, as well as the 4,000 men upon the col, imagined that Hannibal was escaping that way over the hills. But, true to his character, the Dictator would not venture out of his camp till he could see clearly what lay before him; and meantime Hannibal led his army, which had been refreshed by half a night's sleep, quietly up the unguarded pass, and reached Allifæ in safety. Fabius found himself outwitted, and it was natural in the keenness of their vexation, that his men should accuse him of having purposely allowed Hannibal to escape; an accusation which shortly afterwards seemed triumphantly brought home to him, when the crafty Phœnician took occasion to spare his private property, while he wasted all around with fire and sword.

Fabius fails to entrap Hannibal.

Still Fabius clung steadfastly to his purpose. He followed Hannibal northwards to the Peligni, and when his enemy turned southwards again, towards his proposed winter quarters in Apulia, and he himself was called off to Rome to perform some sacrifices incident to his office, he straitly charged Minucius to follow his policy, and on no account to risk a battle in his absence.

<small>Success of Minucius.</small>

Hannibal had long since formed his estimate of Minucius, and when he threw forward a portion of his forces to a hill still nearer to the enemy, a sharp skirmish took place, which ended in the Romans occupying the disputed position. Encouraged by this first success, Minucius made a descent in force upon Hannibal's foragers, and cut many of them to pieces. Hannibal found himself for the first time in his life in the midst of the enemy, yet unable to take the field. He was, so at least his enemies thought, penned within his own camp, and on the morrow he made a hasty retreat to his old position at Geronium, fearing lest Minucius, whose qualities he had apparently underrated, should take it by a *coup de main*, and thus the provisions he had so laboriously got together should fall into the enemy's hands.

It is not to be wondered at, that when the news of this success reached Rome the delight was great, and out of all proportion to its immediate cause. It was the first success which the Roman arms had won in the war, and it seemed to

<small>Minucius co-Dictator.</small>

indicate that the tide had at length begun to turn. The fame of Minucius was in everybody's mouth, and as he rose in popular estimation, so did the Dictator fall. One stroke of good luck had turned the heads of the Romans more completely than had all their previous misfortunes, and they took one of the most incredibly foolish steps recorded in their history They did not try to depose Fabius from the command for which they deemed him unfitted, but they raised Minucius to an equal command with him. For the first time in Roman history were to be seen two co-Dictators, differing alike in temperament and in policy, and the one raised to an equality with the other simply because of the difference! It has been said by a high military authority that one bad general is better than two good ones; and it was apparent to those who had eyes to see that the sword of Hannibal would soon arbitrate between such conflicting claims.

Fabius returned to the army as convinced as ever of the soundness of his policy, and prepared to press upon his colleague by his personal influence what he could no longer enforce upon him by superior power. Seeing that Minucius was bent on fighting, he proposed either that they should take the command of the whole army on alternate days, or that each should have the continuous and unfettered control over his own half of it. Minucius, possibly with a slight distrust of himself, under the new responsibilities of command, chose the latter alternative, and Fabius, doubtless thinking it better to risk the safety of two than of four legions on a single cast, was of the same mind. Hannibal, duly informed by his prisoners or his spies of the arrangement which had been made, directed his attention exclusively to Minucius. Near the camp of the new dictator was a hill with ground below it which presented the appearance of a general level, bare of trees; but in it, as in the level ground near the Trebia, Hannibal's experienced eye had discovered hollows and equalities which might hide a considerable force. Here by night he concealed some 5,000 foot and 500 horse, and at dawn of day he sent a small body of active troops to seize the hill in full view of the Romans. Minucius took the bait. In the engagement which ensued the ambuscade did its duty well; and it would have fared ill with

Great services of Fabius.

the army of the new dictator, had not Fabius, observing from his own camp, at a distance of a mile, what was going on, come up at the right moment and prevented its retreat from being turned into a total rout. Minucius, it is said, frankly acknowledged his error, joined his camp to that of the old Dictator, and descended gracefully once more into his proper post of master of the horse.

The tables were now completely turned. Fabius was the hero alike of the camp and of the city. But his six months of office were drawing to a close, and it remained to be seen whether his mantle would descend on those who were to succeed him. He had done great things in those six months. If he had not, as his admirers said, altogether saved Rome by his delay, he had at least given her a brief breathing space. He had trained raw levies to look the warriors of Hannibal in the face—a feat to which they were quite unequal on the morrow of the Trasimene; and by allowing Hannibal to devastate at his pleasure the Apulian and Campanian plains, he had unintentionally elicited the most conclusive proof of the hopelessness of Hannibal's enterprise. For even now no Italian city had revolted; the serried ranks of the Italian Confederation remained unbroken, and it was clear to the keen-sighted Phœnician that he was still as far as ever from the goal of his hopes. The services, therefore, rendered by the Cunctator to Rome were very real services, even if they were not quite what his admirers represented them. To have escaped from Hannibal without a crushing defeat was in those times, as Livy truly remarks, a victory in itself.

CHAPTER XII.

BATTLE OF CANNÆ. CHARACTER OF HANNIBAL.

(B.C. 216.)

THE Roman Senate, during the winter which followed, gave new and striking proofs of their confidence in their own future by sending legates to expostulate with the Ligurians for having taken the part of Hannibal, and to watch the ever-fickle Gauls. Nor was their horizon bounded by the limits of Italy. With the truest wisdom they despatched reinforcements to their army in Spain; they demanded the arrears of tribute from Illyria, and they sent even to Philip, King of Macedon, ordering him to surrender the intriguer Demetrius of Pharos, who had taken refuge in his court. But party spirit still ran high in the city. In the election for the consulship which had just taken place, other qualifications had been thought of than those which were essential in this supreme hour; perhaps for the simple reason that the Romans did not yet realize that it might be supreme. L. Æmilius Paullus, who had distinguished himself in the Illyrian war, was the successful candidate on the patrican side, but he received as his colleague P. Terentius Varro, the champion of the Plebeians, a man who, if the patrician annalists can be believed, was not only of humble origin, the son of a butcher, but had himself worked in his father's business, and was recommended to the suffrages of the people by nothing but a bullying manner and a vulgar impudence. Varro does not seem, it is true, to have been more of a military genius than Flaminius, or Sempronius, or Fabius; but that most of

Great exertions of Rome.

the accusations laid to his charge are unjust is proved by the fact that he had held high offices before, that he was elected now in what no one could refuse to recognize as a time of danger, and that he was employed in the public service even after the disastrous name of Cannæ had been indissolubly connected with his own.

The spring found the hostile armies still facing each other near Geronium; but Hannibal's provisions were nearly exhausted. Not enough for ten days remained, and the wasted country could yield no more. He began to look out for another Roman magazine which he might convert to his own use; nor had he far to go. The Roman supplies and munitions of war for Apulia were collected in large quantities at Cannæ, a town to the south of the Aufidus, about half way between Canusium and the sea. With strange short-sightedness the Roman generals of the preceding year had neglected to garrison it strongly; and while the consuls of the new year were levying fresh legions at Rome, Hannibal, by one of his rapid marches, seized and appropriated it to his own use, as he had seized and appropriated Geronium before it. When at length Æmilius and Varro assumed the command of the army, they did so under definite instructions from the authorities at home to force on a battle. The Fabian method, they thought, had been tried long enough: it had done all that it could do; and it was apparent that the Italian allies could not stand much longer the strain to which it had exposed them. Every precaution was taken, so far as numbers went, to ensure a victory. A Roman army ordinarily consisted of but two legions, each containing 4,200 infantry and 200 cavalry. The army which was now raised consisted, not of two, but of eight legions, and each legion contained 5,000

Rival armies face each other at Cannæ.

infantry and 300 cavalry. The Romans, therefore, could hardly now be accused of under-estimating, so far as mere numbers went, the gravity of the occasion. The consuls were to act together, and those of the previous year were retained as proconsuls to assist in handling the vast host. Never before had the Romans sent so large an army, at one time and place, into the field, and the contingent furnished by the allies was, according to precedent, equal to that of the Romans. The grand total, therefore, of the force on which the safety of Rome might seem to depend consisted of over 80,000 men. They found Hannibal encamped near Cannæ, on the south side of the Aufidus, and they selected a spot for their own camp on the same side of the river, but six miles higher up its course.

The surrounding country was level and suitable to the evolutions of cavalry, and without doubt had for this reason been selected by Hannibal. Paullus, seeing this, is said to have been anxious to postpone the battle till he should have drawn Hannibal into ground of his own choosing. The historians who have bepraised Paullus for this forgot, in their eagerness to throw all the blame for what happened afterwards on the butcher's son, that the orders of the authorities to fight a battle at once were stringent, and that it was not likely that Hannibal would, by any artifices of the Roman consuls, be drawn off from a position selected by himself, well fortified and well supplied. It was impossible for an army of 80,000 men to linger long in so exhausted a country without striking a blow; and to linger there, or to retreat without fighting, would have been alike fatal to the Roman cause in Apulia. The evils of a divided command were great enough, but they were not created by Varro. They

Paullus and Varro.

were even diminished, to a certain extent, in this case by the arrangement that the consuls should take the supreme command on alternate days; and when Varro, on his day, pushed his camp nearer to the foe he was encouraged in his resolve to force on a battle by a success which he won over some skirmishers and light cavalry who had been sent to bar his progress. Minucius had met with a like first success near Geronium, and Sempronius had done the same at the Trebia. Was it not possible that like effects might be produced by like causes, and that a deep-laid design of Hannibal might have had more to do with each than the prowess of the Romans? But this did not strike—so remarked the Patrician annalists, wise after the event—the mind of Varro. The next day belonged to Paullus, and he signalized his command by throwing a third of his army to the north side of the Aufidus, and by forming a second camp there, some miles nearer to the Carthaginians. By this step he hoped at once to protect his own foraging parties and to annoy those of the enemy. Eager for the conflict, Hannibal, two days after, drew out his forces in battle array on the south side of the river. The offer was declined by the prudent Paullus; and Hannibal, to bring matters to a crisis, sent his Numidians across the river with orders to cut off the Romans, who were encamped on its northern side, from all access to it. It was the middle of June; the country was parched and thirsty, and a dry wind, the Vulturnus, which blows at that time of year, raising clouds of dust, would make a scanty supply of water an intolerable hardship. Even if he had been disposed to postpone fighting, Varro could hardly now have done so.

The delay of the last few days seemed irksome enough to the rural armies; but what must it have seemed to the citizens at home? News had reached the city that the armies were facing each other, and that everything was prepared for a decisive conflict. They had ventured their all, or nearly their all, on this one throw. The stake was laid down, and the throw must be made, but it was hard to have so much time to ask themselves what if they should lose? Omens and portents seemed to fill the air, as before the Trasimene Lake, and busy-tongued rumour passed from mouth to mouth, sending the citizens in crowds to the temples to seek from the gods by supplications what they could no longer gain or lose by any exertions of their own. It was the resource of the destitute, and they knew it, but it helped them to kill the period of suspense.

Once more it was Varro's turn for the command, and as the sun rose he began to transfer his army to the northern side of the river, and, after joining the contingent in the smaller camp there, drew the whole out in battle array, facing the south.

Order of battle.

Nearly opposite Cannæ the Aufidus, whose general course is north-east, takes a sharp bend to the south. Afterwards for some distance it runs east, and then, once more turning northward, reaches the line of its former course. The loop or link thus formed Hannibal marked out as the grave of the Roman army, the grave of 50,000 men; and into it, as a preparatory step, he now threw his own small force, while Varro was crossing the stream higher up. His infantry did not number half that of the Romans; but they were many of them veterans, and all of them men on whom he knew by experience that he could rely. His cavalry were only slightly superior in numbers to the enemy, but how vastly superior in every military quality the result was to prove. In the centre of his line of battle were the Spaniards clothed in white tunics edged with purple, and armed with swords equally suited for thrusting and for striking. Next them were the Gauls who, naked to the waist, and armed with long swords, suited to their gigantic stature, seemed as though they were the warriors of Brennus come to life again with one more terrible than many Brennuses to lead them. This part of his force Hannibal threw forward in the form of a semicircle or a wedge, while on their flanks and some way to the rear he placed the best part of his infantry, the heavy-armed Africans, eager doubtless, many of them to flesh for the first time in Roman hearts the Roman weapons which they bore. Beyond these again and forming the left wing of the whole army were the heavy Gallic and African cavalry, 8,000 strong. On the right wing he posted his light-armed Numidians, reduced by the waste of life attending such campaigns as Hannibal's to 2,000 men all told, but with spirit and fidelity enough to their great leader to fight on to their very last man and last horse. Hasdrubal led the heavy cavalry on the left, and Maherbal the Numidians on the right, while Hannibal, with his brother Mago near him, stationed himself in the centre to direct the general operations of the battle. He had been obliged to leave ten thousand men on the other side of the river to guard his camp against surprise, and was able therefore to put only thirty thousand men into line of battle; thirty thousand against the Roman eighty thousand! The odds were heavy indeed against him in point of numbers; but it must be remembered that his wings rested on the sides of the loop which he had himself selected, and could not be outflanked by the enemy. Varro, whether because he distrusted his raw levies, or because he saw, when it was too late to remedy it, that unless he massed his troops together, half of his whole army would be outside the fray, increased the depth of his maniples from ten to sixteen, hoping by sheer weight to bear down all resistance and drive the Carthaginians into the river. He was, in fact, only penning his sheep more closely for the slaughter.

After the usual preliminary skirmish of the light-armed troops, the 8,000 heavy cavalry on Hannibal's left charged the 2,400 Roman cavalry opposed to them. These last were picked men, belonging, most of them, to the best Roman families, men of Equestrian and Senatorial rank. They withstood the charge bravely for a time, and grappled horse to horse and man to man with the barbarians. But they were overpowered by numbers, and only a small remnant escaped from the field. Unlike Rupert at Naseby, Hasdrubal held his eager cavalry well in hand. He forbade them to pursue those who were already routed, and passing behind the whole Roman line fell on the rear of the Italian cavalry, who were stationed on the other wing, and who had hitherto been held in check by the skilful evolutions of the mere handful of Numidians. Those admirable horsemen had avoided coming to close quarters, in which they must have been crushed by numbers, but had managed to keep their vastly more numerous enemy employed till Hasdrubal came thundering on their rear. Attacked now by the uninjured Numidians in front and by Hasdrubal's cavalry, flushed with success, behind, the Italian cavalry broke and fled. Hasdrubal, not yet sated with victory, left the Numidians to render an account of their flying foes, and turned his attention to the Roman centre. Here, so far, matters had gone well for the Romans; but it was so far only. The semi-circle of Gauls and

Spaniards, whom Hannibal had pushed forward in his centre, had been gradually forced back, or rather had fallen back in accordance with his plan, first to a level with, and then right past, the heavy Africans on their

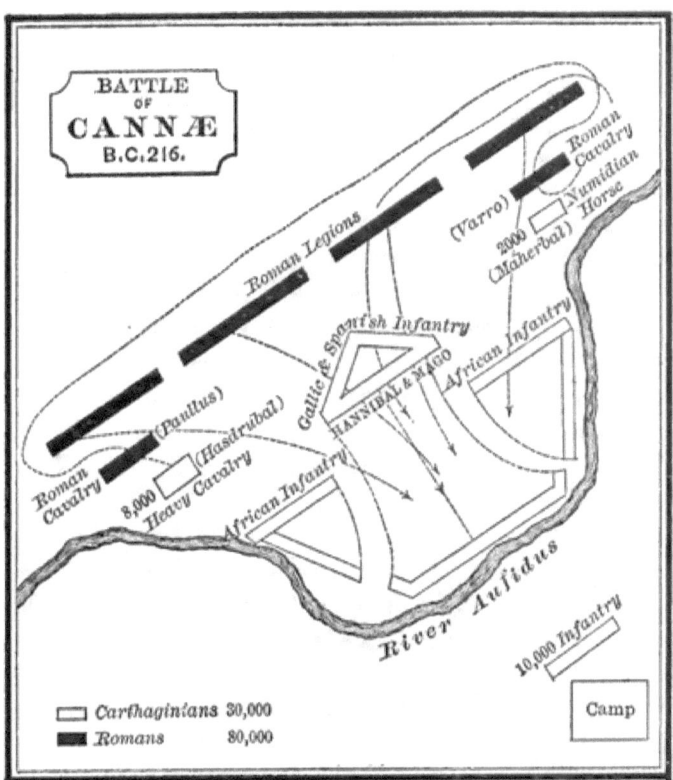

flanks. The convex line of battle had thus become concave, and it seemed that the whole would be driven headlong into the river by the overwhelming masses of the Romans, who, as they yielded, kept pressing on, or were themselves pressed on by those behind and at their flanks, into every inch of ground left· vacant for them.

But just at the critical moment Hasdrubal fell upon their rear, and the heavy Libyan infantry, who had hardly yet taken part in the battle, wheeling inward at the same time from right and left, attacked them on both flanks. Denser and denser grew the mass of terrified Romans, pressed on all four sides at once. Huddled together without room to draw, much less to wield, their swords, they stood or struggled in helpless imbecility, seeing their comrades on the circumference of the fatal circle cut down, one after the other, and doomed to wait in patience till their own turn should come. The question was no longer whether, but simply when, the stroke would fall on each. Few Romans indeed within that fatal ring were destined to escape. As at the Trasimene, it was a simple butchery; but it was a butchery which required treble the number of victims. The Romans were never cowards; but those who stood near the centre of that seething mass must needs have died, like cowards, many times before their death. "The thicker the hay," said Alaric long afterwards, in an outburst of brutality, "the easier it is mown." But not even Alaric's imagination could have pictured such a harvest of death as this of Cannæ, and even the muscles of his brawny Visigoths would have been wearied out before they had slain, as the Carthaginians did on this fatal day, a number of the enemy which, man for man, vastly exceeded their own.

For eight hours the work of destruction went on, and at the end 50,000 men lay dead upon the ground. Æmilius Paullus, the Illyrian hero, who, though wounded by a sling early in the day, had clung to his horse, heartening on his men, till he dropped exhausted from his saddle; the proconsul Servilius; the late high-spirited master of the

Results of battle.

horse Minucius; both quæstors, twenty-one military tribunes, sixty senators, and an unknown number of knights were among the slain. Nearly 20,000 Roman prisoners were taken, whether on the field itself in the pursuit, or in the two camps which were among the prizes of Hannibal's gigantic victory. Of the rest Varro, with a few horsemen only, had the good or ill fortune to escape to Venusia; and it was with difficulty that after some days he managed to rally a few thousand stragglers or malingerers at Canusium—all that now remained of the Roman army. Amidst all this slaughter, the conqueror had lost only 5,500 of his infantry, and but 200 of that matchless cavalry to whom the victory was mainly due. "Send me on with the cavalry," said Maherbal to Hannibal, in the exultation of the moment, "do thou follow behind, and in five days thou shalt sup in the Capitol." He might well think so at the time, for the worst fears of the Romans, the highest hopes of Hannibal, had been more than realized; the double stake had been played and had been lost, lost, it would seem then, irretrievably. So many knights lay dead that, as the story goes, Mago, when sent some time afterwards by Hannibal to Carthage with the tidings of his victory, emptied on the floor of the Senate House three bushels of golden rings taken from Equestrian fingers. It was a trophy of victory which the Carthaginian aristocracy —who, as has been already pointed out, commemorated the number of their campaigns by that of their rings, and who had, many of them, joined the opposition to the noble Barcine gens—could not fail to appreciate.

The news, which was necessarily slow in reaching Carthage, reached Rome apace. It was, as the saying is, "in the air" even before the first courier with his disastrous tidings appeared at the Appian gate, and rumour, as was natural, went even beyond the truth. It was believed that both consuls were dead, and that no portion of the army had survived. Livy, the most graphic of historians or of romancers, fairly shrinks from the attempt to picture the scene of horror which followed. Each flying messenger, as he reached the walls, fancied himself, or was fancied by the Romans, to be but the forerunner of the dread Hannibal himself. He knew not, indeed, as he drew near the city, whether the Numidian cavalry were not even then before him, as their own messengers. A panic-stricken multitude, thinking that all save their lives was lost, made for the gates, and for a moment it seemed likely that Hannibal when he came would find Rome indeed, but no Roman citizens within her.

Reception of news at Rome.

Any other state must have succumbed to such a blow; but now, as after the Trasimene, it was the Senate, or what remained of it, who saved the city from being abandoned by her own children. They alone preserved their presence of mind; and it was the old ex-Dictator, Fabius, who was, once more, the soul of their deliberations. By his advice the gates were closed to prevent the exodus of the inhabitants. The citizens should not be saved, so he willed it, unless the city was saved with them. Messengers were sent along the southern military road to see, as Livy pathetically expresses it, " if the gods, touched by one pang of pity, had left aught remaining to the Roman name," and to bring the first tidings of the expected advance of Hannibal. It was difficult for the Senate to deliberate at all; for the cries of thousands of women outside the Senate House, who were bewailing their absent husbands, or fathers, or sons, as though they were all dead, drowned the voice of those who spoke. Orders

Panic checked.

were issued that the women, if wail they must, should wail within their own houses, and henceforward silence, mournful indeed but dignified, was observed in the public streets. All assemblies of the people were prohibited. M. Junius Pera was named Dictator; the city legions were called out; the whole male population—some eight thousand slaves and criminals among them —were armed, and the angry gods were propitiated, as best they might, by the punishment of guilty Vestals, and by the burying alive of Greek and Gallic men and women in the Roman Forum.

After a few days more hopeful news came. A despatch arrived from Varro himself, saying that he had escaped from the carnage, and was doing his best to reorganize and to rally the ten thousand demoralized fugitives who had at last found their way to Canusium. More important still, Hannibal was not on his way to Rome, but was still encamped on the field of Cannæ. The Romans breathed more freely; but from other parts of the Roman world tidings of fresh danger, fresh disaster, or fresh shame, came pouring in. One Carthaginian fleet was threatening Lilybæum, another Syracuse. The force sent northwards to watch the Gauls had fallen into an ambuscade and had been cut off to a man. Worse still, a body of Roman nobles who had escaped from Cannæ, thinking that all was lost save their honour, had determined, regardless even of their honour, to fly beyond the seas, and would have carried their purpose out had not the young Scipio rushed in amongst them, sword in hand, and sworn that he would slay anyone who would not bind himself never to desert his country.

And why did not Hannibal march at once on the panic-stricken city? Roman historians and Roman generals could not refrain from expressing their thankfulness and their surprise at his dilatoriness or his blindness. In Juvenal's time Roman schoolboys declaimed upon it in their weekly themes. Maherbal, the master of the Numidian cavalry—if indeed the story be true, and not what the Romans imagined ought to have been true—exclaimed, in an outburst of vexation at the chance which was thrown away, that the gods had taught Hannibal how to win, but not how to use, a victory; and the greatest master of modern warfare, Napoleon himself, has joined in the general chorus of condemnation. But perhaps the best and the all-but-sufficing answer to those who say that Hannibal ought to have advanced on Rome, is the simple fact that Hannibal himself, the foremost general of all time, and statesman as well as general, did not attempt it. Moreover, all the arguments which we have seen held good after Trasimene against such an advance, held equally good now. There were still the stone walls of the city. There was still the population of Latium and of the surrounding country, as yet untouched by the war, hostile to him to a man; still—after the first few days of panic, of which Hannibal, laden with booty and with half Italy between him and Rome, could hardly have taken advantage—the unbroken resolution of the citizens themselves. Hannibal never liked sieges, and was seldom successful in those he undertook; he forbore at this moment to besiege even Canusium with its feeble and panic-stricken defenders. Finally, his long-cherished hope of the defection of the Italian allies seemed now at length to be not only within his sight, but, if only he was patient or prudent, already almost within his grasp. The battle of Cannæ had been too much for the resolution of Apulia; Samnium had already in part joined him; Lu-

Why did Hannibal not advance on Rome?

cania and Bruttium rose in revolt. The Greek cities in the south were prepared to hail him as their deliverer! Campania, it was whispered, was wavering in the balance, and ready at the sight of the conqueror to go over to Carthage. Thus deprived of her allies, Rome, he hoped, would fall almost by her own weight.

Never did the self-control and the true nobility of soul of Hannibal, never did the unbending resolution of the Roman Senate, display itself more conspicuously than at this moment. Never, in the very moment of victory, did Hannibal lose his head. The good of his country was even now nearer to his heart—and doubtless it was the only thing that was nearer to his heart—than his hatred to Rome. Thinking that it might be advantageous to Carthage to conclude peace, and that she might now do so almost on her own terms, he called the Roman prisoners together —almost the only occasion in his life on which he brought himself to speak a friendly word to any Roman—and told them that he did not wish that the strife which he was waging should be internecine; he was willing to take a ransom for them, and some of their number might go on their parole to Rome to negotiate the matter. Even in the first flush of his victory he bade Carthalo offer terms of peace, if he saw that the Roman wishes turned in that direction. But the Romans also rose to the emergency. Fifty years before, as has been already related, they had told the victorious Epirot that Rome never negotiated with an enemy so long as he was on Italian soil; and the answer which they had given to Pyrrhus then in words they gave now to a general greater than Pyrrhus, and crowned with a far more overwhelming victory, by their deeds. They spoke no word and thought no thought of peace. Their want of troops was urgent, but they refused, as the story goes, to buy with money men who had disgraced themselves by surrender; and when Varro neared the city, obnoxious though he was to the aristocracy on account of his low birth and of his career, and branded with the defeat of Cannæ, not one word of reproach was uttered against him. His efforts only, not his failures or his mistakes, were remembered, and the citizens went forth in a body to meet him, and thanked him, in words that are ever memorable, for not having despaired of the republic. The Roman historians have a right, here at least, to congratulate themselves that they were not as were the Carthaginians. The defeated Roman general received a vote of thanks for his unsuccessful efforts: a defeated Carthaginian would have been nailed to a cross.

After the battle of Cannæ the character of the war is changed, and it loses something of the intensity of the interest attached to it. Hitherto the tide of invasion has run, as Dr. Arnold has pointed out in an eloquent passage, in one single current and that current so magnificent and so resistless, that it rivets the attention of even the most careless spectators. There has been no reverse, hardly even a check, from the moment when Hannibal left his winter quarters at New Carthage, till he stood victorious on the field of Cannæ. The most vivid of historians can do little by description to make Hannibal's achievements stand out in more startling relief than they do already by their bare recital. The dullest annalist, if only he record them truly, cannot make them seem commonplace. The eye can hardly wander as it sees the great drama develop itself step by step, and sweep irresistibly on towards what seems its legitimate and necessary conclusion. The obstacles interposed by Nature herself

[margin: Unbroken success of Hannibal.]

—rivers and marshes and mountain chains—seemed interposed only to stimulate the energies and to heighten the glory of him who could surmount them all. Each difficulty overcome is an earnest to Hannibal of his power to grapple with the next, and is used by him as a stepping-stone towards it. That they had crossed the Pyrenees, he told his soldiers when they hesitated on the Rhone, was a proof that they could pass the Alps. When they had reached the summit of the Alps, he told them they had already seized the citadel of Italy, and had only to walk down and take possession of the city. Four times over he had now measured his sword with the future conquerors of the world, and each time he had been victorious in an ever ascending series of successes. At the Ticinus he first met the Roman cavalry, and it was their hasty retreat from the field of battle which alone saved them from a rout. At the Trebia, however the consul might try to disguise it, it was no retreat at all, it was a total rout. At the Trasimene it was neither retreat nor rout, it was the extermination of an army. At Cannæ it was the extermination, not of one but of two armies, and each of them twice its usual size. This was the pinnacle of Hannibal's success, and a pinnacle indeed it was.

Almost as wonderful as Hannibal's victories over Nature or his enemies, were his victories over his own followers. Under the spell of his genius, the discordant members of a motley Carthaginian army—disaffected Libyans and Numidians, barbarous and lethargic Spaniards, fierce and fickle Gauls—were welded into a homogeneous whole, which combined the utmost play of individual prowess with all the precision of a machine. No whisper of disaffection or of mutiny was ever heard in Han-

Character of Hannibal.

nibal's camp. Italians deserted by thousands to Hannibal; but no Hannibalian veteran, even when his star was on its wane, ever deserted to Rome. Politic as he was brave, and generous as he was far-sighted, Hannibal could arouse alike the love and the fear, the calm confidence and the passionate enthusiasm of all the various races who served under his standard. The best general, a high authority has said, is he who makes the fewest mistakes; but what single mistake can the keenest critic point out which marred the progress or chequered the success of these three first extraordinary years? They are years, moreover, any one of which might have made or marred the reputation of any lesser general. Unfortunately we know Hannibal only through his enemies. They have done their best to malign his character; they have called him cruel, and, happily, almost every specific charge of cruelty supplies us, even with our imperfect knowledge, with the materials for its own refutation. They talked of "*Punic ill faith*" till they came themselves to believe in its existence, or to think that the name proved itself. But what people or what town, it may well be asked, which Hannibal had ever promised to support, did he voluntarily abandon, or of what single act of treachery can it be proved that he was guilty? They made as light as they could even of his achievements, by attributing to Phœnician cunning, or to the blind forces of Nature, the severity of defeats which no patriotic Roman could believe were due to his individual genius alone, for it was an individual genius such as they had never seen or imagined. A storm of sleet at Trebia, the mist at the Trasimene, the wind and clouds of dust or a *ruse de guerre* of some deserters at Cannæ—such were the transparent fictions by which the Romans attempted to disguise from others, and perhaps even from themselves, that they had found their master. We know Hannibal, let us repeat it once more, only from his enemies; but in what character, even as painted by his friends, can we discern such vivid and such unmistakable marks of greatness? The outline is commanding, imperial, heroic; and there is no detail with which our materials enable us to fill it in at all, which is not in perfect harmony with the whole.

After Cannæ the tide of invasion ceases to flow onward in one irrepressible sweep. It is broken up into a number of smaller currents, which, though they are doubtless each planned by the ruling mind, and conducted by the master hand, are often in the nature of by-play rather than have any direct bearing on the main issues of the war. They are, moreover, always difficult and often impossible to follow. The Romans, taught by the experience which they had bought so bitterly on four battlefields, decline any longer to trust themselves within the reach of Hannibal's arm, or to stake their safety on any single blow; while Hannibal, lacking the reinforcements which he had a right to expect, and which it is impossible to believe that the Carthaginian government, had they been animated by a tithe of the spirit of their general, could not have despatched to him before this, has to adapt the plan of his campaign to his altered circumstances and his ever-straitening means. The Numidian cavalry, as they die off, have to be replaced by Gauls, and the Libyan and Spanish veterans by Samnites or Lucanians, who had long since bowed their necks to the Roman yoke. Isolated sieges, embassies to distant potentates, pressing messages to Carthage, rapid marches and countermarches, ambuscades and surprises, the sudden swoop on Rome, and the doom of Carthage, recognized by Hannibal in the ghastly head of his brother Hasdrubal, thrown with Roman brutality into his camp—these still lend life and variety and a deadly interest to the struggle such as we find in few other wars; but we feel all the time that the war is not what it was. It is not that Hannibal's eye has grown dim or his natural force abated. His right hand never lost its cunning. Invincible as ever in the field, we shall see Hannibal, for years to come, marching wherever he likes, no Roman general—and there were sometimes half a dozen of them round him—daring to say him nay. Following the example of Fabius, they dogged his footsteps, or hung upon the hills above him, while he encamped fearlessly in the plain below; but when he turned his face towards one and the other, they scattered before him in all directions as the jackals before a lion. Yet we feel throughout, what Hannibal must soon have come to feel himself, that fate had at length declared against him. It is a noble, but a hopeless struggle; and we are fain to turn away from the spectacle of so heroic a soul struggling against what it knows to be inevitable. It is indeed a psychological puzzle how any one man—even though he were the greatest product of the Phœnician race—can have combined such opposite, nay such contradictory qualities as must have met in the man who, like one of the world-stormers of more modern times, Attila or Zinghis Khan or Tamerlane, could carry everything before him in one impetuous and overwhelming sweep of conquest, from Saguntum to Cannæ in the three first years of the war, and then for its twelve remaining years could maintain the struggle by a warfare which was, in the main, defensive, hoping against hope, and each year confined to narrower limits with an ever-decreasing force against an ever-increasing foe. It would be well worth the while of the military student to trace, if it were possible with accuracy, the means by which the genius of Hannibal, as great in defence as in attack, and in patience as in impetuosity, prolonged for thirteen years a warfare, which, if only the Romans had been led by a Hannibal, or the Carthaginians by any one but him, must, in one way or the other, have been brought to a close almost at once. But we cannot do so; for at the very time that the war undergoes the change which has been just described, we lose also the guidance of the historian Polybius, who, if any one, could have enabled us to follow closely its vicissitudes.

Although, therefore, we have dwelt at length upon the first three years of the war, wherein victories and defeats are on so gigantic a scale, and where each step can be traced with accuracy, or has a direct bearing on the main result, it seems consistent alike with the scope and object of this book, and with our own views of what is desirable, or even possible, to pass more lightly over its remaining thirteen years, endeavouring mainly to bring into relief those incidents which appeal to the imagination, which are characteristic of the rival nations or of their leaders, and which are of universal or of lasting significance.

CHAPTER XIII.

REVOLT OF CAPUA. SIEGE OF SYRACUSE.

(B.C. 216–212.)

THE victory of Cannæ led almost immediately to the revolt of Capua, a city second only to Rome in wealth and power, and able to put into the field, when disposed to do so, a force of thirty thousand men. But this acquisition was shorn of half its value by the stipulation made by the

Revolt of Capua.

ease loving inhabitants and granted by Hannibal, that no Capuan citizen should be required to serve in his army. It was an arrangement which cost him dear; but cost him what it might, it was ever afterwards religiously observed by him. Naples Hannibal had already tried to capture by a *coup de main*, but, failing in the attempt, he had not cared to besiege it in form; nor was he more successful at Nola, which was prevented from revolting by the energy and skill of M. Claudius Marcellus, the ablest general whom the agony of the last three years had brought to the front; perhaps as able as any whom the Second Punic War produced for Rome at all.

As consul, six years before, Marcellus had slain with his own hand the huge Gallic chieftain Viridomarus, and had, for the third and last time in Roman history, dedicated the *spolia opima* in the temple of Jupiter Feretrius. When, after the battle of Cannæ, Varro was recalled to Rome, it was Marcellus who had taken the command of the 10,000 Roman survivors at Canusium. Like Fabius, Marcellus knew how to avoid defeat, but he knew better than Fabius how and when to strike a vigorous blow. If Fabius deserved to be called the shield of Rome, Marcellus might with equal right be called its sword. He was a rough soldier, uncultured as Marius, and hardly less cruel; but during the next eight eventful years Rome could hardly have done without him. The dread of Hannibal had, at length, taught the city to know a good general, and to keep him when she had found him, and she showed her appreciation of Marcellus by breaking through forever the insane tradition which brought a military command to an end on a predetermined day. For the next eight years his is the name

in the Roman annals which we hear most often, and
that on all the most critical occasions. He served,
in fact, as consul and proconsul in alternate years in
almost continuous succession ; and when, at last, he fell
in an ambuscade, his body was treated with marked
honour by the great Hannibal himself.

Foiled at Nola, Hannibal turned his attention to
Casilinum, a town situated on the Vulturnus, and then
containing a mixed garrison of Prænestines
and Perusians who had taken shelter within
its walls, when they heard of the disaster of
Cannæ. Leaving a sufficient force to blockade the
place, he went with the remainder into winter quarters
at Capua, a few miles to the south. It has been remarked by many writers, modern as well as ancient,
that Capua proved a Cannæ to Hannibal. Given over to
luxury and to Greek vices, it was certainly not the place
best suited for the winter retirement of an overstrained
army; and doubtless the troops, who had ere now
wintered amongst the snows of the Apennines or in the
open plains of Apulia, must have luxuriated in the
easeful quarters which Hannibal's sword had opened for
them. It is true also, as has already been pointed out,
that this year was a turning point in the war; but that it
was so is due to other causes than the luxury of Capua,
and it would not seem to be true that the troops were in
any way demoralized by their winter's comfort. They
were irresistible as ever in the field. The real difference
was that the Roman generals had learned in the school
of adversity not to trust themselves within the reach of
Hannibal's arm, and from this time to the end of the
war in Italy they acted on the Fabian maxim, and never
gave him an opportunity of fighting a pitched battle, or,
what was the same thing, of giving them a crushing defeat.

The consuls for the year 215 were the old Dictator Fabius and Tib. Sempronius Gracchus. Incredible exertions were made by Rome to bear the strain which was put upon her. Double taxes were imposed and paid, and freewill contributions were offered by the citizens, which it was understood were not to be repaid till the treasury was full; in other words, not till the war was over. The year, therefore, which followed the butchery of eight legions at Cannæ saw fourteen new ones raised to take their place, six of them in other parts of the Roman world, and the remaining eight in Italy itself. On his side, Hannibal can hardly have mustered more than 40,000 men, even if we include his recent levies in Samnium. It must be remembered that till towards the close of 216, after fighting four pitched battles, and marching and countermarching through the whole of Italy, Hannibal had received no single soldier and drawn not a single penny from the home government of Carthage. Never before or after was war so made to support itself, and never, even in the hands of the author of that sinister maxim, was it waged with such astonishing results.

Great exertions of Rome.

But if Hannibal's victories had not yet done for him all that he had hoped in Italy itself, might it not be possible to gain his object by taking a wider sweep? If Italy could not be armed against Rome, might not the surrounding countries, whose existence was already threatened, be armed against Italy and Rome alike? Circumstances, at the moment, seemed to smile on the project; for Hiero, the ancient and faithful ally of Rome, was just dead, and Hieronymus, his grandson and successor, straightway joined the Carthaginians. Sardinia, too, was plan-

Hannibal's wide projects.

ning a revolt from the city which had stolen her with such infamous bad faith from Carthaginian rule; and about the same time ambassadors arrived in Hannibal's camp from Philip, king of Macedon, offering to conclude with him an alliance offensive and defensive. But the bright vision rose before his eyes only to vanish away. The revolt of Sardinia was stamped out before it came to a head. Hieronymus was weak and foolish, and, setting himself to imitate the able Dionysius who had once ruled Syracuse, showed that he was able to imitate him only in his arrogance and his vices, and was soon despatched by the well-deserved dagger of the assassin. Finally, the Macedonian ambassadors, when returning with the treaty which had just been concluded between Hannibal and Philip, fell, as ill-luck would have it, into the hands of the Romans, and so gave them a timely warning to prepare for what might otherwise have burst upon them like a thunder-clap.

Amidst such hopes and such disappointments the year passed away. Throughout its course Hannibal had retained Tifata, a hill above Capua, as his headquarters. No better place could have been chosen. Here he could wait in safety the results, if any, of the alliances he was planning; here receive the long-expected reinforcements from Carthage if ever they should come. Here he could protect Capua, his latest and his most important acquisition; here with his one small army he could keep three separate armies, headed by no meaner generals than Fabius, Gracchus, and Marcellus, at bay, and, dealing his blows upon them in rapid succession, could threaten now Cumæ, now Naples, and now Nola; till at last the approach of winter warned him to transfer his troops to his former quarters at Arpi in Apulia.

Hannibal at Tifata.

The elections for the year 214 B. C.—after the consul Fabius had given a solemn warning to the electors to let military considerations alone influence them at such a time of need—ended, as was to be expected, and as Fabius had himself intended, in the re-election of the Mentor himself, Marcellus being chosen as his colleague. Seldom in Roman history had two such men held office at the same time, and the memories of the older citizens had to travel back to the days of Decius Mus, or even of Papirius Cursor, till they found, or thought they found, a parallel to it. In this year, indeed, and for some years to come, Rome was likely enough to need her shield as well as her sword. The fourteen legions which had been thought sufficient in the previous year, were raised now to the still more astonishing number of eighteen; and the wealthier citizens contributed from their private means the sums which were necessary to raise the payment of the sailors of the fleet.

Capua had already begun to tremble for her safety; but she was reassured when the movement of Hannibal showed that it was his intention not only to keep what he had already won in Campania, but, if possible, to win the whole. In vain, however, did he attempt to surprise or to bring over Cumæ, Naples, and Puteoli, seaport towns which would have done good service by opening direct communication with Carthage. Hanno, moreover, on coming to co-operate with him, with the numerous Lucanian and Bruttian levies which he had raised, was intercepted by Gracchus in the heart of Samnium. Gracchus promised freedom, in the event of victory, to the armed slaves of whom his force consisted; and in the battle which ensued, conscious that they were carrying their liberty as well as their lives in their hands, they cut to pieces Hanno's

Tide turns against Hannibal.

army, and received their reward. The word of a Gracchus, in this as in other epochs of Roman history, was his bond ; and a bond which was a first-rate security. These reverses brought Hannibal's plans of Campanian conquest to an abrupt conclusion, and when he received a friendly message from Tarentum, a place more important to him, just then, even than the Campanian towns, from its proximity to Macedon, he paid it a flying visit. But here, too, the Romans had anticipated him, and Fabius, taking advantage of his absence, besieged and recaptured Casilinum. When Hannibal went into his next winter quarters at Salapia in Apulia, the tide of victory had clearly turned against him. He was already waging a warfare which was mainly defensive, and it might have seemed to anyone who had not felt the terrors of his spring, that if only the three armies which lay watching him during the winter had ventured to beard the lion which lay crouching in his den, they would have had a chance of bringing the Second Punic War to a conclusion then.

During the next two years the interest of the war is for the first time, in some measure, diverted from Hannibal. The great Carthaginian, though he had not yet spoken aloud the word "impossible," must have occasionally whispered it to himself. He was still without adequate reinforcements from home ; for the considerable armament, which the news of Hannibal's triumphant progress through Italy had at last shamed the Carthaginians into raising for him, had, when they were on the point of embarkation, been diverted to Sardinia and Spain. In this last country the star of Carthage was not just then in the ascendant, and Hannibal, who had received only a paltry force of some forty elephants and some 4,000 Numidian cavalry from

Hannibal gains Tarentum.

his countrymen at home, was compelled, partly from necessity, and partly, it would seem, from lassitude, to spend the greater part of the summer of 213 in the neighbourhood of Tarentum, without attempting any active operations. With admirable policy, he had, even in the moment of disappointment in the preceding year, abstained from ravaging the Tarentine lands while he harried those of the surrounding towns, and now he reaped the result. In the course of the winter he was half offered, and he half forced for himself, an entrance into the city, though he was unable to eject the recently arrived Roman garrison from the citadel. Other and lesser Greek towns in the south followed the example of this, the greatest of them all; and Hannibal, compelled to relax his grasp upon Campania, made up for its loss by appropriating to himself a large part of Magna Græcia.

Meanwhile the war, which seemed for the moment to have spent its force in Italy, had broken out with fresh fury in Sicily. Marcellus, the best general whom the Romans possessed, was despatched to quell the revolt. The whole island, with few exceptions, had declared for Carthage; and the active emissaries of Hannibal, the desperation of the soldiers who had deserted from Rome, and the cruelties of the Romans in the first towns which they recaptured, cut off all hopes of a reconciliation. The Carthaginian government too, from some unexplained reason, now woke from its sleep, and sent Himilco with considerable reinforcements to Sicily. Had they only sent half the force to Italy in 216 which they sent in 214 to Sicily, the war might have had a different course. They were willing and able, it seemed, to send reinforcements at a time and to a place where they were not much needed; they would not send them at the time

War in Sicily.

and to the place where they would have been all-important.

After massacring the inhabitants of several towns, Marcellus laid siege to Syracuse; but all his efforts were frustrated by the science and by the engines of the famous mathematician Archimedes, and after eight months of chequered warfare, he was obliged to convert the siege into a blockade.

Syracuse was the greatest Greek city in Sicily, possibly the greatest of all Greek cities. It contained within its walls four distinct towns—the island of Ortygia, the oldest and the strongest part of the city; Achradina, or the city proper, crowded with magnificent buildings; and the two suburbs of Tycha and Neapolis. The whole had been recently surrounded by a wall eighteen miles in circumference, which in part abutted on the sea, but was in part carried over rugged hills or low-lying marshes, defensible in themselves, and now rendered doubly strong by art. The city possessed two harbours, in the larger of which the Carthaginian fleet, under Bomilcar, was riding at anchor, while a Carthaginian army, under Himilco, hovered near the walls, or made flying expeditions to other parts of Sicily, thus distracting the attention of the besiegers. The blockade, therefore, was never effective or complete, and it is not to be wondered at that it was nearly three years before the city fell.

Siege of Syracuse.

It was indeed treachery from within rather than force from without, which ultimately enabled Marcellus, in the year 212, to gain possession of the heights of Epipolæ to the rear of the city, and, making these his basis, to conquer in succession its different portions. The two suburbs fell first, and the plunder which they yielded whetted the

Taking of Syracuse.

appetites of the soldiery for the still richer stores which lay behind the walls of Achradina and Ortygia. It was now too late for Bomilcar or Himilco to save the city. Bomilcar sailed away without striking a blow, and the army of Himilco, which lay encamped on the low grounds of the Anapus, fell victims to the fever which had so often before saved Syracuse from a besieging force. By a curious caprice of fortune, the best defence of the city was now turned against its defenders, while it left its assailants on the higher ground unscathed. The Roman deserters and the mercenaries had long established a reign of terror within the city. Having nothing to hope, and little therefore to fear, they were bent on holding the place to the bitter end. But when Marcellus had been admitted by some of his partisans into the island of Ortygia, Achradina could no longer offer resistance. The deserters and the mercenaries, the only portion of the inhabitants who deserved punishment, managed to escape by night, and the remainder threw themselves on the mercy of Marcellus. They might well expect to receive it, for they had been involved in hostilities which were not of their own seeking, and it would be hard if the short-lived folly of Hieronymus should be held by Marcellus to have effaced the recollection of the fifty years' fidelity of Hiero his grandfather. But it seldom suited the Romans to remember past services or extenuating circumstances when they had anything to gain by forgetting them. Marcellus, as Livy tells us, had burst into tears when he first stood on Epipolæ and saw Syracuse, as he fancied, in his power beneath him. But these were not tears of compassion, or, if they were, they were not forthcoming now when they were most needed. The city was given over to plunder, and the death of Archimedes while intent upon a problem, a man whom—just as Alexander bade his troops spare the house of Pindar in the sack of Thebes —even the rough Marcellus had wished to save, gave proof that plunder was not the only aim of the infuriated soldiery.

So fell Syracuse, the virgin city, which had seen two Athenian armaments perish beneath its walls; which had for centuries saved Sicily from becoming altogether, what its greater part then was, a Carthaginian appanage; which had once and again, when its turn came, under Dionysius or Timoleon, almost driven those same Carthaginians from the island; and once, under Agathocles, had threatened the existence of Carthage herself. It fell to rise no more, at least to its former opulence. Its temples were left standing, because they would not pay for moving; and they belonged to the conqueror as much where they were as if they had been transferred to Rome; but the choicest works of art—vases and columns, paintings and statues—were swept off to adorn the imperial city. In so doing Marcellus set an example only too fatally followed by the conquerors who succeeded him. It was a practice new in Roman warfare then, and to be condemned at all times and under all circumstances: a practice cruel and destructive to the states despoiled, and useless for all moral or high artistic purposes to the despoiler.

CHAPTER XIV.

SIEGE OF CAPUA AND HANNIBAL'S MARCH ON ROME.

(212–208 B. C.)

We have hitherto concentrated our attention as much as possible on the main current of the war in Italy; but
Importance of war in Spain. it must not be forgotten that throughout these first six years which we have described in detail, a side conflict was raging in Spain, the result of which might go far to decide that in Italy. To the importance of the Spanish contest the Romans and the Carthaginians were equally alive. It was from Spain, if from any country, that Hannibal must draw his reinforcements; and it was in Spain, if anywhere, that those reinforcements must be intercepted and cut down. The Romans saw that if a second army crossed the Alps and swooped down upon the north of Italy, while Hannibal was at his pleasure overrunning the south, the city would be taken between two fires, and could not long resist. To Hannibal, on the other hand, Spain was the new world which the genius of his family had called into existence. The names of his father, Hamilcar, and of his brother-in-law the elder Hasdrubal, were still names of power among the Spanish tribes whom they had conquered or conciliated, and the younger Hasdrubal, a worthy member of the same family, had been left in Spain by Hannibal when he started on his great expedition, to preserve the family traditions there, and to raise fresh levies for the Italian war

P. Scipio, as we have seen, instead of returning in the autumn of B.C. 218 with all speed and with all his forces from Massilia to Italy, where he might possibly have met and crushed the worn-out troops of Hannibal as they descended from the Alps, had sent the bulk of his army straight to their Spanish destination, while he himself returned to Italy with only a few followers. After his defeats at the Ticinus and the Trebia, and while the memories of the Trasimene Lake were still fresh in the Roman minds, he was sent off to Spain with a naval and military force, which a less courageous and self-reliant people would have been unwilling to spare. There he joined Cnæus, and henceforward the two brothers carried on the war in common, bringing over Spanish tribes as much by their address as by their arms, and winning, if the accounts they sent home were true, an almost unbroken series of successes. After making sure of the country to the north of the Ebro, the Scipios crossed that boundary river, sent to their homes the Spanish hostages which, having been deposited by Hannibal in Saguntum, fell by the caprice of a Saguntine citizen into their hands, and in the autumn of the year 216— the year, it should be remembered, of the battle of Cannæ—defeated Hasdrubal in a pitched battle near a town called Ibera, when he was on the eve of starting for Italy with the large army he had recently raised in Spain or had received from Carthage. Rightly viewed, therefore, the battle of Ibera, though the place at which it was fought is quite unknown, was one of the most decisive in the whole of the war, for it prevented the despatch of reinforcements to Hannibal in the year when they would have made him wholly irresistible.

The two brothers made the most of their success.

They enrolled Celtiberian mercenaries—the first instance of such a practice on a large scale in
Roman history; they won victories which,
if they were not half what their despatches represented
them to be, were yet signal victories; they formed an
alliance with Syphax, a Numidian prince, and seemed
in B. C. 212 to be on the point of ejecting the Carthaginians from Spain, when, in the mid career of their
success, they inadvertently separated from each other.
They were then attacked by Hasdrubal and by Mago,
who had been recently sent thither from Carthage, in
detail, their armies were defeated and dispersed, and
themselves slain. It seemed for the moment as if the
Romans would be driven from Spain in the very year
in which they had confidently counted on driving out
the Carthaginians. But the death of the elder Scipios,
as we shall see, opened a free field for a younger and
still abler member of the family, and one whose high
destiny was to accomplish in Spain what his father and
uncle had been compelled to leave unfinished.

While these events were taking place in Spain, the
flame of war had burst out afresh in Italy. Early, it would
seem, in the winter of B. C. 212, Taren-
tum had fallen into Hannibal's hands, and
in the campaign thus begun the hero seemed
to awake, like a giant refreshed, from his year-long repose. He was needed each moment at Tarentum, where
the citadel still held out; he was needed yet more at
Capua, round which the Roman armies, like vultures
scenting their prey afar, seemed to be gathering for the
last time. The home government of Carthage itself
needed his controlling mind, the war in Sicily needed
it, the war in Spain, and the war in Greece. His spirit
and his influence, if not his bodily presence, were needed

everywhere, and everywhere once again they seemed to
be. Six Roman armies were in the field against him.
By a searching inquisition every free-born citizen—many
of them below the age of seventeen—had been swept
into the ranks, which were intended not, indeed, to face
him, for that they never dared to do, but to harass his
movements; yet he managed, in spite of them all, to
push the siege of the Tarentine citadel on the one hand,
and, on the other, to show himself for a moment when
required on the hills above Capua, where his mere appearance caused the two consular armies which were
threatening it to vanish away before him. One Roman
army of irregulars he annihilated in Lucania; another of
regular troops, under the prætor Fulvius, he annihilated
in Apulia; while a third, consisting of the slaves liber-
ated by Gracchus, as soon as their liberator had fallen
in an ambuscade, dispersed in all directions, thinking
that they had done enough for their step-mother Italy.

But amidst all these brilliant achievements and these
romantic shiftings of the war, the one point of fixed and
central interest was the city of Capua. That
guilty city had long felt that her turn must <small>Siege of Capua.</small>
soon come; she had gone now unpunished
for nearly four years, and the safety and the honour of
the Roman state alike demanded that the day of reckon-
ing should be no longer postponed. The mere presence
of two large armies in her neighbourhood during so considerable a part of these four years had caused a scarcity
within her walls before even a sod was turned of
the Roman lines of circumvallation. But Hannibal,
appearing at Capua while his enemies thought he was
in Iapygia, put the two armies which were threatening
it to flight, and, as it would seem, revictualled it for the
coming blockade. It was not till he had gone far to the

south again, and was scattering the smaller Roman armies there in the manner which has just been described, that they ventured to close in once more around the place, and began the siege in earnest. News of every fresh disaster reached Rome from the track of Hannibal's flying squadrons, and the Senate could only console itself by the reflection that the consular armies of Fulvius and Appius, which had fled before Hannibal's advance, were as yet intact, and were free during his absence, at all events, to prosecute the object which they had most at heart—the punishment of the guilty Capua.

Caius Nero, the prætor, was ordered to co-operate with the consuls, Q. Fulvius Flaccus and App. Claudius Pulcher; and the three armies in their several camps, each with a large magazine established in a town to its rear, settled down before the devoted city. A double line of circumvallation was soon completed, the one to guard the besiegers from the sorties of the besieged, the other to repel the expected attack of Hannibal from without (B. C. 211). The days of Capua were clearly numbered unless help came from him. An adventurous Numidian from the garrison made his way unobserved through the double lines of the Romans and informed Hannibal of the danger of the city. Taking a select band of horsemen and light-armed troops, the Phœnician hero started from Tarentum, and before the enemy dreamed of his approach he appeared on Mount Tifata. According to the plan which had been pre-arranged, a simultaneous attack was made on the Roman lines by the beleaguered garrison and by Hannibal. Some of the elephants, whose bulky frames had been with difficulty forced to keep pace with his cross-country march,

Attempt of Hannibal to relieve Capua.

were killed in the attack. Hannibal threw their bodies into the ditch, and a few of his troops crossing over on the bridge thus formed found themselves within the Roman lines. But it was only for a moment. They were outnumbered and driven back, and Hannibal gave up all hope of thus raising the siege.

One plan alone remained. He might advance on the capital; and the terror of the citizens when the danger which had so often approached them, and had so often been withdrawn, had at last really come, might drive them to recall for the defence of Rome the armies which were besieging Capua. Once more a Numidian messenger made his way through the Roman lines round Capua, and bade the citizens hold out bravely, for Hannibal's departure did not mean that he had deserted them. It rather meant that he was making one more effort for their deliverance, and then he was off for Rome. The news of what was coming reached the city long before Hannibal reached it himself, perhaps before he wished to reach it. A few days' delay would, he knew well, only increase the panic of the citizens. Slowly he advanced along the Latin road, passing each day some Latin fortress, and devastating the country right up to its walls beneath the eyes of its affrighted garrison. Before him fled a panic-stricken throng—women and children, and aged men—leaving their homes like animals when the prairie is on fire, a prey to the destroyer. On he went, through Latium, through the only district of Italy which had not yet felt his dreaded presence, no one daring to say him nay, till he pitched his tent upon the Anio, only three miles from Rome, and the flaming villages announced in language that could not be mistaken that he was really there. He

His march on Rome.

was there in fulfilment of his life-long vow; the hater face to face, at last, with the object of his deadly hate. He was there, the destroyer of every Roman army which had ventured to meet him, to destroy the city which had sent them forth. So thought at least the flying rustics and the mass of the Roman citizens. But so did not think the calm and clear-sighted Hannibal himself; nor yet, after the first days of panic had passed by, so thought the Roman Senate. The imagination, indeed, of the citizens pictured to themselves the total destruction of their armies at Capua. The air was filled with cries of women who ran wildly about the streets, or flocked to the temples of the gods, and, throwing themselves on their knees, raised their suppliant hands to heaven, or swept the altars with their long dishevelled hair.

But the Roman Senate, as after Trasimene and after Cannæ, was once more worthy of itself. When the terrible news of Hannibal's first approach came, they had been disposed to recall the whole of their armies to the defence of the capital; a measure of precaution which would have fulfilled Hannibal's highest hopes and saved the beleaguered Capua. But fresh confidence came. They recalled only Fulvius, who, marching by inner lines, amidst a population who bade him God-speed, managed to reach Rome by the Appian, just before Hannibal reached the Anio by the Latin Way. Two legions which had lately been got together in the country around Rome, when they were joined by the army which had just arrived, gave the city a respectable garrison, and Hannibal made no attack—he probably never intended to make one—on the city itself. Unmolested by the Romans and almost within their view,

Hannibal before Rome.

he ravaged the whole country round, destroying the gardens and the villages, and carrying off into his camp, with stern delight, the crops and the cattle, and the booty of every kind on which he could lay his hand. Then with a body of two thousand horsemen he rode right up to the Colline gate, and passed leisurely along the walls to the temple of Hercules, gazing wistfully at the cruel stones which alone stood between him and his hopes, and alone saved the inhabitants, Romans though they were, from his avenging sword. The fates were against him, but he must have felt that he had nobly kept his vow.

Little wonder is it, when the facts themselves are so dramatic, and when the chief character is so heroic, that the imagination of those who recorded the scene ran riot in the process and filled in the details with what they thought ought to have happened. They pointed, for instance, their eulogies on the faith of the Romans in their own future, by telling us how they put up to auction the ground on which Hannibal's camp was pitched, and how it was bought at its full value; while Hannibal, by way of reprisals, offered for sale to his troops the silversmiths' shops in the Roman Forum, and flung his spear over the walls in token of his contempt and hate. But Hannibal was great enough to know when he had delivered his blow, and he wasted no time in lamenting that it had failed. Accordingly he marched off northward into the Sabine country, which he had only skirted in his first campaign, and then sweeping round to the south he turned fiercely upon the Romans who were making believe to follow him, and after taking one distant look at the unbroken and impenetrable girdle of men, and earth, and iron, which girt Capua in, he left her to her inevitable fate.

Inevitable indeed it was; for the Romans knew no pity, and the citizens themselves must have felt that the murder of all the Romans residing in the city at the time of their revolt would have steeled even those who were naturally pitiful against them. The senators, abandoned to despair, shut themselves within their own houses, and left the responsibilities of the defence to the Numidian leaders. At last, when the surrender of the city was only a question of hours, they met at the house of one Vibius Virrius, the author of the revolt, and after holding high festival on such fare as the besieged city could supply, and could lend them courage for what they were about to do, they passed round the poisoned cup, and, to the number of twenty-seven, balked their Roman conquerors of their long-expected revenge. Of the remaining senators, when, next day, the gates were opened, twenty-five were sent by the orders of the consuls to Cales, and twenty-eight to Teanum; but close behind them followed the victor Fulvius, and by his command they were scourged and beheaded, one by one, before his eyes. When the bloody work was only half finished a despatch from the Senate arrived bidding him reserve for their decision the question of the punishment; but the butcher thrust it into his bosom, and it was not till the last head had fallen that he read the letter which might have postponed, but would hardly have averted, their fate. Three hundred noble Campanian youths were thrown into prison to perish, many of them, later, on a trumped-up charge. The bulk of the citizens were dispersed among the Latin colonies, or were sold into slavery. The city itself was spared, a signal instance, remarks Livy—is he speaking in irony or in earnest?—of Roman clemency. But it was no longer to have citizens or any form of civic life.

Fate of Capua.

Without magistrates, and without a senate, it was to receive year by year a prefect from Rome, who should deal out Roman justice to such waifs and strays of population as might be drawn thither by the incomparable beauty of the situation, or by the fertility of the soil. It was a warning also, Livy remarks—and here he is on safer ground—to any other city which had revolted, or might yet be disposed to revolt, of the amount of protection she might expect henceforward from Hannibal, and of the vengeance which would surely fall upon her from Rome.

In vain did Hannibal endeavour by some brilliant stroke to counteract the fatal impression which the surrender of Capua must produce on his Italian allies. An attempt to surprise Rhegium failed, and all his efforts to capture the citadel of Tarentum failed also. *Hannibal's superiority in the field.* Just now too Marcellus, his worthiest antagonist, returned from Sicily flushed with victory, and eager, so the Romans thought, at last to measure his sword with his ancient foe. Now also an alliance was formed by Rome with the brigands of Ætolia, which cut off Hannibal's last hope that Philip of Macedon would ever be able to join him in Italy. Everything, in fact, seemed to betoken that the end was near; but those who thought so reckoned prematurely. In the year which followed the fall of Capua, the year B. C. 210, Hannibal surprised and slew the Prætor, Cn. Fulvius, before Herdonea. Herdonea itself, which was meditating revolt, he burned to the ground after transferring its inhabitants to Metapontum and Thurii, two of the few towns which were still faithful to him. In B. C. 209, when Samnium and Lucania had already submitted to the Romans, and while one consul, Fulvius, was threatening Metapontum, and the other consul, Fabius was pressing the siege of Tarentum in his rear, he fought two brilliant actions in Apulia, which drove his third antagonist, the sword of Rome, himself, to take refuge in Venusia, and to adopt the more cautious tactics of its shield.

In B. C. 208 and 207 his superiority in the field was as incontestable as ever. Tarentum, indeed, which it had cost him so much to win and so much to keep, had been betrayed by the commander of its garrison into the hands of the Romans, and suffered the fate, or worse even than the fate, of Syracuse and Capua. All the Bruttians found within it were put to death; thirty thousand of its Greek inhabitants were sold as slaves, and all the works of art it contained, except its " angry gods," were carried off to Rome. Yet Hannibal encamped beneath its walls as though the place still belonged to him, and in vain offered battle to its new possessors. When he moved northwards into Apulia and found himself with his ever-diminishing force face to face with two consular armies, there he yet ventured to detach a flying squadron, which cut to pieces a Roman legion on a spot some fifty miles to his rear; and he held his own in the open field, waiting patiently till the moment should come for striking a blow. At last the moment came, and the blow which he struck was a heavy one. The consuls, Crispinus and Marcellus, as fate would have it, had left their camps, each with a small band of followers, and had ridden in company to the top of a wooded hill which lay between their two armies. They were observed by the Numidian cavalry, ready as ever for a surprise or a deed of daring. There was a sudden charge, and Crispinus wounded to the death, staggered back to his camp, while the body of the other consul, the bravest of the brave, was found by Hannibal himself where it had fallen.

Death of Marcellus.

The Phœnician gazed on it for a while in silence, and then remarking, "There lies a good soldier but a bad general," ordered it to be honourably burned and the ashes to be sent to his son.

But dangers greater even than the loss of Marcellus were now threatening the Romans. For in the year 209 symptoms of exhaustion, if not of disaffection had begun to show themselves even within the bounds of the Confederation, amongst the Latin colonies themselves. *Exhaustion of Latin colonies.* Twelve of the thirty colonies, and those some of the oldest and the most important, in the most widely scattered parts of Italy, declared that the Romans must look for no more men and money from them, for they had neither men nor money to give. The news fell like a thunderbolt upon the consuls who were the first to hear it, and the Roman Senate knew that if the example spread all was lost; but they were prudent enough, or generous enough, to require no forced service. Accordingly, throwing themselves on the fidelity and devotion of the remaining eighteen, they prepared to face their redoubtable antagonist with such help as they alone could give her.

CHAPTER XV.
BATTLE OF THE METAURUS.
(207 B. C.)

It seemed to augur ill for Rome that the stress of the war had at length begun to tell on the spirit and the fidelity of the Latin colonies themselves. But, more ominous still, news reached the city in B. C. 208 that after the vicissitudes of the ten years' struggle in Spain, Hasdrubal had at length *Approach of Hasdrubal from Spain.*

eluded Scipio, had entered Gaul by the passes of the Western Pyrenees, was raising fresh levies there, and early in the following summer might be expected in Italy. Rome had been in no such peril since the morrow of the battle of Cannæ; for the approach of Hasdrubal indicated that the great Spanish struggle, to support which Rome had sent out some of her best troops and generals, even when Hannibal was threatening her existence, had at last been played out, and had ended in favour of Carthage. It seemed, indeed, that Carthage by conquering in Spain had assured her victory in Italy also. For the last two years one son of Hamilcar had been overrunning Italy from end to end, and had more than once brought Rome to the brink of destruction; and now with her resources diminished, her population halved, and her allies wavering, she had to face the onset of a second son of the same dreaded chieftain, who would sweep down with new swarms of Gauls and Spaniards from the north, while his brother, for the last time, moved up for her destruction from his retreat in Bruttium in the south. A bitter comment this on the brilliant victory which Scipio was reported to have just won at Bæcula in Spain! For Hasdrubal, his defeated adversary, was not penned, as he should have been, within the walls of Gades, but was collecting allies at his leisure in the heart of Gaul.

A few precious months of winter remained to prepare for the double danger which the spring would bring. C. Claudius Nero, a man who had done fair service before Capua and in Spain, was one of the consuls selected for the year of peril. His plebeian colleague, M. Livius, was one of the few Romans then living who had enjoyed a triumph; but his temper had been soured by an unjust charge of

Preparations of Romans.

peculation, and he was personally hostile to Nero. However, in the face of public danger, he was brought to forget his grievances and to act in concert with his colleague for the public good. Livius, so the Senate arranged, was to await the approach of Hasdrubal near the frontiers of Hither Gaul, while Nero was to impede, as best he could, the movements of Hannibal in the south. Seventy thousand Romans and as many allies were put into the field for this, the supreme effort, as it seemed, of the republic.

As soon as the weather permitted, Hasdrubal started from Auvergne. Everything was in his favour. The mountaineers were friendly, the mountain passes were free from snow, his army gathered strength and bulk as it advanced, *Hasdrubal in Italy.* and was in a more effective condition when it entered the plains of Italy than when it had crossed the Pyrenees. What a contrast to his brother's advance ten years before! Less prudent than his brother, however, Hasdrubal sat down to besiege Placentia when he should have been pressing on towards his destination. When at last he moved forward, the Roman army retreated before him till it reached the small town of Sena to the south of the Metaurus. From this place Hasdrubal sent messengers who were to bid Hannibal meet him at Narnia, only some thirty miles from Rome. But Hannibal the messengers failed to find, and, falling into the hands of the Romans, their despatches were read not by the Carthaginian, but by the Roman general. Since the beginning of the campaign Hannibal had been rapidly shifting his quarters backwards and forwards between Bruttium and Apulia amidst a network of Roman fortresses and armies, always followed and never opposed by his vastly more numerous foe.

The victories attributed by Livy and others to Nero during this period are purely fictitious, and are explicitly contradicted by Polybius himself. Hannibal, as fate would have it, must have gone southwards just before his brother's messengers were despatched to find him. Had it been otherwise, they must have reached him in safety; and in that case we can hardly doubt that the brilliant march northward would have been not Nero's but Hannibal's, and that the Metaurus would have seen the collapse of the fortunes not of Carthage but of Rome.

Nero formed a bold resolution—one almost without precedent at this period of Roman history—to desert the province and even a portion of the troops confided to his keeping by the Senate; with the remainder to march rapidly northward, a distance of 200 miles, to join Livius, to crush Hasdrubal by a combined assault, and then to return again before Hannibal should have discovered his absence. It was a bold step, but hardly bolder than the extremity of the danger required; above all, it was justified by the event. Nero took care not to inform the Senate of what he proposed to do till he was already doing it, thus putting it in their power to co-operate with his later movements, but not giving them the chance of impeding the decisive blow. He had already sent messengers to the friendly cities near his line of march bidding them help, as best they could, the progress of their deliverers. The 6,000 infantry and the 1,000 cavalry selected for the enterprise started, like the 10,000 Greeks before them, in total ignorance of their destination. They believed that they were about to surprise some petty Carthaginian garrison near at home in Lucania; and their enthusiasm, when the momentous

March of Nero.

secret was communicated to them, was only equalled by
that of the Italian provincials who thronged the roadside
with provisions, vehicles, and beasts of burden, and accompanied the army with their blessings and their
prayers. The soldiers declined everything that was not
necessary for their immediate support; and pausing, we
are told, neither to eat nor to drink, hardly even to
sleep, in a few days they neared the camp of the other
consul. Nero entered it at night and distributed his
wearied troops among the tents which were already
occupied, so as to avoid exciting the suspicions of
Hasdrubal till he should meet them in the field. But
next morning the quick ear of the Carthaginian noticed
that the trumpet sounded twice instead of once within
the enemy's camp, and when the Romans offered battle
his quick eye rested with suspicion on the travel-stained
troops and the draggled horses of a portion of the army.
Concluding that the other consul had arrived and that
his brother's army must have been dispersed or annihilated, he remained within his camp throughout that day,
and at nightfall began to retreat towards the friendly
Gaul. He reached the Metaurus in safety, but here his
guides played him false, and instead of crossing at once
by the ford, he wandered hither and thither on the
nearer side, vainly searching for it in the darkness.

Morning light brought the Romans, and Hasdrubal
had now no choice but to draw up his army where it
was, with a rapid and dangerous river in
his rear. The Spanish veterans, his main
strength, he placed on the right, intending
to lead them in person against Livius. The Ligurians,
with the elephants in their front, formed the centre,
while the Gauls, untrustworthy as ever—except when led
by Hannibal—were drawn up on a hill to the left, which,

by the mere advantage of position, they could hardly fail to hold against Nero. The Spaniards, under Hasdrubal's own eye, fought nobly and with every prospect of success, till Nero, unable to dislodge the Gauls, left them to themselves, and by a brilliant manœuvre, passing behind the whole length of the Roman army, fell at once on the Spanish flank and rear. Thus surrounded they were cut to pieces where they stood, and Hasdrubal after doing all that a general could do to save the fortunes of the day, rushed into the midst of the enemy's cavalry, and died as became the son of Hamilcar and the brother of Hannibal. The greater part of the elephants, when they became unmanageable, were killed by their own drivers, who were furnished with weapons for the purpose, and who knew how and where to strike the fatal blow. The Gauls were slaughtered as they lay on the ground, heavy with wine or wearied out by their night's march.

The victory of Rome was not bloodless but it was complete. Hasdrubal's army, whatever its size was annihilated, and some of the Roman annalists, regardless alike of truth and probability, strove to make out that the slaughter of Metaurus equalled that of Cannæ. From the agonies of suspense the Romans passed at once into the exuberant enthusiasm of victory. They had been rudely awakened to the consciousness that there were two Hannibals in Italy. They forgot now that there was still one. That THE Hannibal was still in Italy, still unconquered, and, as far as they knew, unconquerable. A well-deserved triumph was granted the victorious generals. It was the first which the Sacred Way had seen ever since Hannibal had entered Italy, for it was the first time, by the confession of the Romans themselves, that victory had smiled on their arms. **The consuls** triumphed in com-

Barbarism of Nero.

mon; but Nero was the hero of the day. To him was due alike the strategy of the northward march—a mar 'n perhaps only equalled in history by the advance of Marlborough from Belgium to the Danube in the campaign of Blenheim—and the brilliant stroke which decided the battle. To Nero, however, also belongs the act of revolting barbarism which wound up his achievements and must for ever detract from his fair fame. Returning to his army in Apulia as quickly as he had left it, he carried with him the head of Hasdrubal which he had caused to be severed from his body, and, with true Roman brutality ordered this ghastly trophy of victory to be flung into the camp of Hannibal, who, it is said, was still ignorant that the general opposed to him had ever left his quarters. Hannibal recognised the features of the brother whom he had so long and eagerly expected, and in them sadly saw the doom of Carthage.

CHAPTER XVI.

P. CORNELIUS SCIPIO.

(210-206 B.C.)

IT is necessary, now that we have reached this, the decisive point of the war, to direct our attention once more to Spain; for it was on the Metaurus that Spain as well as Italy was lost to the Carthaginians, and it was in Spain, at this very time, that, moving in an atmosphere of mingled war and love, amidst romantic expeditions and hair-breadth escapes, fortunate in what he did, and perhaps more fortunate in what he failed to do, surrounded by devoted friends like Lælius, or by court annalists, who saw all his doings through the bright halo which he or they

Scipio in Spain.

diffused around them, the young general was being nursed by Fortune into fame who was soon to drive the Carthaginians from Spain, then, without striking a blow, was to compel Hannibal to withdraw from Italy, was next to crush that greatest of all heroes in Africa, and, finally, to bring to a conclusion there the long agony of the Second Punic War. P. Cornelius Scipio is one of the central figures of Roman history. His presence and his bearing exercised a strange fascination over all who came within its influence, and his name, with the romances that began to cluster round it even in his lifetime, was a yet more living power with posterity. It turned the head of even the sober-minded Polybius, and has given an air of unreality and of poetry to such fragments of his history of this portion of the war as have, unfortunately, alone come down to us. Let us pause for a while on the antecedents and the surroundings, the virtues and the failings, of so important and conspicuous a personage.

Scipio was the son of that Publius who, by an unlooked-for reverse of fortune, had just been defeated and killed in the field of his numerous victories and in the full tide of his success. But Fortune, so capricious towards the father, was unswerving in her devotion to the son. He was then only twenty-four years of age; but, young as he was, he was already known to fame by his conduct on three critical occasions. As a mere stripling of seventeen he had saved, or it was believed that he had saved, his father's life at the battle of Ticinus at the risk of his own; after Cannæ it was his resolute bearing which had shamed or frightened the recreant nobles of Rome from deserting the fast sinking ship of the state; at the age of twenty-three he had been candidate for the curule ædileship, and when the magistrate objected that he was not yet of legal age, he replied that if all the Quirites wished to make him ædile he was old enough. It was a characteristic reply, a sample of that contempt for the forms of law, and that mingled respect and contempt for popular opinion, which marked his conduct on several occasions of his life, and goes some way to explain alike what he did and what he failed to do ; and now, when his father and uncle had fallen in Spain, and the comitia were being held for the election of some one to fill their place, and, as the story goes, people were looking anxiously one upon the other to see who would offer himself for a task wherein two Scipios had failed, it was the young Publius himself who, with mingled modesty and self-reliance, came forward, and was straightway chosen proconsul amidst the exclamations of all present.

A second secret of Scipio's influence was the popular belief, in part, at least, shared by himself, that he was the special favourite of the gods and inspired by them in all he did. Stories were in the air of his divine descent, and even of his miraculous birth, which he had too much prudence either to affirm or to contradict. Why should the favourite of the gods refuse to avail himself of any help they offered him ? In the existence of the gods and in their special help to him Scipio doubtless implicitly believed; but the ostentatious secrecy of his visits to the Capitol before undertaking any work of importance must have been suggested by the credulity of the multitude rather than his own. At all events, his interviews with Jupiter there never ended in any other way than a careful consideration of the circumstances of the case in the privacy of his own study would have been likely to suggest. He was not, therefore, as has sometimes been said, "a real enthusiast," nor was his a "genuinely prophetic nature;" on the other hand, he was no mere vulgar impostor. He had enough of enthusiasm himself to evoke it towards himself in others, not enough to allow himself, under any circumstances, to be hurried away by it. One of the greatest of Roman heroes, he was himself only three parts a Roman. He was fond of literary men, and was himself not destitute of Greek culture; a weakness which certainly could not be charged against any genuine Roman of the old school. By turns the hero and the enemy of the populace, he knew how to win yet how to despise, how to use yet sometimes how to abuse, popular favour. In Spain, with the air and the surroundings of a king, he had enough Roman feeling to reject the regal gewgaws and the regal title which the Spaniards pressed upon him; at Rome, after his victory at Zama, he showed that he still retained enough of the genuine republican spirit to refuse the invidious honours—the dictatorship for life and the statue in the Capitol—which the citizens in the ecstasy of their joy would fain have given him. But he had not that inborn reverence for law and for authority which had made the Romans what they were, and which would have bidden him cheerfully remain in Italy, even when he knew he had it in him to finish the war in Africa, rather than resist the powers that be. A Roman of the old type would have submitted to an accusation or to a punishment which he knew to be unjust rather than involve himself in the semblance of illegality; but Scipio, when his brother Lucius was called to give an account of the moneys which he had received from King Antiochus, and was about to present to the Senate the document which would have cleared or condemned him,

proudly snatched it from his hands and tore it to pieces
before their eyes. So again, in his last appearance in
public life, when it was his own turn to have his conduct
called in question, he reminded his accusers, by a happy
stroke of audacity which was akin to genius, that this
was the day on which he had defeated Hannibal at
Zama, and called upon them to follow him to the Capitol
that they might there return thanks to the gods who had
given them the victory, and pray that the Roman state
might have other citizens like himself. The appeal was
irresistible, and the Romans once more showed that
they could not judge a Manlius in sight of the Capitol.
These incidents have a grandeur peculiarly their own;
but it is hardly a Roman grandeur. As a young man
Scipio was fond of romantic situations, and fortune
showered them upon him. The charms of his personal
presence, and the moral and material victories which
they won, his adventurous interviews with Spanish or
Berber princes, or with hostile generals, his chivalrous
treatment of captive maidens and their bridegrooms or
their suitors, fill a large part in the histories which
remain to us of his Spanish and his African campaigns.
Much of the setting of these stories may be imaginary;
but the stories themselves doubtless rest on a substratum
of fact, and they reveal to us, however dimly, a union of
gallantry and generosity, of prudence and of passion, of
sensibility to the charms of beauty, and yet of resistance
to their power, which enable us to feel something of the
fascination which made Scipio the idol of his soldiers,
of the natives of Spain and Africa, and of the great
body, and those the more generous, of his fellow-citizens.
Above all, if Scipio had not all the most characteristic
Roman virtues, he was free from the worst Roman vices.
He was not cruel, not faithless, not indifferent to human

life; as times went, he was not self-seeking. He could appreciate virtue in an enemy, he could be generous to a fallen foe. He could observe the terms of a capitulation, he could suppress a mutiny without promiscuous massacre, and could sometimes take a town without slaughtering the inhabitants in cold blood. He could even enter into the peculiarities and characteristics of nations other than his own, and, unlike his younger namesake, could shrink from obliterating a seat of ancient civilization and commerce at one fell blow. In fine, if he was not a worthy antagonist to Hannibal, he was the least unworthy that Rome, the nurse of heroes, could in this sixteen years' war produce; and if he was the favourite of Fortune, it must be admitted that that capricious goddess has seldom conferred her favours on one who did so much to deserve them.

Scipio crossed to Spain with 11,000 men towards the close of the year B.C. 210, and early in the spring of the following year he struck a blow which showed that a general of a new stamp had appeared upon the scene. Finding that the three Carthaginian generals, Hasdrubal and Mago, sons of Hamilcar, and Hasdrubal, son of Gisco, were passing the winter in widely different parts of Spain each more distant from New Carthage than he was himself, and hearing also that the garrison had been reduced to 1,000 men, he determined to make a rapid descent upon that city, the head-quarters of the Carthaginian government and the key to their position in Spain.

New Carthage was a noble city situated on a land-locked harbour, the only good harbour on the south-east coast of Spain. It was surrounded on all sides by water, save where an isthmus only 250 yards wide connected it with the mainland. Its fortifications, strong everywhere, were doubly

Capture of New Carthage.

strong here; but there was one weak spot which fortune or the gods were preparing to reveal to their favourite. The object of the enterprise was entrusted to Lælius, Scipio's lifelong friend, alone; and it was arranged that he should enter the harbour with the fleet just when Scipio with his land force appeared before its walls. Not a whisper of what was coming reached the city till it was already come; and not a misadventure or a hitch occurred from the moment when the adventurous Scipio left Tarraco to the time when New Carthage was in his power. The assault indeed of the Romans on the fortifications of the isthmus was repelled; but Scipio intended it to be so, for it was not the real point of his attack. Taking advantage of the ebb tide which left the waters of the lagoon on the western side so low that they could easily be forded—a fact known to few but himself—and, by a happy inspiration, bidding his soldiers follow him boldly where Neptune himself pointed out the way, Scipio led a select body of his troops to the attack, through waters which besiegers and besieged might well have thought would submerge them all. The walls here proved to be accessible, and they were quite undefended. The attention of the garrison had been called elsewhere, and with the help of scaling ladders and the god of the sea the small band soon found themselves masters of New Carthage. New Carthage—with its mines of gold and silver, its arsenal and its dockyards, its merchant vessels and its stores of corn, its stands of arms and its engines of war, its skilled workmen and its hostages drawn by the suspicious Carthaginians from all the Spanish tribes—all belonged to Rome. The work of slaughter over—and terrible work it was—Scipio addressed himself to the distribution of the booty. If the stories that have come down to us may be trusted, the survivors of the massacre had reason to admire the skill with which their conqueror managed to turn foes into friends, and so, as it were, to arm Carthage against herself. Under promise of their freedom the Punic shipwrights cheerfully transferred their services to Rome. Captive princesses, who might have been given up to the Roman soldiery, or reserved by the young general for himself, were restored to their parents or their betrothed lovers; and the hostages, those standing monuments of Carthaginian mistrust, were dismissed to their homes and converted into so many pledges of Roman moderation and good will.

It seemed once more as if the Spanish war was over; and Lælius was dispatched to Rome to report to the Senate, perhaps to magnify, the achievements of his friend. We are surprised indeed, after so brilliant a beginning, to find that the young general, instead of pressing on at once to Gades, fell back on Tarraco whence he had started, and that Hasdrubal, after he had been conquered by him in a decisive battle at Bæcula, was yet able, as has been already related, to give him the slip and to go off with a considerable force to Italy, thus to all appearance accomplishing the object of the long Spanish struggle. It was not till Hasdrubal had spent the winter months in Gaul, had invaded Italy, and had fallen on the Metaurus, that Scipio ventured to advance into Bætica, and then, step by step, after a decisive victory at Elinga or Silpia, drove the Carthaginians into Gades, "their first and their last possession" in Spain. Nor was it till the year B. C. 205 that Mago, the last of the brood of Hamilcar, passed over into the Balearic Islands, leaving to Rome, or rather to two centuries of half-suppressed revolts against her cruel and treacherous

Carthaginians driven out of Spain.

CHAPTER XVII.

THE WAR IN AFRICA. BATTLE OF ZAMA.

(206–202 B.C.)

ON his return to Rome towards the close of the year B. C. 206, Scipio enumerated to the Senate, which had been assembled for that purpose in the Temple of Bellona outside the walls, the long roll of the actions which he had fought, the towns which he had taken, and the cities which he had subdued. Not a Carthaginian, he proudly told them, was left alive in Spain. He expected to receive a triumph; and, truly, in view of his successes, if not of his intrinsic merits, he deserved it as few Roman generals had done before him. But the Senate, half envious and half distrustful of the young general, determined to abide by precedent where, as in this case, precedent fell in with their own inclinations; and refused an honour which had never yet been granted except to a regularly commissioned officer of the state. Scipio, who had conquered as a mere proconsul, could console himself only with the conquests he had yet in view, when perhaps there might be no such artificial obstacle to the reward which they merited. He had not long to wait; for at the Comitia, to which the people flocked as much to see as to vote for the conqueror of Spain, he was unanimously chosen Consul—though he had not yet filled the office of Prætor, and was still only thirty years of age— and with the purpose clearly understood, even if it was

Scipio elected consul.

not expressed in words, that he should transfer the war to Africa.

But the fathers of the city were full of misgivings. They remembered Regulus. They reflected that Hannibal was still in Italy, that there might be life in the old lion yet, and that even in his death-grapple, he might, like the blind and captive Samson, slay and scatter his foes once more as he had done scores of times in the heyday of his strength. The old Fabius, true to his policy to the end, advised Scipio to reckon with Hannibal and his few soldiers in Italy rather than attempt to draw him off to Africa, where he would have the whole power of Carthage at his back. But Scipio showed clearly enough that, if the Senate refused the leave he sought, he would seek it from the people; and if he failed to get it from them, he would still take it for himself. The Senate, therefore, were glad to save their dignity and to shift a portion of their responsibility from their own shoulders, by assigning the province of Sicily to the newly elected consul, at the same time giving him permission to cross thence into Africa, "if he should judge it to be advantageous to the state." They declined, however, to vote him a sufficient army, and would hardly even allow him to accept the services of those who came to him as volunteers. The army assigned to him consisted of but two legions, and those the two which had survived the defeat at Cannæ, and which had been kept on duty in Sicily, as in a kind of penal settlement, ever since. But the warlike nations of Italy supplied him with seven thousand trusty volunteers; and the Etruscans, those ancient mariners of the Italian waters, eagerly furnished him with the rough materials for a fleet. Once more the fairy tale of the First Punic War is repeated in honour

Proposes to invade Africa.

of the favourite of the gods, and a growing wood was
transformed in forty-five days into a fleet of ten quadri-
remes and twenty quinqueremes.

With this meagre provision for what he was meditating, Scipio landed in his province. There he furnished
three hundred of his army with horses
which he had taken from the Sicilians; a
delicate operation, but so adroitly man-
aged that we are asked to believe that the despoiled provincials, instead of resenting it as an injury, thanked
him as for a benefit. Discharged veterans of the army
of Marcellus came and enrolled themselves amongst his
followers, and supplies of provisions came flowing in
from all the corn-growing lands of Sicily. The ships
which he knew to be seaworthy he sent under the command of Lælius to devastate the African coast; those
which were newly built he laid up for the winter in dry
docks at Panormus, that their unseasoned timbers might
warp or leak in a place where a warp or a leak would
not be fatal to them. He then went into winter quarters
in the pleasant town—too pleasant his critics at Rome
deemed it—of Syracuse. But the inactivity which was
thus forced or seemed to be forced upon him in his own
province he turned to good account by the blow he managed to strike in the province of his colleague. He
threw a small force across the straits of Messana, and
by an arrangement with a party within the town, he
got possession of Locri, an important place near the
southernmost point of Italy. Hannibal thus found himself deprived for the moment of his base of operations in
Bruttium. But the gain was a doubtful one for the
reputation alike of Scipio and of Rome; for the capture
of the town was followed by a series of terrible atrocities
which Scipio, if he did not actually authorize them, took

no measures either to prevent or adequately to punish, and which reflected seriously on the state in whose service the worst offenders were.

Early in 204 B. C., the armament which Scipio had collected in face of the lukewarmness or the opposition of the Senate sailed, amidst all the pomp and circumstance of war, from Lilybæum, that ancient stronghold of the Phœnician race. Accounts differ as to its size. Some of our authorities—they can perhaps in this instance hardly be called authorities at all—place the number of men on board as low as 12,000, while others make it as high as 36,000. But if we take the higher, and perhaps the more likely estimate, we still cannot fail to observe how vastly inferior in numbers this expedition was to those which were again and again despatched against Carthage, or her maritime dependencies, in the course of the First Punic War. Even if the Senate had taken up the project warmly, as a more far-sighted body would probably have done, the waste of life and property occasioned by Hannibal's fourteen years' war in Italy must have made any armament which they were able to raise look small in comparison with that of Regulus; and we are surprised to find that the Carthaginians, who still claimed, in a measure, the empire of the seas, who knew what an invasion of Africa meant, and who had long seen that it was coming, yet offered no opposition by their fleet to Scipio's approach. The small force that was for ever to deprive Carthage of her proudest title, and to make her a mere dependency of Rome, landed on the third day, without seeing a vestige of the foe, near the "Fair Promontory;" and Scipio, according to his wont, drew a not ill-grounded omen of success from the name of the spot to which the gods, or his own care-

[marginal note: Scipio invades Africa.]

fully considered plans, had guided him. Fortune, however, did not smile on his first attempt. Already while in Spain he had prepared the way for his invasion of Africa by opening friendly communications with the two Numidian chieftains from whom, in such a contingency, he might have most to hope or fear. These two chieftains were Massinissa, head of the Massylians, a tribe which dwelt immediately to the westward of the domain of Carthage, and Syphax, who ruled the Massæsylians, a much more important tribe, occupying the region of the modern Algeria. Before we enter on those final operations of the war in which they play so important a part, it is necessary to give a brief account of the antecedents of each of these barbarian princes.

Massinissa had, during many years, fought against the Romans in the Spanish war, and had done good service to Carthage; but, even there, seeing which way fortune was turning, he had, with the astute fickleness of a barbarian, come to a secret understanding with Scipio. Syphax was also bound by treaty to Carthage. But it was a treaty which the Carthaginians well knew that he would break as soon as he should deem it to his advantage to do so; and Scipio flattered himself that by a romantic visit, which, amidst great dangers, he had paid to his court in the midst of the Spanish war, he had secured alike the support of the Berber chieftain and the admiration of Hasdrubal, his Carthaginian antagonist. It was by a strange coincidence indeed that the rival generals, unknown to each other, had abandoned their respective armies in Spain, and, crossing over into Africa, had met with antagonistic objects, but in no unfriendly intercourse, at the court of an African prince. Fascinated by Scipio's address and bearing, Syphax readily promised the alliance which he asked. But the surpassing beauty of Sophonisba, the daughter of his other guest, made a more permanent impression on the amorous barbarian; and on the promise of a marriage with her, Syphax was induced to throw up his newly formed friendship with Rome, and to renew his old one with Carthage. He forthwith drove his nephew Massinissa out of his hereditary kingdom; and when that chieftain, after innumerable adventures and escapes, now presented himself in Scipio's camp near the Fair Promontory, it was only as an outlaw at the head of a few horsemen, whose aid might cost the Romans more than it was worth. This was a keen disappointment to Scipio, and, so far, seemed to augur ill for his African campaign.

It might have been expected that in this, the last period of the war, waged as it was almost under the walls of Carthage, some clear rays of light would have been thrown on the internal state of the city itself. But in this, as in other parts of the long struggle, we look in vain for such a clear and truthful narrative of events as would have enabled us to picture to ourselves the wonderful city from which Hannibal, one of the greatest wonders of all times, came. Here, if anywhere, and now, if anywhen, we might have expected that the Romans would have taken the pains to explain to themselves, if not to others, the condition and the constitution, the fears and the hopes, the strength and the weakness of that great city which had so long contended with them on equal or even superior terms. What a priceless boon, for instance, would Scipio himself, with that taste for literature with which the unlettered Roman senators twitted him, and with his power of understanding, or at least of influencing, nations less civilized than his own, have conferred on all future times, had he cared to tell us exactly what he saw, and what he inferred, about his great antagonists! The facts of these last few years cannot, we should think, have been less instructive, less thrilling, or less strange, than those fictions in which the Scipionic circle appear habitually to have indulged. The glory of Rome would not have lessened, it might even have been increased, had she given her adversaries, now at any rate, that credit which was their due. We might then have been able to judge, on better grounds than those on which most historians have passed so ready and so easy a judgment, as to what elements of civilization and of progress, along with those other elements of weakness, which are admitted on all hands, Carthage might have transported into Europe, had the result of the war been different. We should then have had more data for determining the question, as to what would have been the gain and what the loss to the world at large had the Mediterranean continued, what Nature seems to have intended it to be, the highway of independent nations, each perhaps endeavouring, but, happily, each failing, to conquer its neighbours; instead of becoming a Roman lake, connecting nations whose separate existence had been stamped out of them, and all of them controlled, assimilated, civilized—if we like to call it so—by the all-levelling power of Rome.

The services rendered to civilization by Rome are clear enough; but is not so clear what services might hereafter have been rendered to it by a free Athens and a free Corinth, by the inexhaustible energy of the Greek colonies in Sicily, by a possibly resuscitated Tyre or by the new-born Alexandria; last, not least, by a Carthage freed, as Hannibal was able for a short time at least to free it from its narrow oligarchy, and by a Rome which would have been content with her natural boundaries, content, that is, to assimilate, and to weld into one, the various tribes which were most of them cognate to herself, from the straits of Messana to the Alps. He is certainly a bold historian who with these—so large a part of the conditions of the problem—not before him, will pronounce dogmatically that it was in all respects well for the world that Rome was able utterly to destroy her ancient rival. The phrase, "it would have been," is a dangerous phrase to use in the study of history. It is difficult to avoid using it altogether; but it must always be remembered on what slender grounds we can use it at all, and how infinite are the possibilities of which no account is taken. If it be presumptuous to say, as Napoleon did, that God is always on the side of the big battalions, it is hardly less presumptuous to say dogmatically that in this or that instance He was on the side of the weaker ones. It surely savours of presumption to maintain, as one historian, never to be mentioned without high honour, has, throughout this portion of his noble history, maintained, that Providence must surely have been plotting against Carthage, and watching over Rome, because when Hannibal advanced on the city, two legions which had been raised for the Spanish war happened to be still lingering there and could be utilized for her defence; or again, because the great Carthaginian happened to have turned southwards to Bruttium instead of northwards to Lucania, at the moment when the messengers of his long-looked-for brother were despatched to find him. We know all too little of the nation which produced Hamilcar, Barca, and Hannibal to say what that nation might have done in happier times under the guidance of such commanding geniuses. The Second Punic War ends as it was begun. It is recorded from first to last only by Hannibal's enemies, who neither understood, nor cared to understand, what made him, and what made his city, great. Yet it is the old story. It is the man who paints the prostrate lion. But it is the lion, and not the man; it is Hannibal, and not his conquerors, who, in spite of the painter's intention, rivets all eyes and stands forth alone from the canvas, alike in his military genius and in his patriotism, in his hundred victories and in his one defeat, without a parallel in history.

But the Carthaginians were not more ready to meet Scipio by land than they had been by sea. They were without a sufficient army, and Hasdrubal, the son of Gisco, their best available general was just then at a distance. For nearly fifty years Africa had been free from invasion; and the soldiers of Scipio found the same unwalled towns and villages and the same fruitful and well-watered estates which the followers of Agathocles and Regulus had found before them. From this rich and prosperous country a motley and panic-stricken multitude flocked towards Carthage, driving their flocks and herds before them; and the gates of the capital were shut and the walls manned, as though for an immediate attack. Pressing messages for aid were sent to Hasdrubal and Syphax; and the sense of relief was great when Scipio, instead of advancing on the capital, showed that he intended first to secure Utica. Frequent skirmishes with the Numidian cavalry took place, in which Massinissa, availing himself to the utmost of his knowledge of the Numidian tactics, did good service to the Romans. The ships which Scipio had sent back to Sicily, returned laden with provisions and with his siege train; but

The campaign in Africa.

for forty days the oldest Phœnician colony in Africa resisted, with true Phœnician endurance, all his assaults. Two large armies under Hasdrubal and Syphax advanced to its relief, and on the approach of winter Scipio was obliged, without having won any decisive success, to abandon the blockade, and to transfer his camp to an adjoining tongue of land, which was known for centuries afterwards as the Castra Cornelia.

So ended the year 204. Neither the hopes nor the fears which Scipio's invasion of Africa had called forth had as yet been fulfilled; and so far did the war still seem from its termination, that the Italians were not yet able to look upon themselves as secure from invasion. They even thought it prudent to build ships for the special purpose of protecting their coasts from possible attacks on the part of the Carthaginian navy. Twenty legions were put into the field for the year 203, and the command of Scipio was prolonged, not, as on previous occasions, for a fixed period, but till such time as the war should be brought to a conclusion. From the military point of view this was a step in the right direction. It had already been tried in Spain in the persons of two members of the same illustrious family; but it was also the first step towards the establishment of the military dictatorship, which was destined, after a long agony of civil wars, to overthrow the liberties of Rome.

Scipio's command prolonged.

Fortune or fraud soon gave Scipio the chance of dealing a decisive blow. In sight of his winter quarters was the camp of the Carthaginians, under Hasdrubal, son of Gisco, and at some distance farther lay that of the Numidians under Syphax. The Carthaginian huts were built of dry wood which had been collected from the fields, while

Burning of Carthaginian camps.

those of the Numidians, as their custom was, were made
of wattled reeds thatched with straw. Such materials
suggested to Scipio the way in which they might best be
destroyed. Opening or pretending to open negotiations
for peace, he sent messengers backwards and forwards
with orders to note the shape and the arrangements, the
exits and the entrances, of the hostile camps. This
information obtained, he suddenly broke off the negotiations, and then, with an easy conscience as it would
seem, set out on his night errand. The wily Numidian
chief was told off to the task which seemed appropriate
to him, and which he had perhaps been the first to suggest, the burning of the Numidian camp. The flames
spread with the rapidity of lightning, and when the
Carthaginians hastened to the help of their allies, their
own camp was set on fire by Scipio behind them. The
panic was sudden and universal, and what the flames
spared, the swords of the Romans, who had been stationed at all the outlets, cut down. Forty thousand
Africans fell the victims of this not very glorious exploit.
It was with difficulty that the two generals, Hasdrubal
and Syphax, escaped, the one to Carthage, to keep alive
the spirit of the "Barcine faction" against the faint-
hearted counsels of the peace-party, which now, perhaps
with reason, might make themselves heard ; the other,
to rally the survivors of the slaughter, and to collect new
forces for the defence of the capital.

Another victory of Scipio followed in the so-called
"Great Plains," and on the exiled Massinissa was imposed the congenial task of following up his
rival Syphax, who had deprived him of his *Sophonisba.*
hereditary kingdom. Massinissa's pursuit was as rapid
as it was successful. The Massæsylians were defeated,
and Syphax himself, together with his beautiful wife

Sophonisba, and his capital, Cirta (the modern Constantine), which had been built in the most romantic and impregnable of situations, fell into the conqueror's hands. In times long gone by, so the story went, Massinissa's heart had been touched by the charms of the Carthaginian maiden. Fortune had then thrown her into the hands of his rival, but now his own turn was come. He married her on the spot, and when Scipio, alive to the complications which might follow from such a marriage, and perhaps jealous of his own superior rights, bade him dismiss a wife who might compromise his fidelity to the Romans, he sent her a cup of poison, "the only present which the bridegroom could offer to his bride." Let her see to it that she did nothing unworthy of the daughter of a Carthaginian general and the wife of two Numidian kings. Sophonisba drank off the poison, only remarking that her death would have been more opportune had it not followed so immediately upon her marriage. Massinissa, so the chroniclers rounded off the tragic story, was gently rebuked by his Roman Mentor for having atoned for one rash act by another; but he was consoled for the loss of his bride by the royal title, and by the Roman garments which Scipio solemnly bestowed upon him.

It was an honour never before granted by the proud republic to one who was not a Roman citizen; but Massinissa lived long enough abundantly to justify his privileges. What Hiero had been to the Romans throughout the First Punic War and during the early years of the Second, that Massinissa was to them during its closing years, throughout the long agony of the peace which followed it, and in the short and sharp struggle of the Third. When the "War of Hannibal" was over, Massinissa was planted, as we

Subsequent history of Massinissa.

shall hereafter see, by the Romans as a thorn in the side
of the city with which they professed to have made
peace. He was encouraged to make aggressions on her
mutilated territory, and then to complain to the Romans
if she ventured to defend herself. Carthage was the
lamb in the fable. Whatever excesses she might allege,
or whatever the provocation or the injury she might receive, she knew that the case was prejudged against her
by the wolf, and that she must meet the lamb's fate.

The fall of Syphax was a great blow to Carthage.
Her most powerful friend was gone, and his place was
taken by her deadliest foe. Indeed the whole
power of Numidia was now arrayed against her. In spite of a naval success obtained by *Negotiations for peace.*
the Carthaginians over Scipio's fleet, and the consequent
raising of the siege of Utica, the peace party now came
to the front at Carthage. The able Hasdrubal, the son
of Gisco, they condemned to death in his absence—a
sentence passed, ostensibly, no doubt, as a punishment
for his recent failure, but really, as seems probable, for
his previous energy; and they then opened negotiations
for peace with Scipio. The terms offered by him were
lenient; more lenient, as has been already pointed out,
than those offered by Regulus fifty years before. He
knew that there was a strong party opposed to him at
Rome, and he knew also that an army which had failed
to reduce Utica would not be likely to capture Carthage
by a *coup-de-main*. Ambassadors were sent to Rome
to get the terms to which both parties had agreed in
Africa confirmed by the Roman Senate; and if Livy
may be believed—and he is to a certain extent borne
out by what we know of the state of parties at Carthage
—those who were now in power had the baseness as
well as the folly to try to throw the blame of the war on

Hannibal. Anyhow the proposals were summarily rejected, the ambassadors were dismissed without an answer, and Scipio was instructed to press the war to its natural conclusion.

But for Carthage one chance still remained. The sons of Hamilcar might be recalled to help in the hour of her extremity the state which had done so little to help them, and which now, by the mouths of one party within it, professed to be ashamed of having done even that little. And whether it was the work of the peace party, in the hope that peace might thereby be made more possible, or of the war party, who hoped that Hannibal, the genius of war, might yet strike a blow which would reverse its fortunes, the order was sent to the two sons of Hamilcar to return to Africa (205 B. C.).

<small>Last chance of Carthage.</small>

Driven out of Spain by Scipio, Mago, as we have seen, had crossed to the Balearic Islands, and passing thence from the harbour which still bears his name, Port Mahon, into Northern Italy, had taken Genoa, and during the last two years had been labouring to organize among the unsubdued and ever-savage Ligurians an active coalition against Rome. But it was too late. In the territory of the Insubrian Gauls, he at last measured his sword with the Romans. The battle was well contested, but it was decisive; and Mago, who had received a dangerous wound in his thigh, staggered back by night, as best he could, through that rugged country, to the seacoast. Here he found the message of recall awaiting him. He set sail at once, as became a true son of Hamilcar; but worn out with anxiety of mind and with agony of body, he died, perhaps happily for himself, before he hove in sight of the African shore.

<small>Recall of Mago.</small>

A different, but hardly a less tragic fate awaited his elder and more famous brother. For four years past, ever since the battle of Metaurus had shown him that ultimate success was not to be looked for, Hannibal had been compelled to act simply on the defensive. With his sadly thinned army of veterans, and his Campanian and Bruttian recruits, he had withdrawn into the neck of land to the south of Italy which seemed as if it had been made for his purpose. If it prepared the way for his future retreat to Africa, it was Italy still, and it still for four years enabled him to keep his vow, and to make Rome uneasy. He had withdrawn to the "Land's End," but he lay there with his face to the foe, gathering up his strength, and ever ready to spring upon anyone who should venture to molest him. The Roman vultures gathered indeed around the dying lion; but each, as in the heyday of his strength, demurred to being the first to approach him. Invincible as ever in the field—for Polybius tells us expressly that he was "never beaten in a battle so long as he remained in Italy"—Hannibal had been condemned to see province after province, and fortress after fortress—Consentia and Metapontum, Locri and Pandosia—torn from him, till at last there was nothing left in Italy but the southern corner of Bruttium and the one fortress of Croton which he could call his own. Yet all this time, when he must have been in sore want of provisions, when reinforcements from Carthage were no longer to be thought of, when it became more and more clear that no help could be expected from Philip of Macedon, or from his own heroic brother Mago; when he had already seen the result of the war registered in the ghastly head of his other brother Hasdrubal, there had been no thought of surrender and

Q

no whisper of mutiny in his camp. Without hope, but without fear, he had held on there in his solitary strength; and now when the order came to leave the land of his fifteen years' struggle and of his astonishing victories, he, like his father and like his brother, mastered his feelings and obeyed.

"Leaving the country of his enemies with more regret," says Livy, "than many an exile has left his own," Hannibal made for the smaller Leptis, a place far to the southeast of Carthage. The news of his arrival there at once brought back the war party in the capital to power. Some Roman transports which had been driven ashore in a storm were seized by the excited populace, and hostilities broke out amidst homilies on the part of the Romans against Carthaginian ill-faith, which, owing to the circumstances under which they have come down to us, we can neither refute nor believe. The Romans knew well that the scourge which had been withdrawn from themselves in Italy would fall with redoubled vigour on their countrymen in Africa, and it is all the more to be wondered at that they did not think it worth while to leave to posterity a trustworthy account of the steps which led up to the final catastrophe. Hannibal passed the winter at Adrumetum, the modern Susa, a town nearer to Carthage than Leptis, but still considerably to the southeast of it, and then, instead of advancing on the capital—which he must have yearned to visit, for he had not seen it since he was nine years old—he struck across the southern part of the Carthaginian dominions into Numidia. There he won some successes over Massinissa, he formed an alliance with some Numidian chiefs, and there finally he met or was overtaken by Scipio, who had moved forward from his head-quarters at Tunis, plundering and enslaving as he went.

Hannibal lands in Africa.

After an abortive negotiation for peace, in the year B.C. 202, and probably in the month of October, but on a day and at a place, which, strange to say, are unknown, the two great generals met for the first and last time in the battle which was to decide for centuries the fate of the civilized world. The battle of Zama, like many other battles in history— Arbela, Hastings, and Blenheim—was fought at some distance from the place whose name has been united with it. The battle-field lay probably much to the west of Zama, near the upper Bagradas, and not far from a town called by Livy Naraggara. Hannibal drew up his army in three lines. In the first were his Ligurian, Gallic, and Moorish mercenaries and the slingers from the Balearic Isles. In the second stood the native Carthaginians and their African subjects, with some troops which had recently arrived from Macedon. In the third line were drawn up the tried soldiers of Hannibal's own army, on whom, if on no others, he could rely. These last consisted chiefly of Bruttians. The sixteen years' war had done its work with the veterans who had crossed the Alps, and who had fought at Trasimene and at Cannæ. But the Italians, who had known Hannibal only in the days of his comparative adversity, seem to have been as devoted to him as if they had had a share in winning all his laurels. The cavalry, as usual, were placed upon the wings, and, in front of the whole, marched a magnificent array of eighty elephants. Scipio, as every Roman general did, drew up his army in the three lines of hastati, principes, and triarii. But, observing the number of the enemy's elephants—by a happy thought which alone would distinguish him from the majority of Roman generals, who would have preferred to be conquered by rule rather than try to con-

Order of Battle.

quer without it—he placed the maniples of the second and third lines immediately behind those of the first. Thus, instead of covering his ground chequer-wise, he left broad lanes through the whole depth of his army, of which the sagacious elephants, when they found themselves goaded by the Roman lances, would be likely to avail themselves for their escape.

The plan succeeded; and the whole array of elephants, frightened by the blare of the trumpets, made the best of their way through these open lanes, some to the flanks of their own, and others to the rear of the Roman army, without trampling the legionaries to death or even breaking their line of battle. Those which escaped to the flanks of the army threw into confusion their own cavalry, who were already outnumbered by the Numidians opposed to them. Hannibal thus found on this fatal day that his two most formidable weapons—his elephants and his cavalry—had been turned against himself. Lælius and Massinissa soon drove the disordered Carthaginian horsemen from the field; but the conflict in the centre was much more stubborn. When Hannibal's first line gave way, the second tried by blows to drive them back to the battle. There had not been time for Hannibal to throw over these raw mercenaries that commanding spell which, during his long campaigns in Italy, and under circumstances which looked even more desperate than these, had made desertion or mutiny, or half-heartedness among their Gallic or Ligurian countrymen alike impossible. Some of them, to the number of eleven hundred, now went over to the enemy; but the veterans did their duty well, and withstood the combined attack of Scipio's second and third lines. They stood and fought without flinching, till Lælius and Massinissa, returning

Battle of Zama.

from the pursuit of the cavalry, closed in upon their flanks and rear, and then, like Napoleon's Old Guard at Waterloo, still without flinching, they fought and fell.

Twenty thousand of the Carthaginian army had fallen in the battle. Twenty thousand more had been taken prisoners, and Hannibal himself escaped, with a few survivors only, to Adrumetum. *Hannibal after defeat.* He fled, not because he wished to prolong the campaign, for he had the magnanimity to confess that he was conquered not only in the battle but in the war; still less because he cared for any personal reason to save his own life, but because he felt that the terror of his name and the undefined possibilities which, as in the case of his father at the close of the First Punic War, the Romans still attached to it, might enable him to procure better terms for his unfortunate countrymen. Never did a general return to his native country, after a long absence, under a fate more cruel. The hero of a hundred victories saw his native city for the first time after his one defeat, but that one a defeat so crushing that it could not but, for the moment, obliterate the memory of all that had preceded it. But with true dignity and self-respect, he set himself to accept the inevitable, and to make what he could of it. Scipio prepared as though he would besiege the city, but his heart also inclined to peace. He knew that the consul was already on his way who might rob him of much of his well-earned glory, and with that prudence or that moderation which was habitual to him, he forbore to push his victory to the bitter end.

The terms which he offered were severe enough, and had the Carthaginians only realized what they involved, they would surely have asked to be allowed to meet their fate at once. They were to retain indeed their own laws and their home domain in Africa; but they were to give up all the deserters and prisoners of war, all their elephants, and all their ships of the line but ten. They were not to wage war, either in Africa or outside of it, without the sanction of the Roman Senate. They were to recognize Massinissa as the king of Numidia, and, with it, the prescriptive right which he would enjoy of plundering and annoying them at his pleasure, while they looked on with their hands tied, not daring to make reprisals. Finally, they were to give up all claim to the rich islands of the Mediterranean and to the Spanish kingdom, the creation of the Barcides, of which the fortune of war had already robbed them; and thus shorn of the sources of their wealth, they were to pay within a given term of seven years a crushing war contribution! Henceforward, in fact, they would exist on sufferance only, and that the sufferance of the Romans. Still the terms of peace, heavy though they were, were as light under the circumstances as they could expect; and Hannibal dragged down with his own hands from the rostrum an ill-judging orator who was recommending a continuance of the struggle. The people gave vent to their indignation at this infringement of their liberty of speech; but Hannibal pertinently replied that they must forgive him if, after thirty-six years' service in the camp, he had forgotten the manners of the forum.

Terms of peace.

The terms which had been agreed upon by Scipio and the Carthaginian government were referred to the Roman Senate for their approval; and ambassadors were sent from Carthage, with Hasdrubal, surnamed the Kid, the leader of the peace party, and the bitter opponent of the Barcine family, as their spokesman, to plead the cause of the conquered. The Romans accepted the conditions, for they felt that this time the Carthaginians were in earnest, and they felt also that Hannibal was still at large, and it might not be well, even then, to drive him to despair.

The conclusion of the peace was celebrated at Carthage by a cruel sight, the most cruel which the citizens could have beheld, except the destruction of the city itself—the destruction of their fleet. Five hundred vessels, the pride and glory of the Phœnician race, the symbol and the seal of the commerce, the colonization, and the conquests of this most imperial of Phœnician cities, were towed out of the harbour and were deliberately burned in the sight of the citizens. In the days of the greatest prosperity of Carthage if any signal reverse happened to her—if, for instance, a storm at sea destroyed a portion of her navy, and so touched her in that on which she most prided herself, the command of the seas—the whole state would go into mourning, and the huge walls of the city would themselves be draped in black. It is a strange and touching custom, and the mention of it here may, perhaps, better enable us to picture to ourselves the feelings of the discrowned queen of the seas. Scipio now set sail for Italy, and, landing at Lilybæum, made his way leisurely towards Rome through the cities and the provinces which he had freed from the invader, and which fondly hailed him as their deliverer.

Burning of Carthaginian fleet.

He had delivered them, but from what and to what end? He had delivered them from the immediate scourge of foreign war; but it remained to be seen how far they would be gainers thereby. It remained to be seen, now that their great rival in the western Mediterranean was put out of the way, whether Rome would

What use would Rome make of her victory?

visit the Greek and the Sicilian, the Apulian and the Campanian towns, which had been guilty of coquetting with the invader, with that condign vengeance which she had already wreaked on the unhappy Capua and Tarentum; whether she would hand them over to the more lingering oppression of Roman magistrates and tax-gatherers; or whether, throwing off the narrow municipal conceptions in which she had grown up, she would rise to the imperial dignity which circumstances had forced upon her. In other words, it remained to be seen whether Rome would govern the states which were already, or were hereafter to be, enrolled in her vast empire, in their own interests, encouraging, as far as was consistent with her own safety, their national life, developing their resources, giving them a liberty which was not a license, and a security which was not a solitude. If Rome rose to this, her true dignity, we can hardly regret in the interests of humanity that Hannibal's enterprise ended as it did. But if her conduct was the reverse, or nearly the reverse, of all this, we may at least be allowed to question, as we have already hinted, what most historians have laid down as an axiom too self-evident to be worth discussing, whether it was for the good of the human race that Rome should not only out-top, but should utterly extirpate, her ancient rival. We may believe, on the whole, in the survival of the fittest, and that arms generally come to him who can best handle them; but it is open to us to regret that even the less fit were not allowed to survive as well. There was surely room on the shores of the Mediterranean and on the Ocean beyond for the Phœnician as well as the Roman civilization; and the worst excesses of the Romans, the perfidy and the brutality of their wars in Spain, their grinding and oppressive system of taxation, the destruction of Corinth the eye of Greece, their civil wars themselves, might have been mitigated or postponed, if they could not have been altogether prevented by the salutary knowledge that they had powerful rivals on the other side of the Mediterranean who would not allow them to be judge and jury, council, criminal, and executioner all in one.

CHAPTER XVIII.

CARTHAGE AT THE MERCY OF ROME.

(201–150 B.C.)

THE fifty years which passed between the end of the Second and the outbreak of the Third Punic War were years in which Rome advanced with extraordinarily rapid strides towards the empire of the world; but they witnessed also the incipient decay of all that was best in the Roman character. *Deterioration of Roman character.* Already in the Second Punic War we have seen indications that the Golden Age of Rome was passing away. Whatever the heroic qualities which the long struggle called forth, we feel that the stern simplicity, the simple faith, the submission to law which formed the groundwork of the Roman character, and had marked, at all events, the dealings of Romans with each other, are not what they have been; and now, when the strain of the war is over, and the victorious city has to meet new problems and to face new dangers, we find that except in the one point of her material strength, and her appliances for further conquest, she is unequal to the emergency.

An emergency indeed it was! Three hundred

thousand Italians had fallen in the field; three hundred towns had been destroyed; to the North the Gauls and the Ligurians were still unsubdued; in Central Italy, the Campanians, the Apulians, and the Samnites, who had long dallied with Hannibal, were awaiting their future in ill-concealed anxiety; while in the extreme South, the Bruttians, who had clung to him to the last, abandoned themselves to their fate in dull despair. The Italian yeomen, who had never wavered in their attachment to Rome, torn from their homes for years, and demoralized by the camp, were unable or unwilling to settle down into the quiet routine of agricultural life. They went as settlers to those disaffected towns which Rome, according to her practice, selected as new military colonies, or were content to swell the city rabble, which now began to rise into importance and was kept in good humour by largesses of corn, or by cruel and degrading public spectacles. Their farms passed into the hands of capitalists, and were cultivated by foreign slaves whom the frequent wars with the half-subdued provinces brought in shoals to Rome. "Sardinians for sale," was the sorry jest which rose to people's lips when they saw a batch of these wretched creatures landed at Ostia, or exposed for what little they could fetch in the Roman Forum. "The more slaves, the more enemies," was the grim proverb which forced itself on their minds in all its stern reality, when they awoke to the danger, which it was then too late either to prevent or to cure. The rich arable lands of Italy fell back, as might be expected under such keeping, into pasture; and half-naked slaves tended herds of cattle where Roman consuls or dictators had been content to plough and dig before them. When the slaves asked their masters for clothes to cover them, they were

Condition of Italy.

met by the suggestion, half question and half answer, whether the travellers who passed through their solitudes were wont to pass naked?

In Rome itself the old aristocracy, which, it must be admitted, with all its faults, had been, on the whole, an aristocracy of merit, had given place to a new nobility of wealth, who were as exclusive, and certainly were not more farsighted or more public-spirited, than their predecessors. Rule was no longer looked upon as its own reward. It was valued for what it brought, and high office lost half its dignity when it was won by a reckless display of wealth, or was used as a means of acquiring more. Religion was no longer the simple and childlike faith of the early commonwealth, but tended to become an affair of titles and of priests, of auguries and of ceremonies— of ceremonies which became more stringent and more vexatious exactly in proportion as they were felt to be less real.

Condition of Rome.

Beyond the confines of Italy Proper, Rome was mistress indeed of the four provinces which she had torn from Carthage in her fifty years' war, of Hither and Further Spain, of Sicily and Sardinia. But of these, Sicily alone was unlikely to give her further trouble; and that, not because she was well-affected, but simply because she was exhausted. Sardinia supplied Rome with the living chattels which were to be so perilous a property; while Spain entailed upon her a yet more disastrous heritage of petty wars—wars incessantly ended and incessantly renewed; wars waged on the part of the Romans with a baseness and a cruelty such as have characterized few wars before or since. The wholesale murder of a tribe which had submitted, and the assassination of a for-

Of Roman provinces.

midable but honourable foe, were the weapons with which the Roman generals managed to retain their hold over their Spanish provinces.

It does not fall within the scope of this work to trace in detail the steps by which, in the interval between the First and the Second Punic Wars Rome acquired a universal supremacy as undisputed in the East as in the West; to show how Philip, who had scornfully remarked that the Roman general " thought he might do anything with Macedon because he was a Roman, and that if war was what he wanted, war he should have," found in a few short years, when the Macedonian phalanx first measured its strength with the Roman legion in the open field at Cynoscephalæ, that the Roman general was not far wrong, and, being thus driven to sue for peace, was able, out of all his conquests or dependencies, to retain only his hereditary kingdom ; how the Greeks, delivered from the Macedonians, received at the hands of the Romans their nominal liberty, and greeted with short-sighted acclamations the Phil-hellenic Flamininus who was in fact giving them only a change of masters ; how " the fetters of Greece," first adjusted by Philip, were now riveted on that unhappy country by a firmer hand, and how its petty cities and blustering confederations, the degenerate representatives of those states to whom the world owes Hellenic art and culture, after being allowed for a brief space to air their importance and their imbecility, settled down peaceably under the Roman protectorate, and avenged themselves by corrupting by their manners, or subduing by their arts, those whom they could not meet in arms ; how Antiochus the Seleucid, the successor, as he fondly thought, of the king of kings who rejoiced in the self-assumed name of the Great, was driven by the Romans first out of Greece and then out of Asia Minor, eighty thousand of his Asiatic troops flying like chaff before the onset of less than half that number of Roman legionaries at Magnesia; how the Asia Minor that he had overrun gradually passed under the control of Rome while the puppet monarchs of its various portions humbly registered her decrees, and even the hordes of Gallic invaders learned to stop their ravages, or at least to keep at a respectful distance from her all-powerful arm; how the grand schemes of a greater than Antiochus the "Great," now a friendless exile at his court, were crushed, not so much by the wisdom or courage as by the good fortune of Rome which found her best ally in the jealousy and the incapacity of the empty-headed monarch who flattered himself that he was Hannibal's protector; how the Egyptian Ptolemy himself became the ward of Rome, and the chief naval power of the Eastern Mediterranean was saved from the ambitious schemes of Macedon and Syria only by the upstart naval power of Rome in the West; how, lastly, by the defeat of Perseus at Pydna, and the taking of Corinth by Mummius, Macedon and Greece disappeared for ever as independent powers from history, and became part and parcel of the Roman Empire. All these events, and many more, are crowded into the fifty years of existence which it still suited Rome by a cruel kindness to allow to her Carthaginian rival. But they belong to the general current of Roman history, rather than to that special episode of which this book treats.

The year B.C. 146, which witnessed the fall of Corinth, witnessed also, by a strange coincidence, the destruction of Carthage; and to the chain of events which led directly up to that catastrophe we now turn.

Beaten in the war by his cruel destiny, Hannibal made the best of his altered circumstances. He had lived many lives in what he had achieved and suffered; but he was still comparatively a young man, and he set himself, as though he had been born to be a statesman, to reform those abuses in the state which had done so much to mar his patriotic aims. His apology for his ignorance of the manners of the forum was hardly needed. He triumphantly refuted the accusations which the peace party were impudent enough, or base enough, to bring against him, that he had spared Rome, and had appropriated to his own use the public money! Whether by the help of his veterans, or by the voice of the citizens, he was appointed Shofete, or chief magistrate; and he used his power to overthrow the narrow and selfish oligarchy whose strength lay in the council of "the Hundred Judges." Henceforward this council was to be filled up, not, as heretofore, by co-optation, but, in part at least, by free annual election. Lastly, Hannibal reformed the financial system, made those who had thriven on the plunder of the treasury disgorge their ill-gotten gains, and applied the proceeds to the payment of the war indemnity. So admirable were his measures, that at the end of thirteen years his successors were able to offer to pay up the whole of the instalments of the forty millions due to Rome, and that without imposing any additional taxes on the subjects of Carthage.

Hannibal as a statesman at Carthage.

These reforms stirred up a nest of hornets round the ears of their great author, and his new enemies joined his old ones in denouncing his projects to the Romans. Rome, indeed, hardly needed such an invitation; she had made peace with Carthage, but not with Hannibal.

If she no longer feared the city, she feared one of its simple citizens; and in spite of the protest of Scipio Africanus, Hannibal's noble-minded foe, an embassy was sent to demand the surrender of the man whose bare existence disturbed her equanimity. From the crowning disgrace of complying with this demand, Hannibal saved his fellow-citizens by going into voluntary exile. The greatest of the Phœnicians first visited Tyre, the cradle of his race, and passed thence to Ephesus, whither, as chance would have it, Antiochus had gone before him, that he might prepare for war with Rome. He was received with the highest honours; and, striking while the iron was hot, he asked the great king to place at his disposal a small fleet and army. If this boon were granted him, he undertook to sail to Carthage; to renew the struggle with Rome in Africa; thence once more to cross to Italy, and there meeting Antiochus himself—who was to advance overland and draw fresh contingents as he advanced from Macedon and Greece—to bear down with him on their common enemy.

Hannibal driven into exile.

It was a magnificent scheme, and one which did not seem altogether impossible of realization, for just then a general rising in Spain gave the Romans enough to do in the West alone. But it was proposed to deaf ears. In vain did Hannibal reveal, perhaps for the first time in his life, the secret which had been the mainspring of his achievements, the story of his early vow. The courtiers were jealous of the lonely exile, and the great king himself had no mind to be told by a suppliant and a refugee what his interests or his duty called for, or, if he was told, to do it. Against his own urgent entreaties, Hannibal was carried into Greece, in the wake of the Syrian army, there to be

Wanderings and death of Hannibal.

asked for fresh advice, which Antiochus took care again ostentatiously to reject. When his warnings turned out true, he was carried back into Asia, and Antiochus having, as it would seem, nothing for the greatest soldier of his age to do by land, sent him off to sea to escort some ships from Phœnicia. The small armament was met, as might have been expected, by the large Rhodian navy, and was overpowered in an engagement which took place off Sidé. Hannibal himself fought well and escaped to Ephesus just in time to see the huge force which, as Antiochus imagined, was to sweep the Romans out of Asia. This force was itself annihilated at Magnesia, and the conquerors demanded, as one of the conditions of peace, that Hannibal should be surrendered to them. Once more he anticipated the demand. He fled to Crete, and thence returning to Asia, wandered from land to land, till at last he found refuge with Prusias, the petty king of Bithynia. There he lived for some years; but even there the Roman fear, or hatred, pursued him; and at last, at a place called Libyssa, the Phœnician hero disappointed his implacable enemies—who were headed, it is sad to say, by no less a person than Flamininus, the conqueror of Macedon—in the only way which was now left to him, by taking the poison which, as the story goes, he used to carry about with him concealed in a ring. The oracle which had foretold that "Libyssian soil should one day give shelter to Hannibal," was fulfilled, not by his return in his old age to his native country, but by his death in this remote corner of the Sea of Marmora, and for centuries afterwards a huge mound of earth was shown to travellers which was called "the tomb of Hannibal."

So died the last and the greatest of Hamilcar's sons; and it may be doubted—or may we not rather say, after such study as we have been able to give to their lives and actions, that it hardly admits of doubt—whether the whole of history can furnish another example of a father and a son, each cast in so truly heroic a mould, each so worthy of the other, and each proving so brilliantly, in his own person, through a lifelong struggle with fate, that success is in no way necessary to greatness?

In the same year with Hannibal died his great rival, Scipio Africanus, the victim of a like reverse of fortune. Like Hannibal, the victor of Zama had tried his hand at politics, but, like many other great generals who have followed his example, in politics he does not seem to have been at home. *Death of Scipio.* He longed for literary repose, and when the tide of popular favour turned against him, he retired into a kind of voluntary exile at Liternum. "Ungrateful country," he cried, with his last breath, "thou shalt not have my ashes."

The great Carthaginian leader was gone, but something of his handiwork still remained in the prosperity which his reforms had secured for his native city, in spite of the ever-increasing depredations of Massinissa. *Delenda est Carthago.* The Second Punic War had hardly been concluded, and the terms of peace agreed to, when that wily Numidian, lord, by the favour of Rome, of the dominions of Syphax as well as of his own, began to justify his position by encroaching on the Emporia to the south-east of Carthage. This was the richest part of the Phœnician territory in Africa; it contained the oldest Phœnician colonies, and had belonged to Carthage by a prescription of at least 300 years. The Carthaginians, as by treaty bound, appealed to Rome for protection; and Scipio, the best judge of its provisions, as well as one of the most honourable of Roman citizens, went over to Africa to decide the matter. But he decided nothing, and Massinissa was left in possession of his plunder. This led to fresh encroachments on the other side of the Carthaginian territory along the river Bagradas, and these again to fresh commissions from Rome, which always ended in the same way. At last the trampled worm turned on its oppressor; but fortune was on the side of the chartered brigandage of Massinissa. Hasdrubal, at the head of the patriotic party, was completely defeated, and Carthage itself was in danger. The Carthaginians, by neglecting to ask leave of Rome to defend themselves, had at length given the Romans the very pretext which they wanted for interfering actively and giving them the *coup de grâce*. Already before this a new commission had been sent out with old Marcus Cato at its head. It proved to be an evil day for Carthage. The Censor had passed through the rich districts which still remained to her. He had been amazed at the wealth, the population, and the resources of the city, which he had believed was crushed; and he returned home with his narrow mind thoroughly impressed with the belief that if Rome was to be saved, Carthage must be destroyed. Cato brought to the consideration of every subject a mind thoroughly made up upon it. No one ever reasoned him out of an opinion he had formed. He exhibited in the Senate some figs as remarkable for their freshness as their size; and telling the admiring senators that they grew in Carthaginian territory only three days' sail from Rome, he ended his speech that day, and every speech which he delivered in the Senate afterwards, whatever the subject under debate, with the memorable words—Carthage must be blotted out.

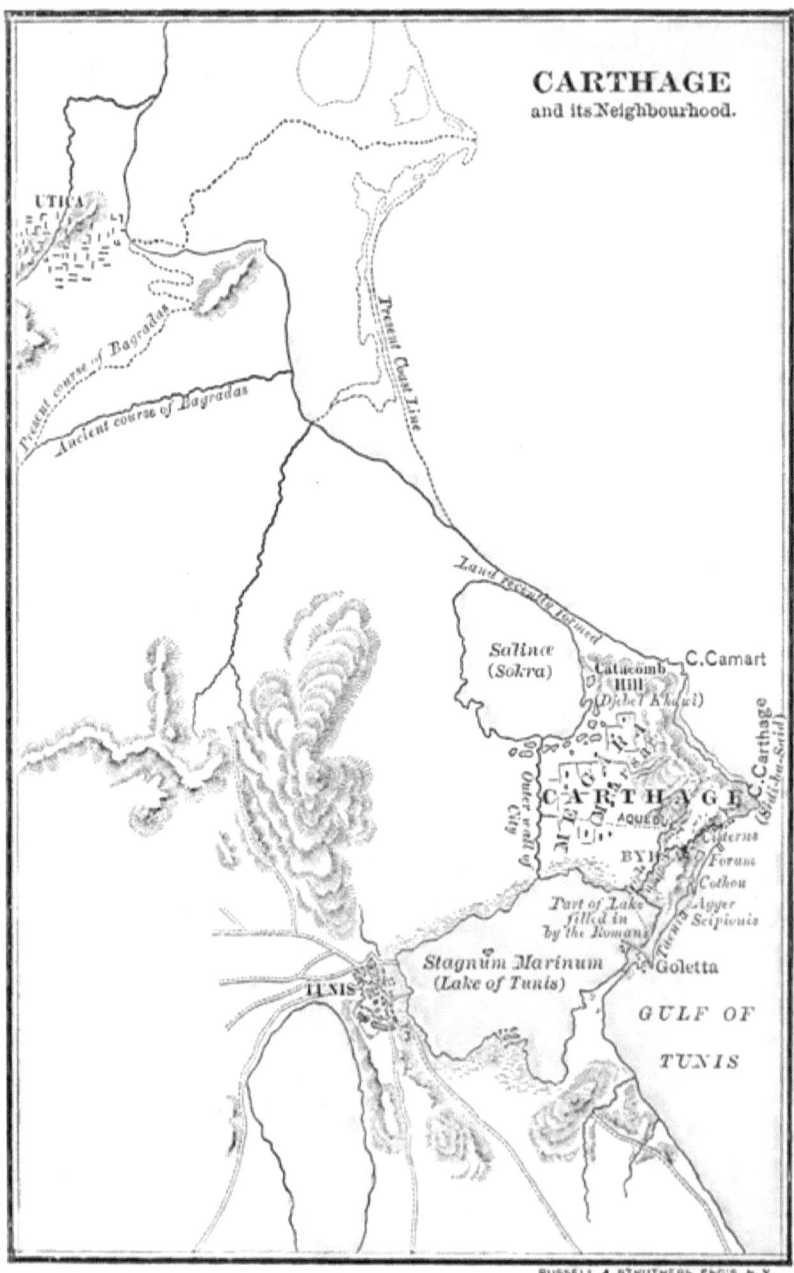

CHAPTER XIX.

DESTRUCTION OF CARTHAGE.

(149–146 B.C.)

OUR knowledge of the Third Punic War is derived almost exclusively from Appian, a mere compiler, who did not live till the time of the Emperor Hadrian, and whose accuracy, where he draws upon his own resources, may be judged from the fact that he places Saguntum to the north of the Ebro, and makes Britain only half a day's sail from Spain. Fortunately for us, however, there is good reason to believe that his account of the fall of Carthage is drawn directly from Polybius, who not only stands in the highest rank as an historian, but was himself present and bore a part in the scenes which he described, and here, perhaps, before we look upon the last scene of all, will be the place to describe, as c'early as we can, the position, the fortifications, and the appearance of the imperial city. We noticed, at the outset, the strange obscurity which hangs over the origin, the rise, and the internal life of a city whose influence was for centuries so wide-spread and so commanding. The same obscurity unfortunately extends also to its topography. The blind forces of Nature, and the ruthless hand of Man, have conspired to efface even its ruins. It is not merely the identification in detail of its walls, its temples, and its streets, for these might have been expected to disappear; but it is those more permanent features of its citadel and its harbours, nay, it is the position of the city itself, which is in some points open to dispute. How this has come about requires explanation.

To the north of the city the tempests of two thousand years, and the alluvial deposits of the river Bagradas, which now enters the sea several miles to the north of its former mouth, have turned much which, in the palmy days of Carthage, was open sea into dry land or into land-locked lagunes; while along the whole west and north front of the city the sea has revenged itself by encroaching on the land, and the massive substructions of fortifications which, perhaps, turned Agathocles aside and long baffled even Scipio, may still be seen engulfed beneath the waters at the distance of a furlong or more from the present coast. Nor has man been less destructive than Nature. On the same or nearly the same spot have risen successively a Phœnician, a Roman, a Vandal, and a Byzantine capital. Each was destroyed in whole or in part by that which was to take its place, and each successive city found ample materials for its own rise in the ruins which it had itself occasioned. The Byzantine city was finally destroyed in 698 A. D. Since that time its site has been almost uninhabited, and Berbers and Bedouins, Fatimite Kalifs and Italian Republics, German Emperors and French Kings, have all had a share in the work of obliteration. The *débris* of so many cities have formed a vast quarry out of which neighbouring hamlets and towns have been built and rebuilt, and, if we except the aqueducts and reservoirs, which, even to the most cursory observer, tell the tale of its former population and prosperity, he who would see any remains of the once imperial city must dig deep down through fathoms of crumbling masonry, or through mosaic pavement laid above mosaic pavement,

Changes made by nature and man.

sometimes three in number, till, perchance, he lights upon a votive tablet covered with Punic characters and scored with rude figures of a triangle and an uplifted hand, or, it may be, with the two horns of the Moon-goddess, Astarte ; or brings to view the basement of the mighty temple which witnessed the bloody offerings to Baal-Moloch.

The isthmus connecting the peninsula on which Carthage was built with the mainland was three miles across, and the whole of the widening ground to the east of it, embracing a circuit of about twenty-three miles, would seem, at one time, to have been covered by the city proper, its suburbs, its gardens, and its burying-ground. The peninsula terminates towards the north and east in two bluff headlands, now called Cape Ghamart and Cape Carthage. Whether these were included in the city fortifications or were left to defend themselves as outlying forts by their own inherent strength, is not quite clear. *Size of Carthage.*

The city proper was adequately defended on the three sides which touched the water by ordinary sea-walls; but on the side towards the land, the side from which alone the mistress of the seas and islands could dream of serious danger, ran a triple line of fortifications, of which the remains have only very recently been brought to light. The outer wall which would have to bear the brunt of an attack, was six or seven feet thick and forty-five feet high, and it was flanked throughout its length by towers at equal distances of two hundred feet. Between this and the two similar walls which rose behind it, and somehow forming part of them so as to make the whole one compact mass of masonry were casemates capable *Its fortifications.*

of containing three hundred elephants, with their vast stores of food. Above these rose another story with stabling for four thousand horses. In close proximity there were barracks for their riders, as well as for twenty thousand infantry. These magnificent fortifications ran up from near the lake of Tunis to the hill on which the citadel was built, and here were dovetailed into the wall of the citadel itself, but, it would seem, were not continued on the same scale to the sea to the north of it. The nature of the ground appears to have made the prolongation of such elaborate defences unnecessary, and the only point which was really weak in the whole line of defence was the bit of wall at the south angle of the town, just where a narrow tongue of land, called the Tænia, which plays an important part in the siege, cut off the open gulf from the lake which lay within it. This spot, lying as it were between land and water, was especially open to attacks from both, but seems never to have been sufficiently protected against either.

Besides the Lake of Tunis there were two landlocked docks or harbours, opening the one into the other, and both, it would seem, the work of human hands. *Hic portus alii effodiunt*, says Virgil, and in this instance, at least, he speaks historical truth. The outer harbour was rectangular, about fourteen hundred feet long and eleven hundred broad, and was appropriated to merchant vessels; the inner was circular like a drinking cup, whence it was called the Cothon, and was reserved for ships of war. It could not be approached except through the merchant harbour, and the entrance to this last was only seventy feet wide, and could be closed at any time by chains. The war harbour was entirely surrounded by quays, containing separate docks for 220 ships. In front of each dock

Its harbours.

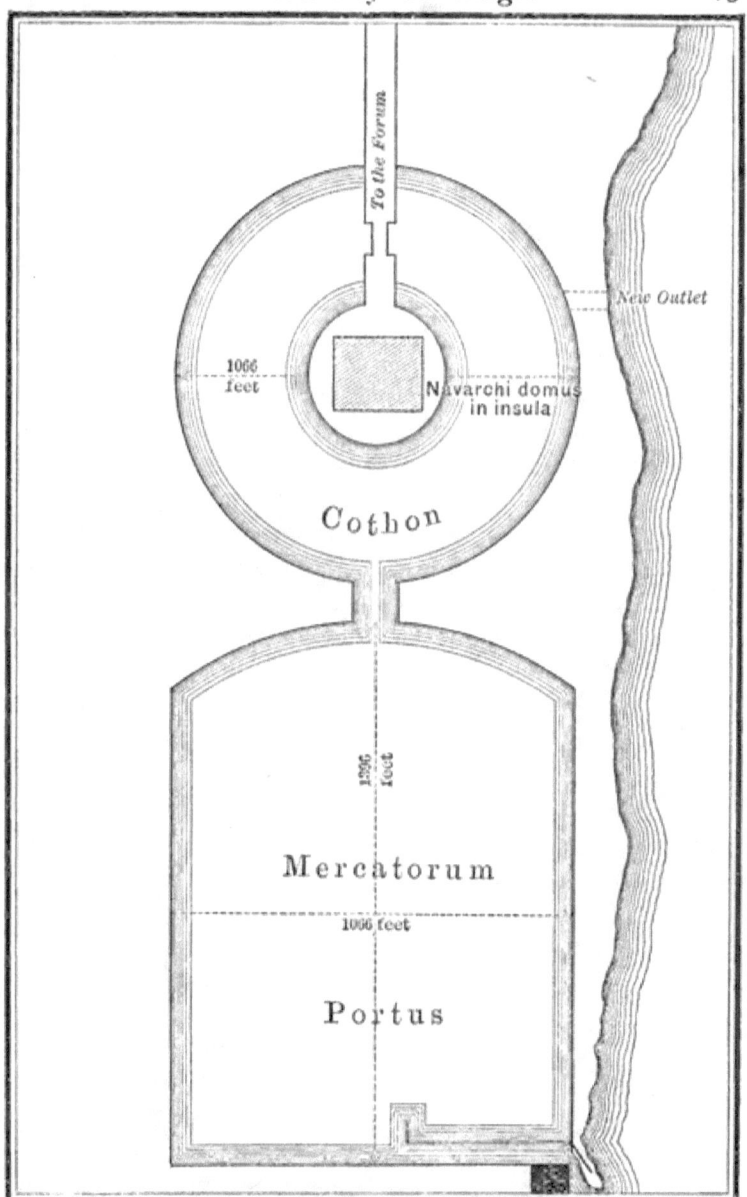

PLAN OF HARBOURS AT CARTHAGE

were two Ionic pillars of marble, so that the whole must have presented the appearance of a splendid circular colonnade. Right in the centre of the harbour was an island, the headquarters of the admiral. Here he could superintend all the operations of that thriving and industrious population; here his orders were proclaimed by the voice of the trumpet, and from its most elevated point he could oversee the intervening strip of land, and keep himself informed of all that was going on in the open sea beyond. In time of war he could view a hostile fleet approaching and watch all its movements, while the enemy could know nothing of what was being done inside. We have no full description of the merchants' harbour; but in time of peace the spacious Lake of Tunis, which was much deeper then than now, would afford safe anchorage to the myriads of merchant vessels which no artificial harbour could contain, and which, sweeping the whole of the Western Mediterranean, were not afraid in very early times to tempt the dangers of even the Ocean beyond. Such was the general aspect and position of the city whose last struggle we have now to relate. That struggle was heroic, desperate, and superhuman, but the conclusion was foregone; and he who gazed on the free and the imperial, may well be excused from dwelling at length on the agonies of the doomed city.

The resolution of Rome was taken. The question of time was the only one that remained, and the straits to which Carthage had been already reduced by Massinissa demonstrated to the few dissentients alike the guilt of the city and the fitness of the present moment. In vain did P. Cornelius Scipio Nasica, a man worthy of his name, protest against the idea that it was necessary, in order that Rome might be

War declared.

strong, that her rival must be destroyed ; and point out what a useful check upon the growing tide of luxury and corruption the bare existence of her ancient foe might prove. In vain did the Carthaginians condemn Hasdrubal and Carthalo, the leaders of the patriotic party, to death. In vain did they send embassy after embassy to Rome, proffering the amplest compensation and the most unlimited submission. The Romans replied that they wanted only "satisfaction ;" to the natural question as to what "satisfaction" meant, they rejoined that the Carthaginians knew that best themselves. Just then too the rats began to leave the sinking vessel ; for there arrived an embassy from Utica, the mother-city of Carthage herself, surrendering the city absolutely to the Romans. This was just what the Romans wanted, for it gave them an unimpeded landing, and a second base of operations in Africa, only ten miles from Carthage. An armament of eighty thousand men had already been raised, and it was at once despatched under the Consuls, Manilius and Censorinus, to Lilybæum, on its way to Africa. War was thus declared and begun on the very same day.

To a final embassy which, even after this, was sent to Rome, and was instructed to avert the invasion by any and by every means, the Romans replied, that the Carthaginians had now at length done well, and that Rome would guarantee *Perfidia plus-quam Punica.* to Carthage "her territory, her sacred rites, her tombs, her liberty, and her possessions," if three hundred hostages, drawn from the noblest families, were delivered to the consuls at Lilybæum within thirty days. Long before the thirty days were out the demand was complied with, by the obsequious zeal of the Carthaginians, who were then told that the further demands of the Romans would be made known in Africa. This secured the Romans from all opposition in crossing or in landing; and when the ambassadors again presented themselves in Utica, they were told that, as Carthage was henceforward to be under the protection of Rome, they would need no other protection at all. All arms and all engines of war were therefore to be given up. After some remonstrances this demand too was complied with, and long lines of wagons brought to the consuls two thousand catapults and two hundred thousand stands of arms. Then Censorinus rose, and all possibility of resistance having, as he thought, been taken away, revealed the final orders of Rome—the orders which, it must be remembered, had been secretly committed to him and his brother-consul from the very beginning—that Carthage was to be destroyed, but that the citizens might build a new city in any part of their territory they pleased, provided only it was ten miles from the coast.

The Consul was interrupted in the few words he had to say by an outburst of grief and indignation on the part of the assembled senators and ambassadors. They beat their breasts, they tore their hair and clothes, they threw themselves on the ground in their agony. The Romans were prepared for this, and kindly allowed their grief to have its way. When the first outburst was over, and the ambassadors found that all their appeals to the treaty and to the recent understanding with Rome were alike unavailing, they begged, in the extremity of their distress. that the Roman fleet might appear before the walls of Carthage at the same time with themselves; a step which they deemed would make resistance seem doubly hopeless, and would save the lives which, in the paroxysm

Scene in Roman camp.

of their fury, the inhabitants would otherwise be likely to throw away. Many of them, even so, were afraid to face the reception which awaited them in the city, and remained behind in the Roman camp. Those who had the courage to bear the fatal message gave no answer to the citizens who thronged out to meet them as they neared the city walls; but, keeping their eyes on the ground, made their way, as best they could, in imminent danger of their lives, to the council chamber.

The cry which burst from the assembled senators when they learned the Roman ultimatum was taken up by the multitude outside; and then was seen a sublime outburst of frenzy and despair, to which history affords no parallel. The multitude wreaked their fury on the senators who had counselled submission, on the ambassadors who had brought back the message, on the gods who had forsaken them. All the Italians found within the walls were put to death with torture. There was a rush of the infuriated citizens to the armoury; but they found there only the empty stands, which a few days before had been laden with arms. They adjourned to the harbour, but the docks were empty; there were only vast supplies of timber there, which, but for their blind fidelity to the very treaty which the Romans had set at nought, might ere now have been converted into ships-of-war. They called by name on the elephants whose horse-shoe stalls still stood beneath the shelter of the huge triple wall, and whose deeds of prowess in the last war were still remembered, but alas! were matters of remembrance only. The matrons whose sons had been taken to serve as hostages rushed about like furies, upbraiding the magistrates who had disregarded their remonstrances, and the gods who could look on unmoved at their grief. Meanwhile the

Scene at Carthage.

Senate, or what remained of it, declared war; the gates were closed; stones were carried to the walls; all the slaves in the city were set free; messages were sent to the outlawed Hasdrubal, who was at large at the head of twenty thousand men, begging him to forgive and forget, and to save the city, which, in his just indignation, he was even then preparing to attack. A second Hasdrubal, the grandson of Massinissa, was made commander-in-chief; and while leave was being humbly asked, and refused, to send once more to Rome, before the irrevocable deed was done, the whole city was turned into one vast workshop. Its buildings—public and private, sacred and profane alike—resounded with the workman's hammer and anvil. Lead was stripped off from the roofs and iron torn out of the walls. Men and women worked day and night, taking neither rest nor sleep; the matrons cut off their long hair and twisted it into ropes for the catapults; and while the Romans were hesitating, partly perhaps from pity to their victims, partly from the belief that a few days would demonstrate even to these frenzied Phœnicians the hopelessness of resistance, arms were extemporized for an adequate number of the citizens, and the city was somehow put into a position to stand a siege.

When at last the executioners approached to receive its submission, they found, to their surprise, that the gates were closed, and that the walls were fully manned and armed with all the engines of war. There was nothing for it but to try force. But force they tried in vain. Manilius attacked the city on the land side where it was strongest, for a wall and ditch ran right across the isthmus from sea to sea; Censorinus from the side of the Tænia, between land and water, where it was weakest. To their dismay both at-

Failure of Romans.

tempts failed; and each had to go through the humiliating process of fortifying his camp. Censorinus now proceeded to bring up wood and woodcutters from the other side of the lake of Tunis, and filled in with stones and soil that portion of it which lay behind the Tænia, so that he might bring his battering rams to bear upon the weakest part of the wall. A portion of it fell beneath a gigantic ram, propelled by 6,000 soldiers. But the damage was partially repaired during the night, and the besieging engines themselves were disabled by a sudden sortie. On the following day the Romans ventured through the part of the breach which was still open; but they were glad enough to make their way out again under the protection of the young Scipio, who was then serving in their army as a simple military tribune. With the rising of the dogstar pestilence broke out in the ranks of the besiegers, and when Censorinus transferred his ships from the fetid waters of the lake to the open sea, they narrowly escaped being destroyed by the Carthaginian fire-ships.

The year B.C. 149 drew towards its close, and when Censorinus returned to Rome to hold the elections for the ensuing year, he had no progress to report. Operations were not suspended during the winter, and once and again, if our authorities are to be trusted, it would have fared ill with the other consul if Scipio had not come to the rescue. Hasdrubal and Himilco Phameas, who were in command of the Carthaginian army outside the city, showed themselves to be skilful generals; and Massinissa himself, not liking to see the game taken out of his hands, when he thought it was his own, declined to supply the Romans with the aid which they asked. A rupture seemed imminent, but the wily old Numidian was spared the humiliation of seeing what he looked upon as his predestined booty appropriated by the Romans. It must have been a drop of consolation, the only drop of consolation in the cup of misery which the Carthaginians had now to drain, that neither the honest Roman Censor nor the grasping Numidian king lived to see the deed for which they had so long worked and plotted. Cato and Massinissa died in the same year, after the destruction of Carthage had been finally resolved on, but, thanks to the heroism of the inhabitants, before it had been fully carried out.

The generals of the year B.C. 148, the Consul Calpurnius Piso and his legate Mancinus, were not more successful and were less energetic even than their predecessors. The siege of Carthage was practically raised, and their term of office was frittered away in aimless and desultory attacks upon smaller places—such as Clypea and Hippo Zarytus—wherein success could have done them little service, and defeat, which was the more common result, entailed much discouragement and disorganization.

So things might have gone on for years, and the Romans, by their unprovoked aggression, well deserved that it should be so. But one man there *Scipio Æmilianus.* was serving in a humble capacity in the Roman army, whom his exploits and his parentage, alike lineal and adoptive, marked out even then from his professional superiors. Even Cato, who was opposed on principle to his family and his mode of life, had applied to him what Homer says of the Seer Teiresias, amidst the airy phantoms of the nether world, "He alone is flesh and blood, the rest are fleeting shades." P. Cornelius Scipio was the youngest son of Æmilius Paullus, the conqueror of Macedonia. When quite a youth he had fought by his father's side at Pydna, and he was afterwards adopted into a still more illustrious family, that of the Scipios. Like his grandfather, the great Africanus, he had early shown a taste for other arts than that of war; and his fondness for literature was cemented by the friendship which he formed, while still a youth, with the more distinguished of the Achæan exiles, above all with the historian Polybius. Not that he was, in any sense of the word, as Polybius himself and his contemporaries generally, not unnaturally, thought him, a man of genius. He was inferior in all respects to his grandfather by adoption, the elder Scipio. Yet his friendship with the best men of his time was a pure and noble friendship, and was worthy of being immortalized by the song of Horace and by the *De Amicitia* of Cicero. It was well for Rome that to a man so born and bred, and so richly endowed amidst the blunders and the incapacity of his nominal superiors, the eyes of the Roman soldiers, and the Roman citizens alike, were now instinctively turning for safety. Three times over, so it was said, during the absence of Censorinus, by his address or valour, had Scipio saved the army of the other consul, Manilius, from destruction. He had even induced the ablest of the Carthaginian generals, Himilco Phameas, to cross over to the Romans with 2,500 cavalry. But the most that he could do in his capacity of mere military tribune was to anticipate or undo the blunders of his superiors ; and it seemed more and more possible that Carthage might yet weather the storm, when, fortunately for himself and for Rome, Scipio left the army to stand for the Ædileship. He was accompanied to the ship by the soldiers, who did not conceal their hope that he would soon return as their commander-in-chief; and as their commander-in-chief he soon did return. Now as on one or two other occasions in their history, notably as when the elder Scipio had volunteered to take the command in Spain, the Romans, wedded though they were to constitutional forms, saw that there was something more important even than those forms, the safety of the state itself; and in spite of his age, which was still six years below the legal age, and of his not having filled any other curule office, the young Scipio was elected not to the Ædileship, but to the Consulship, with the implied understanding, as in the case of the elder Scipio, that his command was not to come to an end except with the end of the war.

The new consul arrived in Africa at a critical moment. He first rescued from imminent destruction Mancinus, one of the outgoing generals, who had allowed himself to be cut off from all supplies and reinforcements on a high cliff in the suburbs, and then brought back the other army of the consul Piso which was still carrying on a make-believe warfare amidst the inland towns, to its proper work, the siege of the capital. Having restored discipline by clearing his camp of the ineffectives and of the birds of prey of various species which had accumulated in it with amazing rapidity, during the exploits of the last two years, he managed to take the vast suburbs of Megara by surprise, and thus compelled Hasdrubal to abandon his open camp and to take refuge in the Byrsa. The siege of the city proper now began in earnest, and now also began, if we may believe our authorities, a reign of terror for the unhappy Carthaginians who were pent up within it. Having got rid of his namesake, the commander of the garrison, by false charges, Hasdrubal installed himself as commander-in-chief. But he proved to be as vain as he was cruel, and as weak as he was pretentious. His first act was to bring all the Roman prisoners to the battlements, and,

Fresh incursions of Scipio.

after torturing them cruelly, to throw them over the wall in sight of the Roman army. When expostulations were addressed to him by some of the citizens, he vented his rage on them in a similar manner.

Scipio bridled his indignation, caring little if his revenge were slow provided only it were sure. He carried a double line of fortifications right across the isthmus within a bowshot of the city walls, thus at once protecting himself from a surprise and effectually cutting off the Carthaginians from all succor on the land side. But the sea was still open to its own children, and fearless blockade-runners kept entering the narrow mouth of the merchant harbour right under the eyes of the Romans. Scipio therefore began to construct a mole of huge stones, which, starting from the Tænia, should block up for ever the mouth of the harbour. This operation, if it was feasible, would make the surrender only a question of time. At first the Carthaginians thought it was not feasible. But it progressed rapidly, and in two months it was all but completed, when, to the infinite surprise and chagrin of the Romans, a fleet of fifty triremes, hastily built of materials which had been accumulated before the war began, sailed out, as it were, through dry land, into the open sea, and that at a point where the waters were so deep and the surf so angry that it was hopeless to think of closing the exit by any further prolongation of the mole.

Scipio's mole.

How so gigantic a work can have been accomplished —new ships built, and a new passage opened—without even a suspicion being roused in the minds of the Romans as to what was going on, it is difficult to say. Deserters, indeed, had reported that the workman's pickaxe and hammer were to be heard day and night within the harbour quarter,

The new outlet.

s

which was itself surrounded by a wall. But the secret had been kept; and kept, it would seem, not merely from the Romans, but from the mass of the citizens themselves. It is another illustration of that suspicious shrewdness which marked the policy of the ruling Carthaginian oligarchy throughout its history—a shrewdness which often, indeed, outwitted itself, but sometimes, as in this supreme crisis of their fate, did good service, and which explains in part what is otherwise so inexplicable —that alternation of caution and of rashness, of ebullient enthusiasm and of much enduring patience, of long-sighted provision and of short-sighted *laissez faire*, of sordid selfishness and of sublime self-abnegation, which baffles calculation and defies analysis, refusing to be accounted for by any ordinary combination of motives or to be tested by any of the received maxims of morality. The Romans found that all their labour had been thrown away; and if only the newly-fledged vessels had joined battle with them at once, instead of airing in childish but natural glee their untried powers of flight in the open gulf, they must have surprised and overpowered them. But this was not to be; and after an evolution or two, they returned into the harbour through the passage by which they had left it. Three days after they sailed out again, and this time they offered battle. But the Romans had recovered from their dismay. The conflict was waged on equal terms, and on returning at nightfall to their harbour, the Carthaginian ships, jostling against one another at its narrow entrance, were exposed to the attacks of the enemy and suffered much loss.

Baffled in his attempt to block up the harbour by sea, Scipio now attacked its fortifications by land from the side of the Tænia and from the newly constructed mole.

A part of its walls fell; but the Carthaginians, wading or swimming through the water by night, made an attack on the besieging lines, and then, suddenly kindling the torches which they carried, withstood, with the fury of maniacs or of wild beasts at bay, the darts which were rained on their naked bodies till they had effected their object, the destruction of the engines by fire, and had scattered panic throughout the Roman army. In the morning they repaired the breach in the fortifications at their leisure, and raised lofty towers along the harbour wall, to face the lines of circumvallation and the mounds with which the Romans were endeavouring to approach it. So the summer passed away and still Carthage stood.

During the winter months Scipio attacked Nepheris, a town on the other side of the lake, the head-quarters of a relieving army, and the place from which provisions and supplies had been most systematically forwarded to the beleaguered Carthaginians ever since the siege began. Lælius, having received the chief command of the expedition, took the large fortified camp outside the town, and put to the sword a mixed multitude of seventy thousand soldiers and peasants. Soon afterwards the town itself fell into Scipio's hands; and all the isolated garrisons which had hitherto remained true to Carthage, together with the country which they commanded submitted to Rome. And so one more winter passed away, and still—without a foot of ground which she could now call her own except that which her buildings covered, and without a soldier or a citizen save those who were penned within her walls—the grand old city held bravely out.

But now her hour had come. At the beginning of the spring Scipio delivered his final attack. He first

took by storm the quarter of the merchants' harbour;
then, with the help of a surprise planned
and carried out by Lælius, the war harbour;
and thence he passed without opposition
into the adjacent market-place.

The final assault.

The city might now have been thought to be in his hands. Three streets led up from the market-place to the citadel, and the citadel alone, it might have been anticipated, would now give any further trouble. But those three streets meant six days of fighting and of massacre. They were held by frenzied and despairing Phœnicians, and were well adapted for such a defence as frenzied and despairing Phœnicians alone could make. They were narrow, and above them rose houses six stories high with overhanging eaves; and from these such darts and missiles as came to hand would be hurled down in one continuous shower on the advancing foe. From such a downpour even the Romans shrank. They hesitated for a moment; but it was for a moment only. Storming the first house to which they came, they put its inhabitants to the sword, and then, passing step by step, and inch by inch, from building to building, or from roof-top to roof-top by planks laid across the intervals, they massacred every living thing they met. Each house was a castle, and a castle defended by its garrison to the last extremity. The battle raged on the housetops, within the houses themselves, and in the streets below. Many of the inmates were hurled down from the windows or the roofs and caught on the pikes of the assailants.

Desperate resistance.

At last the citadel was reached and the fighting was at an end. But the most piteous scene of all was still to come. Scipio gave the order to fire the streets which it had cost the Romans so much to gain, to level the ruins, and so to open the approaches to the Byrsa which still frowned in front. It was a natural order, and one which did not appear to imply unnecessary cruelty or loss of life. But, unknown to Scipio, a number of old men and women and children had concealed themselves only too skilfully in the cupboards or the cellars of the houses in which the fighting had been going on, and these were now burned alive, or fell with the falling buildings; while others, half roasted or half suffocated, flung themselves headlong from the windows into the streets. There they lay, and thence they were shovelled, dead and dying alike, amidst charred beams and crumbling masonry, into any hollows which required filling up. Heads or legs might be seen protruding from the reeking and the smouldering mass till they were trampled into nothing by the oncoming cavalry. This fearful scene Polybius himself witnessed and recorded.

The three streets.

The six days of the struggle and the massacre were at last over. The Roman troops had frequently relieved each other during its progress, but Scipio had allowed himself to take no rest. He snatched his food only in the intervals of giving orders, and he now at last sat down on an "elevated place" to see what had been done and what yet remained to do. The Byrsa was not so much a citadel or any single building, as that quarter of the city which was on the highest ground and was most strongly fortified. Within that quarter all who had escaped the starvation of the siege, and the tyranny of Hasdrubal, and the sword and fire of the Romans, were now huddled together; and on the following day a deputation came forth, with suppliant branches and fillets taken from the temple of Æsculapius in their hands, begging

The Byrsa and Hasdrubal's wife.

Scipio to spare their lives. Their lives, but nothing else, the conqueror spared them, and fifty thousand men, women, and children came forth through the gate of the citadel. The nine hundred deserters from the Romans remained behind with Hasdrubal and his wife and children. For them no mercy was either asked or granted. They withdrew, first from the sixty steps which led up towards the citadel, to the level ground at the top; thence into the temple of Æsculapius itself, and thence, once more, to its roof, determined to sell their lives as dearly as possible. But there was, it is said, one coward soul even amongst them. Alone and trembling, Hasdrubal, the commander-in-chief, the murderer of his predecessor, the man who had tortured and massacred the Roman prisoners, who, if our reports speak true, had starved the citizens while he himself feasted and drank—the Marat and the Robespierre in one of the reign of terror which he had established—crept forth in suppliant guise, and threw himself at Scipio's feet begging for his dear life. It was contemptuously granted him amidst the curses, loud and long, of the deserters who were crowded together on the roof, and who saw the dastardly deed. Worn out with fatigue they now set fire to the temple, and Hasdrubal's wife, arraying herself, like her majestic compatriot Jezebel, in her best attire, came forth, it is said, upon the roof with her two sons, and after complimenting Scipio as a noble foe, and heaping reproaches on her recreant husband, she first slew her sons with the sword, and then, flinging herself and them together into the flames, died as became, not indeed the wife of Hasdrubal, but as became the wife of the last commander-in-chief of Carthage and the last of the free Phœnician race.

All resistance was now over, and Scipio was master

of a heap of smouldering ruins. But to him, at all events, the victory did not seem, even in the exuberance of the moment, to be matter for unmixed congratulation. He burst into tears, and was overheard by his faithful friend Polybius repeating to himself in ominous tones the words of Homer, "The day will come when sacred Troy shall fall, and Priam and Priam's people too." The work of butchery over, it was time for that of plunder to begin. The gold and silver and temple ornaments were reserved to grace Scipio's triumph; but the sculptures and the paintings and other works of art which had been stolen from the Sicilian cities were freely restored to them; an act of grace and moderation otherwise unknown in the Roman annals, and, doubtless, due to the refined soul and Hellenic sympathies of the general himself. Many of these works of art were unfortunately, as Cicero remarks, restored to the Sicilians by Scipio only that they might be taken from them by Verres; but for this the Roman people at large are, happily, not responsible. The joy at Rome when Scipio's galley, laden with the trophies of his victory, arrived, was boundless; and it was some time before the citizens could fully realize the fact that their ancient rival, the rival which had once and again brought them to the brink of destruction, was no more.

Much of the city still remained standing, and it was the wish of Scipio and of a small minority of the noblest Romans that that part should still be spared. But what had been granted even to the hated Capua was denied to Carthage. The spirit of old Cato seemed even from his tomb to rule the day, and the orders of the Senate were peremptory that every vestige of their hereditary foe was to be effaced. When every building had been levelled with the ground, the plough was driven over its remains, and a solemn curse was pronounced by Scipio on anyone who should attempt to rebuild the city, or even to dwell upon its site. The rest of the inhabitants were, with few exceptions, sold as slaves. The one Carthaginian who, if the tales told of him are to be trusted, was least worthy of his liberty and life, the miserable Hasdrubal himself, was—perhaps, by an act of cruel kindness on the part of the Romans—allowed to retain them both, and after adorning Scipio's triumph, to end his days in peace in Italy. Utica was rewarded for her desertion by an addition to her territory; while all the towns which had remained faithful to Carthage were condemned to share her fate.

Thus happened what, happily, has rarely happened in history before or since. An ancient seat of civilization, together with the race which inhabited it, with its arts and its sciences, its laws, its literature, and its religion, was swept away at a single stroke, leaving hardly a wrack behind; and with it vanished the last rival whom Rome had to fear, the one state which ever met her on equal terms, and therefore alone stood between her and universal empire; the one possible check upon the evils which the decay of the republican spirit, the increase of wealth, the abuse of conquest, and the temptations of absolute power were sure to bring in their train. It is a thrice melancholy picture. It is the second book of the Æneid in stern and simple fact. The great Roman poet needed not to draw upon his imagination for a single detail of his splendid picture of the fall of Troy. The burning and the slaughter, the crash of falling houses, the obliteration of a wealthy and an ancient city which had held imperial sway for many, nay, for seven hundred years—it was all there, written in letters of blood and fire, in the record of his own country's most signal achievement! It was a loss not to be replaced. The territory of Carthage, indeed, for the century or two that the republic was yet to last, supplied Rome with corn for her markets, and with wild beasts and gladiators for her arena. It gave, in fact, to the populace their bread and their Circensian games, all that when the republic had fallen they would ever want, and all that they would ever have. A poor equivalent this for the mighty city, the queen of the Mediterranean and its islands, the explorer of the Ocean beyond, the nurse of commerce and colonization, the mother of Hamilcar Barca and Mago, of Hasdrubal and Hannibal!

The curse of Scipio rested upon its site. Yet not many years afterwards Caius Gracchus, unmindful or, perhaps, resentful of it, and moved doubtless by the noblest motives, proposed to relieve the wants of the poorer Roman citizens by planting six thousand of them on the spot. But African hyenas, it was said, tore up and scattered the boundary marks which had been laid down, thus demonstrating to the hostile Senate alike the efficacy of the curse and the guilt of the people's friend who had set it at naught. The proposed colony of Junonia cost its originator his noble life before he had done more for it than give it its name. It was reserved for the greatest of the Romans, for Julius Cæsar himself, some forty years after Caius Marius had so theatrically taken his seat amidst its ruins, to revive the project of Caius Gracchus. His death anticipated this, as it anticipated other cosmopolitan projects of his imperial and ultra-Roman mind. But Augustus carried out with filial reverence this and other provisions of his uncle's will, only attempting, it is said, to evade the letter of Scipio's curse by building his town not on, but near, the site of the Phœnician city. He must have failed in this, for, as we have seen, the whole of the peninsula had been more or less covered by the original Carthage, its suburbs, its gardens, and its burial ground. Anyhow, the natural advantages of the spot overcame the curse and soon made the new city the capital of Northern Africa and the headquarters alike of Roman civilization and of African Christianity. After connecting itself with the great names of Augustine and Tertullian and Cyprian—names and characters different indeed from those of their Phœnician predecessors—and passing through the hands of the Vandals, it fell under the sway of the new Rome, and "shed or received a last ray of lustre" from the great name of Belisarius.

Finally, by a destiny stranger still, it was destroyed by the Arabs, a race nearly akin to its first founders. The hurricane of their invasion swept away all that remained of the city, and though the Arabs founded or developed at various times in other parts of Africa rich commercial or literary capitals, such as Cairo and Cairwân, Fez, Tangiers, and Morocco, they did nothing for Carthage. A straggling village, indeed, sprang up later on its site and dragged on a wretched existence for some centuries, and at the present moment, by another caprice of fortune, the citadel of Carthage is occupied by a chapel dedicated to a French crusader, king and saint in one. But ever since the Arab chief Hassan gave, in A. D. 689, the Byzantine city to the flames, the memorable words in which the author of the "Decline and Fall" has described Palestine as it has been ever since the Crusades, may, with at least equal truth, be applied to Carthage: "A mournful and a solitary silence has prevailed along the coast which had so long resounded with the world's debate."

CHAPTER XX.

CARTHAGE AS IT IS.

IT was early on the morning of April 1, 1877, that we cast anchor off the Goletta, a tumble-down fort which commands, or does not command, the narrow entrance to the Lake of Tunis, and found ourselves in full view of the bold promontory and the low coast-line, the undulating hills and the fertile plain, which mark the site of ancient Carthage. It was a moment not easily to be forgotten, a moment into which the interests of half a lifetime—of half my lifetime at all events—seemed to be compressed. There was that tumult of feelings, that mixture of satisfaction and of unrest, of melancholy and delight, of enthusiasm and of disappointment, which it is, perhaps, not easy adequately to explain, but which needs, I imagine, no explanation at all to anyone who has seen for the first time in his life a spot which has long filled a large place in his imagination ; to the poet or the scholar who has seen for the first time the Acropolis of Athens ; to the historian who has at last set foot in Rome ; to the pilgrim who, after traversing, perhaps half a continent, amidst burning deserts or eternal snows, has caught sight—his whole nature strung to the highest pitch of tension - of some storied mountain or some holy city, the goal of all his aspirations and his passionate religious yearnings, Mount Sinai or Mount Elburz, Kapalivastu or Benares, Mecca or Jerusalem. It is more, perhaps, than he has hoped for, but it is also less.

Quæsivit cælo lucem ingemuitque repertâ.

In a work of this kind, anything in the shape of a journal, even though it be a journal of a visit to the city of which it treats, would be obviously out of place. But it may not be out of place to gather up within the compass of a single chapter some of the impressions made upon my mind, by what I saw of the site of Carthage, of its remains, and of its present inhabitants. First impressions of a place, it has been often said, may make up their freshness for what they lack in point of accuracy and completeness; but I am not sure that my own record can lay claim to even this merit. If, in one sense, they are my first impressions, in another they are my ultimate conclusions; and it may well be, therefore, that they may lack the freshness of the one without possessing the value or solidity of the other. Deep and varied though the interests of my visit were, it seemed to me throughout as though I was taking a last rather than a first view of the site of the city, and was driving home impressions which had been made long before rather than forming new ones. Be that as it may, I will endeavour to record some of them here, for what they may be worth.

Nature of impressions thence derived.

Everyone who has given even the most cursory attention to the topography of Carthage knows what diametrically opposite views have been held respecting it; and it was with a feeling of interest not unmixed with anxiety, that I took that first glance at the general outline of the place, which, if it proves nothing at all, may yet seem ominous or suggestive of the result. It might well be that on a personal inspection of the spot I might come to conclusions very different from those which I had drawn from books and maps, and which had hitherto seemed to harmonize best with the history of the final siege. I might be driven by

Topography.

the evidence of my own eyes to agree with those who put the Byrsa where I had imagined the Megara, and the Megara where I had imagined the Byrsa, and transfer the harbours, the Tænia, the Forum, and all the thrilling operations of which they were the scene, from the south to the north of the city. *Tum labor effusus:* much at least of my labour would have been thrown away, and it would only have remained for me to beat a retreat while it was still possible, and to make my views bend to the facts, since the facts would not bend to them. The critical moment came and it passed. Feeling that I could not be an altogether disinterested witness in the matter, I believe I put considerable strain upon myself to see if I could fall in with the views expresssed by Dr. Davis, the energetic excavator and explorer, as regards the position of the Byrsa, and the triple wall, and of Ritter or Mannert, as regards the position of the ports.*
But I came to the conclusion that, on these particular points, the balance of the evidence lay strongly in other directions, and that the inferences on which I had based my account of Carthage were, on the whole, correct.

But if the first view of the place, as seen from the deck of a steamer, is so far satisfactory, it must be ad-

---

* Dr. Davis places the Byrsa on Burj Jedeed, a hill near the sea, considerably to the S. E. of the hill of St. Louis, while he throws back the triple walls to the isthmus behind the Megara. Ritter identifies the Byrsa with Djebel Khawi or the Catacomb Hill on the N. W. of the city, and necessarily therefore also places the Tænia and the artificial harbours in the same locality on the ground now occupied by the Salt Marsh. Mannert places the harbours much in the position which I have indicated in the accompanying plan of Carthage, but conceives the entrance to them and therefore also Scipio's Mole to have been inside the Tænia ; that is, not in the open gulf, but in the Lake of Tunis.

mitted that in other respects it is somewhat disappointing. There is nothing, at first sight, to delight or to charm; there are no bold outlines, nothing, in fact, in the physical features of the spot to suggest the mighty part which it played in ancient history. The Byrsa is an ordinary-looking hill, scarped, it is true, in some portions, but anything but commanding in itself. There is no frowning rock—such as you cannot help picturing to yourself beforehand—like the Acropolis or the Acro-Corinthus, like Edinburgh or Stirling Castle; nothing, in fact, which could put to shame even the supposed Tarpeian rock at Rome. Rough grass, acres of beans and barley, and ploughed fields do not delight the eye; they are not naturally suggestive of anything beyond themselves; moreover the whole thing lies or appears to lie within so small a compass. There does not seem room at first sight for the vast operations of the siege, for the myriad merchantmen and ships of war, for the teeming population who, we are told, and truly told, throve and trafficked here for centuries. A partial explanation of this, no doubt, lies in the fact that the distances are altogether foreshortened, and it is not till you begin to walk over the ground from the Goletta to the Byrsa, from the Byrsa to Cape Carthage, from Cape Carthage to the Necropolis, and so round the whole circuit of twenty-three miles, that the first impression of want of space and want of dignity is even partially removed.

Let me now, without attempting to adhere to any definite order of place or time, say a word or two on some of the spots which interested me most. I had felt somewhat sceptical beforehand as to the existence of that extraordinarily shaped neck of land which I had seen in the larger maps

Goletta and the Tænia.

of Carthage, with its tiny opening now called the Goletta
or gullet. My doubts on that score were set at rest at
once, for, as I have said, we dropped anchor off it, and
were rowed up the channel along which only a few
boats could pass abreast. This was a good omen for
what was to follow, and by walking some half mile to the
westward along the narrow bar of sand which cuts off
the Lake of Tunis from the outer sea, we found ourselves
standing on the broadening ground whence Censorinus,
as I believe, delivered his first, and Scipio his last attack
on the doomed city. On one side of us was the land
which owed its very existence to the operations of the
siege, for it must have been from this point that Censorinus threw those vast masses of soil and ballast into the
lake which gave him standing room for his forces, and
so enabled him to bring his gigantic battering rams to
bear on the weak angle of the wall. On the other side
of the bar was the spot from near to which Scipio must
have begun to carry that cruel mole which was to cut
off from the beleaguered citizens their last hope of relief
from without.

To the extreme north-west of the ground once occupied by the Phœnician city, is the promontory of Râs
Ghamart, 200 feet high, and the line of rounded hills,
called Djebel Khawi, which runs thence in
a southerly direction for the distance of a
mile or so, is "one vast Necropolis." Everywhere, a few feet beneath the surface of the ground are
labyrinths of low vaulted chambers, often communi-
cating with each other or separated only by narrow walls
of rock; perhaps the quarries from which the Punic city
was originally hewn, certainly used afterwards as sepulchres for its dead. They are now, for the most part,
hidden from view or filled with rubbish; and wild fig

Djebel Khawi and the Ne-cropolis.

tree which, as the Roman poet remarked, was able to cleave the costly marble sepulchres of Messala, pushes its sturdy roots in every direction through these humble tenements of the Phœnicians.

All traces of the original occupants have long since disappeared, and the vacant space is often tenanted by the jackal and the hyena.* When the Romans had exhausted their fury on the city of the living, they turned their attention, as it would seem, even to this city of the dead. It was their practice not to bury but to burn their dead, and it is not likely that they used at first the vast Necropolis which they had rifled of its contents, for their own small cinerary urns. But when the Roman Carthage became the metropolis of Africa, and the head-quarters of African Christianity, the Pagan practice of cremation was replaced by Christian burial, and the ancient mortuary chambers were filled, after the lapse of centuries, by new occupants. These, when the impetuous flood of Arab invasion had spread over the country, were, in their turn, dispossessed by marauding Bedouins. For centuries the Bedouins have ransacked them for any treasures to be found within them, and they visit them to this day for the chalk which they contain. Accordingly we are not surprised to hear that out of some hundred sepulchres, examined by Dr. Davis and M. Beulé, only one contained a skeleton. In another was found a relic of even greater interest, though it belongs to the Vandal or the Byzantine rather than the Roman era, a representation on the rock of the seven-branched candlestick.† The seven-branched candlestick, carried off by Titus from Jerusalem to Rome, was, in the strange vicissitudes of human fortune, car-

---

* Davis, *Carthage*, p. 472. † Ibid. p. 486.

ried off again from Rome to Carthage by the terrible Genseric, the lame Vandal king; and so, probably, it comes about that the sacred ornament of the Jewish temple—the exact shape of which is known to all the world from the sculptures on the arch of Titus—has been found engraven also within a Phœnician sarcophagus at Carthage. Some of the sepulchral chambers measure twelve by fifteen feet, and contain as many as ten niches, or columbaria, hewn out of the solid limestone as receptacles for the dead.*

With what deep pathos as one looks at Djebel Khawi —its hill-sides riddled, as they are, with myriads of Phœnician sepulchres—do the words of the Carthaginian legate Banno come back to the mind! " Kill," replied he to the Roman consul who cruelly ordered the now disarmed and helpless Carthaginians to destroy their beloved city and build another ten miles from the coast, " kill, if it be your good pleasure, all the citizens, but spare the city, spare the temples of the gods, spare the tombs of the dead. The dead, at least, can do you no harm; let them receive the honours that are their due." † The appeal might have moved a heart of stone, but it touched no chord in the breast of the Romans.

Deep in the sanctuary of the human heart, civilized or uncivilized alike, lies the feeling of reverence for the last resting-place of the individual, the family, or the nation. For the tombs of their fathers, even the Nomad Scythians told Darius, when he was wearied out by his vain pursuit of an enemy, who always fled before him and always eluded his grasp, that they would stand

<small>Sanctity of burying-places among the Semitic races.</small>

---

* See Beulé, *Fouilles à Carthage*, p. 129 *seq.*, and the plans of the sepulchres in the Appendix. † Appian, viii. c. 84.

T

and fight to the death.* But nowhere, probably, does the feeling lie quite so deep as in the hearts of the various branches of the Semitic race. The voice of the Phœnician Banno is the voice of human nature; but in a more special sense it is the voice which seems to speak to us in each deed of heroism which marked the last agony of Carthage, and which does speak to us from each successive page of the sacred literature of the Hebrews who are next of kin to the Carthaginians. It is the voice of the patriarch himself that we seem to hear: "Bury me with my fathers in the cave that is in the field of Machpelah which Abraham bought for a possession of a burying-place; there they buried Abraham and Sarah his wife; there they buried Isaac and Rebekah his wife, and there I buried Leah."

The other promontory which is included within the circuit of the ancient city, Râs Sidi Bu Said, or, as it is called in our maps, Cape Carthage, outtops Râs Ghamart by a hundred feet. It is of red sandstone, and is the most commanding eminence within the precincts. It is crowned at present by an Arab village of peculiar sanctity, so sacred that, as we were told, no Christian is allowed to sleep there. The venerable Sheikh of the village, however, courteously allowed us to enter and to enjoy the superb view from the summit. It is inhabited by a large number of Marabouts or Muslim Saints, living and dead; men who, by their austerities, their theological learning, or their charity, have earned a reputation for sanctity, and have come to live where other saints have lived before them, and to lay their bones in death by the bones of those whose virtues they have emulated.

Râs Sidi Bu Said.

By a curious caprice of fortune, or, may we not rather

---

* See Stanley's *Jewish Church*, vol. i. chap. 2, p. 24.

say, by a theological Nemesis, the Saint who is supposed to give to Sidi Bu Said its special sanctity is no less a personage than St. Louis of France himself. The crusading king died in 1270 of a pestilence which broke out in his army near Tunis, as he was on his way to Egypt. His heart lies buried near Palermo, and his body rests in the sanctuary of the French kings at St. Denis; but his virtues and his sanctity are still a living power on the plains of Carthage. So widely were his virtues recognized among those whom he came to exterminate, that with true Muslim charity they believed, or wished to believe, that he had died a good Muslim, and "the Village of the Saint" is believed, even to this day, to be blessed by his body, and by a special portion of his spirit. It is an homage, even if an all-unwitting homage, paid by his followers to the teachings of the Prophet, who told them, what Muslim and Christian have proved alike so apt to forget, that the God of Muslims and Christians is one.*

It must have been near to this commanding eminence, and above the remains of the ancient sea gate which is still to be seen on the beach beneath, that the incompetent legate, Mancinus, effected a landing with a small force during the final siege, hoping to take the town by assault, and it was from this spot, when entirely isolated, without a sufficiency of arms or of provisions, that he was rescued from total destruction by the prompt succour of Scipio.

Scene of misadventure of Mancinus.

Scipio sent him off in disgrace to Rome, and we can hardly believe, what we are gravely told by a Roman writer, that he had the face to assert, in virtue of his very brief and very uncomfortable occupation of this one spot in the suburbs, that he had been the first Roman

---

* Koran, Sura v. 73: "Say unto the Christians their God and our God is one," and cf. Sura ii. 59 and v. 52, 53.

to enter Carthage; that he caused pictures to be painted representing the city and the various assaults made on it by the Romans—in which his own, doubtless bore a conspicuous figure; that he exhibited them in the Forum to all comers with copious explanations; and that he became so popular thereby that, to the extreme disgust of Scipio, he was elected consul for the year which followed the fall of Carthage.* We can share Scipio's disgust! but we feel as we stand upon the spot and look upon the red sandstone cliffs, the straggling cactus hedges, and the bare hill-sides, with perhaps a sedate Arab or two picturesquely grouped upon them, that we could pardon the impudence of Mancinus, if only one of those pictures had been preserved to us, or had been so described by any one of the eager multitude who thronged to look at them, as to enable us better to reclothe in our imagination the landscape with the walls and the towers, the palaces and the gardens, of the mighty city which must have lain full within his view.

From Sidi Bu Said runs in a south-west direction, parallel to the line of the coast, and at a distance of three-quarters of a mile from it, a broken line of hills which terminates abruptly in that which, since its purchase by the French and the erection of a small chapel on its summit, bears also the name of St Louis. This hill, although it is in no way striking or precipitous, and although there are some difficulties connected with the large number of fifty thousand souls said by Appian to have taken refuge within its precincts, when the last hours of Carthage came, yet, unquestionably, dominates the plain, the harbours, and the isthmus behind it, and there can be no reasonable

Hill of St. Louis, the ancient Byrsa.

---

* Pliny, *Nat. Hist.* xxxv. 4, 7. Cf. Cic. *Lælius*, xxv. 96.

doubt that it formed the Byrsa or citadel of the palmy days of Carthage. At all events, it was its most commanding eminence.

It is at a moderate distance from the coast, as the ancient citadels almost invariably were. It lies, as Appian expresses it, "towards the isthmus" * which connected Carthage with the mainland, and, alone of all the hills within the circumference of ancient Carthage, it answers to the description of Strabo, as being "a brow sufficiently steep lying in the middle of the city, with houses on all sides of it." † On this spot stood the famous temple of Esmun or Æsculapius. Under its protection the infant settlement grew up to maturity and to empire; against its fortifications discontented mercenaries and hostile Libyans, Sicilian Greeks, and Roman generals spent their strength, for centuries, in vain, and on its summit the last scene of the sad tragedy, the heroic death of Hasdrubal's wife, is said to have been enacted. The view from the Byrsa is, therefore, one which, for its historical and tragic interest, if not for its intrinsic beauty, has few equals in the world. It may be well, therefore, taking the Byrsa hill as our central standpoint, to describe something of what we saw from thence or from points in its immediate neighborhood.

To the south and east, almost beneath one's feet, is the broad and beautiful gulf of Tunis, stretching away to the open Mediterranean between the far-famed Promontories of Mercury and Apollo. Beyond the gulf is the Peninsula of the Dakhla, whose majestic mountains—Hammam-el-Enf, the most commanding among them—by their shape, their silence, and their barrenness, recall what one has read of the "Alps unclothed," as they have been well described,

<small>Gulf of Tunis and Peninsula of the Dakhla.</small>

---

* Appian, viii. 95, ἐπὶ τοῦ αὐχένος.   † xx. 9.

of the Peninsula of Mount Sinai. Hidden from view behind the mountains at the end of this peninsula, and looking straight across towards Sicily, of which, in prehistoric times, it must have formed a part, is the Promontory of Mercury, sometimes called also the "Fair Promontory," the point which, in times of peace, was named by the proud and jealous republic as the *ne plus ultra* of all foreign—especially of all Roman—merchantmen, the point where Regulus halted his ships of war, where the greater Scipio first landed, and from which, with characteristic adroitness, he drew his first omen of success.

To the west and north is a sandy plain, flanked by the Lake of Tunis, with its flamingo-haunted waters, and by the ancient city, whose glaring houses and whitened roof-tops, relieved a little by its Moorish mosques and minarets, still recall the name of "the white," given to Tunis by Diodorus Siculus eighteen centuries ago.* The plain is dotted here and there by houses of the wealthy Tunisians, by olive plantations, by one or two solitary palm trees, and by huge hedges of the Barbary fig, whose sharp fleshy leaves afford sure protection against every animal except the camel. Part of it is under cultivation, and yields to its cultivators—if those who just scratch the surface of the earth may be so called—no longer, indeed, the hundred-and-fifty fold of Pliny's time ; † but still in ordinary years

<small>Lake of Tunis and plain of Carthage.</small>

---

* xx. 9.

† Pliny, *Hist. Nat.* xvii. 3, cf. v. 3. Sir Richard Wood, K. C. M. G., Her Majesty's Consul-General at Tunis, to whose hospitality and kindness, as well as to that of his family, we owe much of the success and comfort of our stay there, told us of exceptional instances within his knowledge in which even Pliny's estimate of the fertility of the soil had been largely exceeded.

a large return. Large tracts of country which we know
were, till very lately, covered with forests, are now entirely bare. Trees are cut down but new ones are never
planted. Even the olive plantations seem to be dying
away for want of tending or renewal. There is nothing,
therefore, to help the thirsty soil to retain even that
modicum of rain from heaven which falls upon it, while
scientific irrigation with the help of the rivers, which was
carried to such a wonderful pitch in ancient times alike
by the Phœnicians and by the Romans, is now entirely
neglected. What wonder, then, if in seasons of exceptional drought Nature revenges herself and that the crops,
having no deep roots, wither away, while the inhabitants
perish by hundreds? The cultivated portions of the
plain, at certain times of the year, swarm with quails,
vast numbers of which are snared in nets by the natives
or knocked down by sticks when they are tired out—as
was the case when we were there—by their annual mi-
gration. Wandering over the pasture-lands may be seen
the flocks and herds of the Arabs and the long lines of
their camels. Here and there are their black tents,
which may be shifted at convenience. But some of the
natives, passing gradually from the nomadic to the agricultural stage, have found a more permanent, if not a
more congenial abode, in the numerous subterranean
cisterns or magazines which the forethought of their more
civilized predecessors constructed; and the domestic
animals of the Arabs are found stabling in the very
buildings which may once, perhaps, have sheltered the
Carthaginian elephants.

Stretching right across the plain, "like the bleached
vertebræ of some gigantic serpent," as they have been
well described by Sir Grenville Temple, may be seen
great blocks of masonry, the remains of the noble Ro-

man aqueduct,* which brought from the mountains of Zaghouan (Mons Zeugitanus) and Djebel Djougar (Mons Zuccharus)—from a distance, that is, of over sixty miles — those perennial streams of fresh water which not only supplied the inhabitants of the city, but sufficed to irrigate its suburbs and its gardens, and made much even of the intervening arid country to smile as the Garden of the Lord.† It was the handiwork of that Roman emperor who has left behind him traces of his truly imperial passion for building and for travelling in every province of his vast empire. The aqueduct of Carthage is not unworthy, either in the magnificence of its design or in the completeness of its execution, of the man who could rear at Rome the mighty mass of buildings once called "Hadrian's Pile," and at Tivoli that museum of art which is still known as his "Villa;" who, at one end of his dominions, could carry a wall from sea to sea, from the mouth of the Tyne to the Solway Firth, still called Hadrian's Rampart, and at another could complete the colossal temple of the Olympian Zeus, which had been begun by Pisistratus seven centuries before, and had waited seven centuries to find anyone who had the means and the will to finish it.

The arches of the aqueduct which were once visible from the Byrsa have been destroyed, not by the hand of time, but by the barbarism of the inhabitants. The basements alone remain, and we saw bands of Arabs

The aqueduct.

* Procopius, *Bell. Van.* ii. 1, τὸν ὀχετὸν ἀξιοθέατον ὄντα ὃς ἐς τὴν πόλιν εἰσῆγε τὸ ὕδωρ. Perhaps even more "worthy of admiration" it still is in its decay and ruin.

† It has been calculated that the aqueduct conveyed seven millions of gallons of water a day, or eighty-one gallons per second! See Playfair's *Travels in the Footsteps of Bruce*, p. 131.

in the act of carrying away such blocks even of these as their pickaxes could break off, to build a new palace for the Bey of Tunis. Further away man has been more merciful, or, at all events, less powerful to injure, and its arches, rising to the height often of sixty, and sometimes, it is said, of a hundred and twenty-five feet,* march across the valleys from hill to hill in stately procession. Those who are fond of birds may be interested to know that a large owl, of a species which I had never seen before, was building its nest on one of the highest of these arches, while on the other side of the same arch a raven was sitting on its young in undisturbed repose, and its mate flew croaking round—a curious mixture of associations, ornithological and religious: the bird of Pallas and the bird of Odin nestling together on what is doubtless the handiwork of those master builders of antiquity, the Roman worshippers of Jupiter and Juno, but which supplied the wants of those who, after the lapse of centuries of foreign conquest, still clung desperately to their ancestral worship of Baal-Moloch and Astarte!† The channel which conveyed the water from Zaghouan sometimes penetrates deep beneath the ground, sometimes runs along the top of single arches, or of tiers of them, one above

---

* Davis, i. 460.

† The deep channels full of water mentioned by Appian as intersecting the Megara in every direction seem to necessitate an artificial conduit from a distance even in the time of the Phœnician city: Appian, viii. 117, τὰ Μέγαρα .... ὀχετοῖς βαθέσιν ὕδατος ποικίλοις τε καὶ σκολιοῖς κατάπλεων ἦν. In like manner the description of the country round Carthage given by Diodorus (xv. 8) as it appeared to the soldiers of Agathocles, implies a vast system of tanks or cisterns, as well as scientific irrigation. πολλῶν ὑδάτων διοχετευομένων καὶ πάντα τόπον ἀρδεόντων.

the other. It is broad enough and deep enough for a man to walk upright within it, and in many parts it is still so perfect as to be utilized for the water-supply which modern enterprise has, within the last few years, brought to Tunis from the same distant and perennial fount.

Far away to the north of the plain we could see the hill, on the top of which the citadel of Utica was perched, the parent city and the one trusted ally of Carthage, the point where the Romans so often landed in their invasions of Africa, and whence they must have caught the first glimpse of the city which they had so perfidiously doomed to destruction.

Utica.

But if the view from the Byrsa is impressive from what it contains within it, how infinitely more impressive is it from what it can only suggest! It was long, indeed, before we could fully realize, what we knew well enough before we went there, that on the ground immediately beneath our feet so many cities—Phœnician, Roman, Vandal, Byzantine—had been founded, had risen to opulence and power, and had vanished again, leaving barely a trace of their existence behind. A lively German, indeed, a resident in Tunis, whom we met on board the steamer on our way to Africa, could hardly suppress his surprise or his merriment, perhaps even his contempt, when we told him that we were actually coming all the way from England to see Carthage. "*Carthage! c'est rien!*" he exclaimed; and nothing, indeed, in one sense of the word, there was; but in another, and perhaps a truer sense, how very much!

One trace, however, of the ancient city there is which one would have thought that even our matter-of-fact German friend would hardly have called "nothing."

About a quarter of a mile from the Byrsa and nearer to the sea, is a huge mass of masonry embedded in the soil, the low vaulted roofs of which, rising side by side in pairs only a few feet above the level of the hillside which has been excavated around them and are actually below its level where it has been undisturbed, look like the graves of some gigantic prehistoric race. "There were giants in the earth in those days," were the words which rose involuntarily to the mind; but these vaulted roofs turned out to be the coverings of the vast reservoirs which stored up water for the teeming population of the city. They are eighteen in number; the masonry and cement are still all but perfect. Each reservoir is nearly one hundred feet long by twenty wide, and the water still stands in many of them to the depth of seventeen feet. A narrow gallery, hollowed out of the face of the hill beside them, enables the visitor to pass beneath the surface along their whole length, and to realize the silence and the solitude which reign supreme around this, the one remaining monument of the vanished ancient city.

The smaller cisterns.

I say advisedly of the *ancient* city, for though the facings of the cisterns and perhaps nearly everything which meets the eye may, very possibly, be Roman, yet, as M. Beulé, one of the highest authorities on ancient architecture, as well as an indefatigable excavator, has pointed out, the plan on which they are constructed is undoubtedly more ancient, and the Roman architects have only copied their Punic predecessors. It seems likely, I would rather say, that they have only repaired their work. If the aqueduct is admitted to be Roman, it will follow that a huge collection of rain-water cisterns would have been an absolute necessity in the Punic city. Nor is it easily credible that the Romans would have taken the trouble

to destroy what lay deep hidden beneath the ground
We have seen that they did not destroy the Necropolis,
they only pillaged and profaned it. Why then should
they have destroyed, at an infinite expenditure of labour,
the huge reservoirs which in that arid country would be
of untold value to the scattered cultivators of the ground,
or to their flocks and herds, and which did not disturb
that dead level to which it was their pleasure and their
practice to condemn alike the house or the city of an
offender?* The low vaulted roofs of the cisterns were
probably then covered with soil, to lower the temperature
and to prevent evaporation, and the Roman plough might
therefore have well been driven by the Roman destroyers
almost inadvertently across them. M. Beulé well points
out, moreover, that the definition which exactly hits off
the series of undoubtedly Punic fortifications which he
has disinterred beneath the Byrsa, hits off with equal
precision the range of cisterns themselves. Each consists of a "series of chambers equal and parallel, and
opening on a common corridor."†

Behind the Byrsa and beyond the precincts of the ancient city proper, there is another group of cisterns of
still larger proportions. These probably belong to the
Roman city, and they were fed not by rain water but by
the aqueduct of which they formed the termination.
They are called the "large cisterns" to distinguish them from the other group, which
certainly could never be called "small" except by comparison with them. They are said by the
traveller Shaw to have been in his time twenty in number,

The Large Cisterns.

---

* Cf. Livy, iv. 16, for the Æquimælium or Mælian level; the place on which the house of Sp. Mælius, the presumed traitor, had stood.

† Beulé, *Fouilles*, p. 61.

each measuring not less than a hundred feet in length by thirty in breadth. Gigantic as they are, they are not so imposing either in associations or in appearance as the smaller group which I have just described, partly because they do not lie so well together, and partly because the deposits and accumulations of successive ages have filled them to within a few feet of the roof. Even so, they are of considerable value to the inhabitants; for, giving shelter as they do to a whole settlement of Arabs with their wives and children, their stores of grain, their agricultural implements, and their domestic animals—which are never few in number—they form in themselves the whole hamlet of Moalka, home and homestead in one!

All the other buildings of the city, whether Punic or Roman, have long since disappeared. Whole hamlets and towns have been built out of their materials. We saw huge slabs of Carthaginian marble embedded in the palaces of Tunisian nobles; and some have found their way even into Italian and Spanish cathedrals. Innumerable small fragments, however, which were not thought worth carrying away, still linger on the site of the city. The ground beneath one's feet teems with them; nay, rather it is composed of them. Bits of tessellated pavement, of porphyry, of the famous Numidian marble—green, white, and red—everywhere meet the eye, or are turned up by the spade and the ploughshare. These belong, I believe, almost exclusively to periods later than that of the Phœnician city. The Romans did their work of destruction on their hated rival too thoroughly. For seventeen days its ruins burned,* and at the end not one stone was left standing on another, at all events above the surface of the ground.

* Florus, ii. 17, 18.

The Manes of old Cato must have been more than satisfied by the way in which his countrymen carried out his grim resolve.

The work of excavation has been attempted in recent times, with such means as were at their disposal, by Dr. Davis, an English, and by M. Beulé, a French archæologist, whose names I have already had occasion to mention. Dr. Davis, in a series of explorations, which he has carried on for many years, partly at his own expense, and partly at that of the English Government, has disinterred a large number of marbles and mosaics, many of which, of course, belong to the Roman period. But he has also opened out to view the basement of a large temple to Baal, which, if it is not Punic itself, is in all probability—as we know the Romans in their new-born enthusiasm for the city of Dido and Venus made a point of doing—built upon the exact site, and, as nearly as possible, after the model of its Punic predecessor; and, what is more important still, he has discovered a very large number, over 120, of genuine Punic inscriptions. That some of the mosaic pavements also found by him belong to the Phœnician city, we may not unreasonably conclude, when we are told that he has sometimes found three successive layers of mosaics placed one above the other at considerable intervals; that the cement in which the lower stratum was laid was of a wholly different character from those of the upper; that it was easily detached from the mosaics and was very friable in itself, having lost all its adhesive power by long lapse of time.*

Excavations of Dr. Davis.

M. Beulé, on the other hand, who is well known for his excavations in the Acropolis at Athens, expended

* Davis, p. 202.

much labour in sinking deep shafts, some of which happily still remain open, at various points near the circumference of the Byrsa, and he was fortunate enough to bring to light considerable remains of the great triple wall so accurately described by the ancients.

There he came upon the foundation of the outer wall, which, as we have already stated, was six feet thick and forty-five feet high, strengthened by towers at intervals which rose twenty feet higher still. There, before his eyes, were the basements of the semi-circular chambers —the shape so much affected by the Phœnicians as we see in their remains at Malta and at Gozo—which contained stabling for three hundred elephants below, and for four thousand horses above; and there too, at the depth of fifty-six feet below the present surface of the hill, he worked his way through a layer of ashes five or six feet thick, some of which still blackened the hand which touched them, and were mixed with half-charred pieces of wood, with small bits of iron twisted into strange contortions by the fury of the Roman flames which had attempted to consume them, with fragments of pottery and glass—the invention of the Tyrians—and with projectiles which must, all too probably, have been collected together in the citadel when the last assault was imminent, to be thrown thence by the Balearic slingers, or to be launched from the very catapults which had been equipped for service by the free-will offerings of the long hair of the frenzied Carthaginian matrons.*

Some of these remains are preserved in a small museum near the chapel of St. Louis, and one of the projectiles Père Roger, the custodian of the chapel, was kind

*Beulé, p. 55.

enough to give me, when he found that I was specially interested in the history and topography of Carthage. It is heavy for its size, and is made of terra-cotta, that is to say, of clay which had been moulded into an oval form, and then baked to a red heat, exactly answering to the description given by Cæsar of the acorn-shaped bolts used by the Romans, and hence called "acorns." *Ferventes fusili ex argillâ glandes*,* he says in his "Gallic War," and this is one of precisely the same shape and material used by the Phœnicians.

There is one feature of the ancient city which in spite of all I had heard and read about it I was surprised to find in such perfect preservation. It will doubtless be remembered that ancient Carthage had two docks or harbours, both the work of human hands—one oblong for the use of merchant vessels, the other circular for the use of vessels of war—and our pleasure may be imagined when on suddenly reaching the summit of the Byrsa from behind we saw them both immediately below us, each, of course, much diminished in size by the ever-shifting soil, and by the débris of the buildings which had perished around them, but each preserving its characteristic shape. There, before our eyes, was the circular war-harbour, once surrounded by 220 different docks, each fronted by two Ionic marble pillars. There was still the island in the middle, on which, in the days when Carthage was the mistress of all known seas and islands, was the residence of her lord high admiral, the spot from which he could superintend all the operations of that busy hive of industry, and could issue his orders by the sound of the trumpet; and there was the intervening strip of land, narrower now than then, owing to

* Cæsar, *Bell* Gall., v. 41.

the encroachment of the waves, looking across which—himself unobserved the while—he could see all that went on in the open sea and concert his measures against any state which dared—and few ever dared—to measure her strength against that of the Queen of the Ocean. And there, too, was something—though I believe it is really much more modern—which looked like the traces of the outlet opened by the beleaguered Carthaginians in the days of their distress, when they were thus able, for the time at least, to laugh to scorn all the labours of Scipio.

We bathed close to the supposed outlet. The water was deliciously warm, early though it was in the month of April, and as far out as we could swim, we could rest once and again on the blocks of masonry which once formed the quays, or the sea wall, or it may be even the buildings, of the Phœnician city, but which are now encrusted by shell-fish and seaweeds, and have long been covered by the waves.

It will readily be believed that the first and great charm of a visit to Carthage is the *religio loci*, the place itself, and the associations which cluster round it; but a second and hardly inferior attraction to my mind, is the character of the people who inhabit the plains where Carthage once was. Comparatively few travellers have as yet visited Cothon or the Byrsa. Of tourists in the ordinary sense of the word, there are none; and Tunis, I have reason to believe, is at the present day the most Oriental of all Oriental towns. The wave of Western civilization or its counterfeit, which has done so much to transform Constantinople and Cairo, nay even Bagdad and Damascus, has not yet swept over Tunis. A few shopkeepers, indeed, and most of the voituriers are Italians, while the boatmen and the porters who quarrel for the honour

<small>Oriental character of Tunis.</small>

of carrying your portmanteau, and nearly carry you off
in the process, are Maltese, who, it is said, do most of
the crime, and certainly seem to carry it in their for-
bidding countenances. But beyond these outliers of
civilization, and the few Europeans attached to the con-
sulates, there are no sights visible, and there is no
influence felt, but those of the East.

And what a mixture of Eastern races there is, and
what gorgeous costumes! Grave and dignified Osmanli
Turks with their pride of race, their scarlet fezes, and
their yellow slippers; Jews with their bagging panta-
loons and their blue coats and head-dresses; Arabs with
their long beards, their white turbans and burnouses,
and their many-coloured tunics; descendants of the
prophet, "Grand Scherifs" as they are called, rejoicing
in their green robes and green turbans—the size of which
is not unusually exactly proportioned to the degree of
their sanctity and their dirtiness; swarthy Moors from
the desert, and Negroes from the Soudan—not such
sickly and cringing hybrids as you see in Oxford Street,
clad in European dress and aping European manners—
but real downright Negroes, half-naked, black as ebony;
all jostling one against the other, and all rejoicing in the
brotherhood of Islam.

The streets of Tunis are narrow and unpaved, and
are often very dirty. The houses—as in their counter-
parts, the three narrow streets leading from
Streets of Tunis. the Forum to the Byrsa in ancient Carthage—often all but meet across them over-
head, and few of them have any pretensions to archi-
tectural beauty, yet, as you walk up and down, you
have endless and ever-varying subjects of interest and
amusement. Every man and woman you meet, and
still more every shop or stall you pass, with its owner

sitting in the middle of it cross-legged and barefooted in dignified repose, waiting patiently till it pleases Allah to send him a customer, is a study in itself.

You seem to have the "Arabian Nights" before your very eyes. There, for instance, is the barber's shop with a bench all round it, on which sit rows of customers divested of their turbans and their fezes, listening to the barber's chatter and each waiting till his turn comes to have his head operated upon. There is the Court where justice—Eastern justice, of course, I mean—is administered by a Turkish Pasha, who sometimes despatches the cases brought before him at the rate of two a minute, but to the equal satisfaction, as it would seem, of both plaintiff and defendant. There is the prison, the doors of which are never closed but guarded only by one shabby policeman armed with a blunderbuss which looks as if it would never go off, and a yataghan which is so rusty that you would think it could never leave its scabbard; the prisoners squatting complacently inside, smoking, or knitting, or wrapped in contemplation, and all submitting quietly to their incarceration, because it, too, is the will of Allah—or of the Bey. There is the Arab coffee-house, where grave and sedate revellers sit almost in the dark playing draughts and sipping strong black coffee, of course without sugar and without milk, from minute saucerless cups. There is the College, founded by the Prime Minister Kheir-eddin—a Turk and a Pasha and yet a genuine reformer, who is loved and honoured the whole country through *—where little boys learn to repeat by rote the Koran from end to end at the top of their voices before they understand a word

---

* See his book on "Necessary Reforms of Mussulman States:" Athens, 1874.

of its meaning, while some reverend Moullah sits in the midst of the circle and, holding his wand of office, chastises them gently, not if they are not quiet, but—oh! what a paradise of boys!—if they do not make noise enough. The higher classes, meanwhile, are answering questions in Euclid, or arithmetic, or geography, describing by memory, for instance, the sea passage from St. Petersburg to Stamboul through the Cattegat, and the Skaggerack, and all the rest of it, with a precision and a readiness in which I am not quite sure that all, even in the highest forms in English schools, would be able to keep pace with them. There again are the mosques, visited five times a day by throngs of worshippers, who reverently put off their shoes before they enter them, and into which Christians—since the European element in Tunis is happily small and unaggressive,—rightly forbear to claim an entrance. There are the minarets, from which, at stated intervals throughout the day and night, and, above all, at daybreak, comes that strange and beautiful call to prayer—the very same which is heard from Sierra Leone to Sumatra, and from Astrakan to Zanzibar—" *Allahu Akbar, God is most great; prayer is better than sleep, prayer is better than sleep; there is no God but God, and Mohammed is his prophet.*" And there, once more, are the caravanserais, filled at evening with groups of camels kneeling in a circle, their old-world heads pointed inwards, sullenly crunching the heap of green barley which their owners with characteristic improvidence have gathered for them, and tended all night long by some swarthy Arab squatting on his haunches. All these and many more such sights were crowded into the few days that we were enabled to spend in Tunis and its neighborhood.

And when you pass the city wall—for Tunis, it must

be made known to all, is a fortified city, and possesses something which may by courtesy, indeed, be called a wall, but which would, I verily believe, like the walls of Jericho, tumble down, *en masse*, at the bare report of a heavy gun,— when you pass the gates and find yourself in the country, what a delight, irrespective of the Roman remains which are so thickly strewn over it, at Utica, for instance, and at Uthina, at Hippo Zarytus and at Tysdrus, to see, not the Turk, or the Moor, or the Negro, or the Jew, interesting, though each is in his way, but, what is still more interesting, the genuine Bedouin of the desert.

The Neighborhood of Tunis.

There you have, not the "Arabian Nights" but what is better still, the Book of Genesis itself before your eyes. There, for instance, is the gaunt figure of the Arab against the clear horizon as from the hill-top, wrapped in his white blanket, he stands like Joseph or like Moses watching his flocks, or as he walks magnificently—for who has a walk that can be named with that of the Arab?—over the plain. There is the encampment of black tents, the very same in colour and materials, in shape and in size, as that which heard the laugh of Sarah, or witnessed the last long sleep of Sisera. There is the venerable Sheik, the Abraham of his tribe, with his long white beard, his grave courtesy, and his boundless hospitality; there his dark-eyed princess, with tattered garments perhaps and bare feet, but richly decorated with glass beads and amulets, with ear-rings, which hang not through but round the ear, and with ankle-rings which are often of silver and richly chased; such jewelry, doubtless, as struck the fancy of the grasping Laban, and helped to win the heart of his sister to a stranger in a far distant country. There, again, is a young Rebekah, a damsel of olive complexion but of strange beauty, going with her pitcher to the well. Within the tent are stone jars of water of patriarchal make and shape, curtains and coverlets of camel's hair, churns for butter, kids' skins, and sheep skins, while near its entrance is the rude circular stone oven about the size of a basin, within which the scanty fuel may be husbanded to the utmost and yet a cake may be baked hastily and well for the tired wayfarer. Round about the encampment roam the Bedouin's wealth, the only wealth he possesses, his sheep and his oxen, his goats and his dogs, his mules and his asses, while here and there, crossing the plains, may be seen those ships of the desert, the long lines of his camels, each one, perhaps, carrying a whole house and household on his back, each grunting and grumbling as he shambles along, every line in his ungainly figure, and every feature of his countenance, even his gentle eye, looking like what it really is, a never-ceasing, but, alas, a bootless protest against the advance of civilization.

And, then, what lavish hospitality you meet with everywhere, what courtesy, what simplicity of heart and life! On one occasion we stopped for a few moments before a Bedouin encampment, and after partaking of their simple fare, their milk and their butter, from a dish which was not a lordly one, only because they had none such in their possession, we were about to depart when one of their number was sent off to a point half a mile away, and returned bringing on his shoulders a present which, it will be believed, it was equally difficult for us to refuse or accept—a live lamb. They would not take a refusal, still less would they take any return for it

The Arab is, in a sense in which it can hardly be said of any European nation, an inborn gentleman. If he is not the noblest, he is yet, in my opinion, a truly noble specimen of humanity. He is, and herein lies one of his chief charms, as unchangeable as the deserts in which he has his home. What he was in the time of Abraham and Moses, that he was in the time of Christ, and that, in spite of the vast religious impulse given him by Mohammed, which carried him in one sweep of unbroken conquest over half the world, he is, in all essentials, down to the present day. He is, indeed, such a living bit of antiquity himself that we are disposed to make rather more allowance for the thoughtless way in which, unconscious of his past and careless of his future, he destroys, and has for centuries past destroyed the remains of a less venerable antiquity than his own which lie scattered so thickly around him. But I must forbear to enter further here upon the fascinating subject of the Arab; for though he forms one of the chief attractions of a visit to Carthage and its neighbourhood, I have treated of him fully elsewhere, and his history and characteristics lie beyond the proper scope and object of this volume.

Characteristics of the Arab.

It was a revelation, doubtless, to the Roman senators that the splendid figs which Cato showed them grew in a country only three days' sail from Rome; but I am inclined to think it was a greater revelation to me that the remains of the great imperial city, whose history had so long occupied my thoughts, lay within six days' journey of England, and that they could be enjoyed, if not to the full, at least, I hope, to some good effect, within the narrow limits of an Easter holiday.

Conclusion.

INDEX

ACHRADINA, 179, 180.
Adherbal, Carthaginian admiral, 79; defeats Claudius at Drepanum, 80; causes the destruction of the third Roman fleet, 82.
Adis, battle of, 58, 62.
Adrumetum, 10, 222, 225.
Ægatian Islands, 9; battle of, 92.
Ægusa, 92.
Africa, 9.
  invasion by Romans, 56.
  Romans driven from, 66.
  Scipio invades, 210.
  researches in, 265.
Agathocles, 21, 30, 31, 56.
Agrigentum, 15, 36; besieged, 37; captured, 38.
Aleria, 47.
Alps, 117; Hannibal's passage of, 118, 121, 124.
Anapus, marshes of, 35, 180.
Antigonus, 114.
Antiochus, the Great, 109, 232; defeated at Magnesia, 233.
Aosta, 124.
Apennines, 110, 129, 133, 135.
Appian, 239.
Archimedes, 179; death of, 181.
Argyrippa, 145.
Ariminum, 112, 127, 129, 136.
Arno, 134.
Arpi, 145; Hannibal's quarters at, 175.
Arretium, 133, 135.
As, 86.
Asina, Cn. Corn. Scipio, consul, 66.
Aspis, 55.
Astarte, or Tanith, 17, 277.

Atilius, A., consul, 66.
Aufidus, 153, 155.
Autaritus, 98.

BAAL-MOLOCH, 7, 16, 63, 241, 277.
Bagradas, 10, 58, 68, 223.
Balearic Islands, 9, 19, 206, 220.
Balearic slingers, 139.
Barcine gens, or, "Lion's brood," 14, 84, 110, 161.
Barcine faction, 217.
Battles of, Adis, 56, 62.
  Ægatian Islands, 92.
  Cannæ, 158.
  Drepanum, 80.
  Ecnomus, 50.
  Ibera, 183.
  Lake Trasymene, 140.
  Metaurus, 197.
  Mylæ, 45.
  Panormus, 69.
  Telamon, 111.
  Ticinus, 127.
  Trebia, 130.
  Zama, 224.
Beneventum, 146.
Berbers, 10.
Beulé, M., researches of, 263, 279, 283.
Boetis, 108.
Boii, 110, 111.
Bomilcar, 179.
Borghetto, 138.
Bostar, a Carthaginian, 73.
Bovianum, 27.
"Bride of the Sea," 66.
Bruttians, put to death, 192.
Bruttium, 42, 221.
Byrsa, 6, 251, 257, 265, 268, 272.

CAR.

CARTHAGE, topography, 5; relation to Sicily, 6; few records of, 7; spread of influence on the Western Mediterranean, 8; constitution, 11; the 100 judges of, 12; oligarchy of, 13; social life at, 14; wealth and agriculture of, 15; military spirit, 16; religion, 17; proper names, 17; literature, 17; mercenaries, 18; the poor of, 20; sources of weakness, 21; contrasted with Rome, 23; first war with Rome, 29; backwardness of, 36; naval supremacy of, 39; prosperity and short-sightedness of, 55; terms of Regulus rejected by, 59; "Bride of the Sea," 66; sends embassy to Rome, 71; negligence at, 76; armies of, 88; supreme efforts of, 91; makes peace with Rome, 94; gains and losses by the First Punic War. 95; sore distress of, 98; mercenaries revolt against, 97; war and peace parties at, 103; war declared against Rome, 113; news of victories of Hannibal sent to, 134; lack of zeal at, 169; lose Spanish possessions, 206; threatened by Scipio, 210; last chance of, 220; makes peace with Rome, 226; destroys her fleet, 227; topography of, 239; changes by nature and man, 240; siege of, 240; fortifications, 241; harbours, 242; third war wi h Rome, 244; "peace at any price" offers of, 245; grief of, 246; scene at, 247; besieged by Romans, 247; repulse of Romans, 248; new outlet of, 253; closely besieged by Scipio Æmilianus, 255; final assault, 256; desperate resistance, 256; set on fire, 257; fate of, 259; ruins of, 263; impressions, 264; topography, 265; modern researches, 266; plan of. 274; aqueduct of, 276; smaller cisterns, 279; large cisterns, 280.
Camerina, 65.
Cannæ, 153; battle of, 158; results of the battle, 160.
Canaanites, 1, 16.
Canusium, 153, 161, 163.
Capua, 171; siege of, 185; capture of, 190; cruelty of the Romans at, 190.
Carthaginian proper names, 18.
Carthalo, Carthaginian admiral, 82, 245.

ETR.

Casilinum, 177.
Catana, 89.
Cato, 238, 250.
Catulus, C. Lutatius, consul, 91; defeats Hanno at Ægatian Islands, 92, 93; makes peace with Hamilcar, 94.
Caudex, A. Claudius, 32, 33, 34.
Censorinus, consul, 245, 246, 249, 251.
Chevelu Pass, 120.
Claudius, P., 79; defeated at Drepanum, 80; sister of, 81; punished 82.
Clypea, 55, 59, 63, 64, 65, 250.
Columna Rostrata, 46.
Consentia, 221.
Corsica, 4, 6, 9, 47, 59; seized by Hamilcar Barca, 102.
Corinth, 233.
Cortona, 138.
Corvus, 44, 45, 46.
Cothon. 6, 244.
Cremona, 111, 128.
Crispinus, 192.
Croton, 221.
Cumæ, 89.

DAKHLA, 273.
Davis, Dr., researches of, 265, 268, 283.
Diecplus, 43.
Dionysius, the tyrant, 30.
Djebel Khawi, 267, 269.
Dora Baltea, 127.
Drepanum, 48, 75, 79; battle of, 80, 84, 90, 91.
Duillius, defeats the Carthaginians at Mylæ, 45; honours bestowed upon, 46.
Duum viri navales, 41.

EBRO, 112, 116, 117.
Ecnomus, battle of, 50.
Egesta, 47, 48.
Elba, 9.
Elinga, 206.
Embole, 43.
Embolon, 52.
Epipolæ, 179.
Epirus, 28.
Eratosthenes, 9.
Erbessus, 37, 38.
Ercte, captured by Hamilcar, 85.
Eryx, Mount, 83; captured by Paulus, 84; captured by Hamilcar, 70.
Etruscans, conquest of, 25, 116.

HAN.

FABIUS Q. MAXIMUS, 11, policy of, 145; called the Lingerer, 146; continued inaction of, 147; fails to trap Hannibal, 148; instructs Minucius, 149; divides the command with Minucius, 150; great services of, *ib.*; restores confidence after Cannæ, 162; shield of Rome, 172; consul, 174, 176; advice to Scipio, 208.
Fæsulæ, 134, 137.
Flaccus, M. Fulvius, 32.
Flaccus, Q. Fulvius, consul, 186.
Flaminia, Via, 111, 112.
Flaminius, C., 110; captures Mediolanum, 111; character of, 134; disliked by the patricians, 135; elected consul, 136; defeated at Trasymene, 140; death of, 141.
Fulvius, Cn., prætor, 190, 191.

GADES, 18, 106, 206.
Gallic tribes join Hannibal, 128.
Gaul, 117.
Gela, 15.
Geronium, 149, 153, 155.
Gerusia, or council of ancients, 12.
Gescon, 97, 98.
Giuliano, St., 83.
Goletta, 266.
Gracchus, T. Sempronius, 174, 175; promises freedom to the armed slaves, 176.
"Great Plains," 217.

HAMILCAR, 206, 215.
Hamilcar, a Carthaginian, 73.
Hamilcar Barca, 75, 84; greatness of, 87; plans, 88; achievements, 89; siezes Eryx, 90; magnanimity 94, 95; makes peace with Rome, 96; his patriotism, 99; crosses to Spain, 105; character and death, 107.
Hamilcar, defeat and death at Himera, 11.
Hamilcar; a Carthaginian general, 48, 52; defeated at Ecnomus, 53.
Hannibal, son of Hamilcar, 108; his vow, 109; besieges Saguntum, 112; his surrender demanded, 113; his preparations for the expedition to Italy, 114; determines to go by land, 115; size of his army, 116; passes the Rhone, 117; defeat of the Gauls, 117; passage of Alps selected, 118; difficulties encountered, 120; crosses the Alps, 120; speech of, 122; in Italy,

HER.

125; defeats Romans at Ticinus, 127; advances, 128; defeats Romans at Trebia, 130; passes the Apennines, 133; passes the marshes, 134; marches through Etruria, defeats the Romans at Trasymene, 140; overruns Italy, 144; rests his army in Picenum, 145; marches into Campania, 146; escapes from Fabius, 148; defeats the Romans at Cannæ, 164; unbroken success of, 166; his character, 167; his genius, 169; foiled at Nola, 173; winters at Capua, 173; his wide projects, 174; at Tifata, 175; tide turns against, 176; gains Tarentum, 177; renewed successes of, 184; attempts to relieve Capua, 186; marches on Rome, 187; before Rome, 188; his superiority in the field, 191; defeats Fulvius, *ib.*; messengers from Hasdrubal captured, 195; recalled to Africa, 221; lands in Africa, 222; defeats Massinissa, 222; defeated at Zama, 224; escapes to Adrumetum, 225; advises peace, 226; as a statesman, 234; driven into exile, 235; wanderings and death, *ib.*
Hannibal, son of Hamilcar, 77; reinforces Lilybæum, 77.
Hannibal, son of Gisco, 37, 39; defeated by Duillius, 47, 66.
Hanno, Carthaginian admiral, 34.
Hanno, Carthaginian general, 34; sent to Sicily, 38, 52; defeated at Ecnomus, 53; sails for Carthage, 55; defeated by Catulus at Ægatian Islands, 92; enmity to Hamilcar Barca, 99, 104, 116, 117.
Hasdrubal, son of Gisco, 204, 206, 216; condemned to death, 219.
Hasdrubal, son-in-law of Hamilcar, 108.
Hasdrubal, grandson of Massinissa, 248.
Hasdrubal, son of Hamilcar, 114; encounters the Romans, 183, 184; advances from Spain, 193; in Gaul, 194; in Italy, 195; defeated by Nero, 197; death, 198.
Hasdrubal, Carthaginian general, 248; usurps authority, 252; cruelty, 253; cowardice, 258; his wife, 258.
Hasdrubal, Carthaginian general, 68; defeated at Panormus, 69.
Hasdrubal, Carthaginian general, 160.
Hastati, 223.
Heraclea, 28, 38, 50, 82.
Hercules, pillars of, 104.

MAN.

Herdonia, 19.
Hermæan promontory, 6, 55, 75.
Herodotus, 5, 17.
Hiero, 31, 36, 79, 82.
Hieronymus, 174, 175, 180.
Himera, 11, 15, 48.
Hill of St. Louis, 272.
Himilco, 76. 78, 179, 180.
Himilco Phameas, 249, 251.
Hippo Zarytus, 10, 98, 100, 250.
Horace, 126.

IAPYGIA, 185.
Ibera, 183.
Iberians, 108
Isère, valley of, 119.
Island of the Allobroges, 119.
Italy, Gallic war in, 110; Hannibal in, 118.

JUDGES, The hundred, 12, 47, 234.

KARCHEDON, 5.
Keleustes, 4?, 44.
Kirjath-Hadeschath, 5.

LAKE TRASYMENE, battle of, 140.
Lælius, 199, 209, 224.
Latins, conquest of, 25.
Leptis, 10.
Libyans, 55.
Libyssa, 236.
Liguria, 36; joins Hannibal, 128.
Lilybæum, 29, 36, 50, 66, 68; siege of, 75; relieved, 77; threatened by Carthaginians, 163.
Liparean Islands, 9.
Lucca, 134.
Livy, 109, 162, 190, 219, 222, 223
Livius, M., 194, 196, 197.
Locri, 34, 85, 221.
Lombardy, 128.
Lipari, 59.
Lucanians, 116.

MAGO, brother of Hannibal, 130, 132, 134, 157, 161; returns to Carthage, 161; in Spain, 204; recalled to Africa, 220; death of, ib.
Mago, family of, 13.
" a Shofete, 18.
Maherbal, 141, 157, 161.
Malta, 4, 9.
Mamertines, 29, 31, 35, 101.
Mamilius, Q., consul, 37.
Manilius, consul, 245, 248, 251.
Manlius, Q., 37.
Manlius, L., 52, 56.

OST.

Marca, 134.
Marcellus defeats the Gauls at Telamon, 111, 172; in Sicily, 178; besieges Syracuse, 179; captures Syracuse, 180; spoils Syracuse, 181; death of, 192; Hannibal's treatment of, 193.
Marcinus, 252, 271.
Marsalia, 116.
Massinissa, 211, 217, 218; routs the Carthaginian cavalry at Zama, 224; king of Numidia, 228, 244; death of, 249.
Matsæsylians, 211.
Massylians, 211.
Matho, 97, 98.
Mediolanum, 111.
Megara, 6.
Melcarth, 17, 106.
Melicertes, 17.
Mercenaries, 21; treatment of, 97; revolt of, 97, 100; destroyed, 101.
Messana, straits of, 63, 95.
Messana, 29, 31, 50.
Metagonitæ urbes, 106.
Metapontum, 191, 221.
Metaurus, battle of, 197.
Metellus, Cecilius, 69; defeats Hasdrubal at Panormus, 70.
Minucius, Marcus, 146; success of, 149; co-dictator, 149; beaten by Hannibal, 150; death of, 16.
Monte Pellegrino, 85.
Murviedro, 112.
Mummius, 233.
Mylæ, battle of, 45, 47, 52.
Mylitta, 17.

NAPLES, 175.
Naraggara, 223.
Narnia, 195.
Nasica P. Cornelius Scipio, 244.
Naval tactics, 43.
" armaments, 49.
Neapolis, 34.
Necropolis, 267.
Nepheris, 255.
Nero Caius, prætor, 186.
Nero C. Claudius, 194, outgenerals Hannibal, 196; defeats Hasdrubal at Metaurus, 197; barbarism of, 198
New Carthage, 108, 115, 116, 166; taken by Scipio, 205.
Nola, 172, 175.
Numidia, 19; cavalry of, 38, 120, 128.

OCTACILIUS, M., 35.
Ortigia, 189.
Ostia, 230.

RAS.

PACHYNUS, 36, 65, 83.
    Panormus, 48; Romans take, 66; battle at, 70; Hamilcar lands at, 85.
Passignano, 138.
Paullus, L. Æmilius, consul, 152, 153, 154; defeated at Cannæ, 160; death of, 161.
Paullus L. Junius, consul, 82, 83, 84, 86.
Pavia, 127.
Pænulus, 8.
Peace negotiations, 219.
Pera, M. Junius, Dictator, 163.
Periplus, 20, 43.
Perseus, 233.
Perugia, 139.
Philip, 175.
Phœnicians, characteristics of, 1; commercial enterprise, 2; size of territory, 3; found Carthage, 5.
Phileni, 19.
Phintias, 50.
Picenum, 145.
Pisa, 116.
Piso, Consul, 252.
Pityusian Islands, 9.
Placentia, 111, 127, 128, 132, 195.
Plautus, 8.
Pliny, 15, 86.
Po, 110, 111, 112, 127.
Polybius, 38, 50, 52, 56, 63, 73, 83, 90, 94, 101, 111, 119, 133, 137, 196, 251, 259.
Postumius, L., 37.
Principes, 223.
Prosbole, 43.
Prusias, 236.
Punic faith, 109, 168.
Punic wars, first, 20; end of, 94; second, 112; end of, 227; third, 244; end of, 259.
Pulcher, A. Claudius, consul, 186
Puteoli, 176.
Pydna, 250.
Pyrenees, 116, 117.
Pyrrhus, war with, 28; discomfiture of, 29.

RAS SIDS BU SAID, 270.
    Regulus, M. Atilius, 52; defeats Hanno at Ecnomus, 53, 54; invades Africa, 56; defeats the Carthaginians at Adis, 58; offers terms to the Carthaginians, 59; defeated at Adis, 62; embassy to Rome, 71; death, 72; wife of, 74; her cruelty, 74.

SCI.

Rhegium, 30, 32.
Rhodian, mercenary, 77; baffles the Romans, 78; is captured, *ib.*
Rhodian ship, u ed as a model by Romans, 91.
Rhone, 116, 119, 126.
Rome, 23; compared with Carthage, 23; advancement, 27; war with Pyrrhus, 28; and Carthage face to face, 29; political questions, 33; first fleet, 39; difficulties in creating a fleet, 41; naval affairs *ib.* fleet sails, 43; joy over first naval victory, 46; attacks Sardinia and Corsica, 47; victory at Ecnomus, 52; efforts of Rome, 64; destruction of Roman fleet, 65; destruction of second Roman fleet, 67; destruction of elephants at, 71; destruction of third Roman fleet, 83; despondency at, *ib.*; during the mercenary w. r, 102; seizes Sardinia and Corsica, *ib.*; defeats the Gauls, 110; Senate, 126; news of Trasymene at, 142; great exertions of, 152; news of Cannæ, 162; greatness of, 165; great excitement of, 174; condition of, 231; in the Eas , 232; joy at, over capture of Carthage, 259.
Roman Legion, 28; character deteriorated, 229.
Roquemaure, 119.
Rubicon, 110.

SACRED BAND, 16.
    Saguntum, 112.
Salapia, 177.
Samnium, 146.
Sardinia, 4, 5, 59, 67, 102.
Sardinia, Island of, 4, 9, 101.
Sardinians for sale, 230.
Scipio, P. Cornelius, 126; defeated at Ticinus, 128; successes in Spain, 183; defeat and death, 184.
Scipio, C., 126; defeat and death, 184.
Scipio, P. Cornelius, Africanus, son of P. Cornelius, 128, 199; early history, 200; character and influence, 201; captures New Carthage, 204; elected consul, 207; in Sicily, 209; invades Africa, 210; rebukes Massinissa, 218; moderation of, 219; defeats Hannibal at Zama, 224; returns to Rome, 227; death of, 237.

TEM.

Scipio, P. Cornelius, Æmilianus, 249; 250; consul, 252; attacks on Carthage, 253; mole, 253; final assault on Carthage, 256; takes Carthage by storm, 257; destroys Carthage, 259.
Scipio, L. Cornelius, epitaph of, 48.
Selinus, 15, 69.
Sempronius, consul, 127, 129; defeated at Trebia, 130.
Servilius, Cn., 133, 135, 141.
Shaw, researches of, 280.
Shofete, 13, 18.
Sicily, 6; a battle-field, 30; Carthaginians driven from, 95; war in, 178.
Sidon, 1.
Siculus, Diodorus, 73, 274.
Silpia, 206.
Sophonisba, 212, 217; drinks poison, 218.
Spain, 24; Phœnician settlements in, 9.
Spendius, 97, 98, 100, 101.
Spoletium, 144.
Spolia opima, 111.
Strabo, 273.
Suffetes, 11, 12.
Syphax, 184, 211, 217; fall of, 219.
Syracuse, 31, 34, 35; siege of, 37; capture, 38; threatened by Carthaginian fleet, 163; besieged by Marcellus, 179; captured by Marcellus, 180; fate of, 181.
Syrtis, 67.
Syssitia, 14, 15, 16.

T ÆNIA, 248, 249, 254, 266.
Tagus, 108, 112.
Tarentaise, 120.
Tarentines, 28, 34.
Tarentum, 34, 133, 177; captured by Hannibal, 184; besieged by Fabius, 192.
Tartessus, 106.
Taurini, 127.
Telamon, battle of, 111.
Telesia, 146.
Temple, Sir Grenville, researches of, 275.

ZAM.

Tiber, 144.
Trasymene, battle of Lake, 140.
Thurii, 191.
Ticinus, battle of, 127.
Tifata, 175.
Trebia, battle of, 130.
Tripolis, desert of, 10.
Triton, 10.
Triarii, 50, 223.
Timoleon, 30, 37.
Tunis, 58, 97, 99, 101; gulf of, 273; oriental character, 285; streets of, 286.
Tycha, 179.
Tyndaris, 52.
Tyre, 1; merchants of, 3, 11, 17, 106

U MBRIANS, 116.
Utica, 5, 10, 98, 99, 100, 246, 260, 278.

V ALERIUS, M., consul, 35.
Valerius, Q., prætor, 92.
Varro, P. Terentius, consul, 152, 154; divides command with Paullus, *ib.*; defeated at Cannæ, 160, 163, 166.
Valerius, Q., prætor, 92; at battle of Ægatian Islands, 93.
Velia, 34.
Venusia, 16.
Venus Cœlestis, 17.
Verbanus, lake of, 127.
Volscians, 26.
Vulturnus 156, 173.

W AR, the truceless, 100, 101.
"White rock," 121.

X ANTHIPPUS, 60; the commander of Carthaginian army 61; defeats Regulus at Adis, 62.

Z ACYNTHUS, 112.
Zama, 223; battle of, 224.

"*The volumes contain the ripe results of the studies of men who are authorities in their respective fields.*"—THE NATION.

EPOCHS OF HISTORY

EPOCHS OF ANCIENT HISTORY	EPOCHS OF MODERN HISTORY
Eleven volumes, 16mo, each $1.00.	Eighteen volumes, 16mo, each $1.00.

The Epoch volumes have most successfully borne the test of experience, and are universally acknowledged to be the best series of historical manuals in existence. They are admirably adapted in form and matter to the needs of colleges, schools, reading circles, and private classes. Attention is called to them as giving the utmost satisfaction as class hand-books.

NOAH PORTER, *President of Yale College.*

"The 'Epochs of History' have been prepared with knowledge and artistic skill to meet the wants of a large number of readers. To the young they furnish an outline or compendium. To those who are older they present a convenient sketch of the heads of the knowledge which they have already acquired. The outlines are by no means destitute of spirit, and may be used with great profit for family reading, and in select classes or reading clubs."

CHARLES KENDALL ADAMS, *President of Cornell University.*

"A series of concise and carefully prepared volumes on special eras of history. Each is also complete in itself, and has no especial connection with the other members of the series. The works are all written by authors selected by the editor on account of some especial qualifications for a portrayal of the period they respectively describe. The volumes form an excellent collection, especially adapted to the wants of a general reader."

The Publishers will supply these volumes to teachers at SPECIAL NET RATES, and would solicit correspondence concerning terms for examination and introduction copies.

CHARLES SCRIBNER'S SONS, Publishers
743-745 Broadway, New York

THE GREAT SUCCESS OF THE SERIES

is the best proof of its general popularity, and the excellence of the various volumes is further attested by their having been adopted as text-books in many of our leading educational institutions. The publishers beg to call attention to the following list comprising some of the most prominent institutions using volumes of the series:

Smith College, Northampton, Mass.
Univ. of Vermont, Burlington, Vt.
Yale Univ., New Haven, Conn.
Harvard Univ., Cambridge, Mass.
Bellewood Sem., Anchorage, Ky.
Vanderbilt Univ., Nashville, Tenn.
State Univ., Minneapolis, Minn.
Christian Coll., Columbia, Mo.
Adelphi Acad., Brooklyn, N. Y.
Earlham Coll., Richmond, Ind.
Granger Place School, Canandaigua, N. Y.
Salt Lake Acad., Salt Lake City, Utah.
Beloit Col., Beloit, Wis.
Logan Female Coll., Russellville, Ky.
No. West Univ., Evanston, Ill.
State Normal School, Baltimore, Md.
Hamilton Coll., Clinton, N. Y.
Doane Coll., Crete, Neb.
Princeton College, Princeton, N. J.
Williams Coll., Williamstown, Mass.
Cornell Univ., Ithaca, N. Y.
Illinois Coll., Jacksonville, Ill.

Univ. of South, Sewaunee, Tenn.
Wesleyan Univ., Mt. Pleasant, Ia.
Univ. of Cal., Berkeley, Cal.
So. Car. Coll., Columbia, S. C.
Amsterdam Acad., Amsterdam, N. Y.
Carleton Coll., Northfield, Minn.
Wesleyan Univ., Middletown, Mass.
Albion Coll., Albion, Mich.
Dartmouth Coll., Hanover, N. H.
Wilmington Coll., Wilmington, O.
Madison Univ., Hamilton, N. Y.
Syracuse Univ., Syracuse, N. Y.
Univ. of Wis., Madison, Wis.
Union Coll., Schenectady, N. Y.
Norwich Free Acad., Norwich, Conn.
Greenwich Acad., Greenwich, Conn.
Univ. of Neb., Lincoln, Neb.
Kalamazoo Coll., Kalamazoo, Mich.
Olivet Coll., Olivet, Mich.
Amherst Coll., Amherst, Mass.
Ohio State Univ., Columbus, O.
Free Schools, Oswego, N. Y.

Bishop J. F. HURST, *ex-President of Drew Theol. Sem.*

"It appears to me that the idea of Morris in his Epochs is strictly in harmony with the philosophy of history—namely, that great movements should be treated not according to narrow geographical and national limits and distinction, but universally, according to their place in the general life of the world. The historical Maps and the copious Indices are welcome additions to the volumes."

EPOCHS OF ANCIENT HISTORY.

A SERIES OF BOOKS NARRATING THE HISTORY OF GREECE AND ROME, AND OF THEIR RELATIONS TO OTHER COUNTRIES AT SUCCESSIVE EPOCHS.

Edited by

Rev. G. W. Cox and Charles Sankey, M.A.

Eleven volumes, 16mo, with 41 Maps and Plans.
Sold separately. Price per vol., $1.00.
The Set, Roxburgh style, gilt top, in box, $11.00.

TROY—ITS LEGEND, HISTORY, AND LITERATURE. By S. G. W. Benjamin.

"The task of the author has been to gather into a clear and very readable narrative all that is known of legendary, historical, and geographical Troy, and to tell the story of Homer, and weigh and compare the different theories in the Homeric controversy. The work is well done. His book is altogether candid, and is a very valuable and entertaining compendium."—*Hartford Courant.*

"As a monograph on Troy, covering all sides of the question, it is of great value, and supplies a long vacant place in our fund of classical knowledge."—*N. Y. Christian Advocate.*

THE GREEKS AND THE PERSIANS. By Rev G. W. Cox.

"It covers the ground in a perfectly satisfactory way. The work is clear, succinct, and readable."—*New York Independent.*

"Marked by thorough and comprehensive scholarship and by a skillful style."—*Congregationalist.*

"It would be hard to find a more creditable book. The author's prefatory remarks upon the origin and growth of Greek civilization are alone worth the price of the volume."
—*Christian Union.*

EPOCHS OF ANCIENT HISTORY

THE ATHENIAN EMPIRE—From the Flight of Xerxes to the Fall of Athens. By Rev. G. W. Cox.

"Mr. Cox writes in such a way as to bring before the reader everything which is important to be known or learned; and his narrative cannot fail to give a good idea of the men and deeds with which he is concerned."—*The Churchman.*

"Mr. Cox has done his work with the honesty of a true student. It shows persevering scholarship and a desire to get at the truth."—*New York Herald.*

THE SPARTAN AND THEBAN SUPREMACIES. By CHARLES SANKEY, M.A.

"This volume covers the period between the disasters of Athens at the close of the Pelopenesian war and the rise of Macedon. It is a very striking and instructive picture of the political life of the Grecian commonwealth at that time."—*The Churchman.*

"It is singularly interesting to read, and in respect to arrangement, maps, etc., is all that can be desired."—*Boston Congregationalist.*

THE MACEDONIAN EMPIRE—Its Rise and Culmination to Death of Alexander the Great. By A. M. CURTEIS, M.A.

"A good and satisfactory history of a very important period. The maps are excellent, and the story is lucidly and vigorously told."—*The Nation.*

"The same compressive style and yet completeness of detail that have characterized the previous issues in this delightful series, are found in this volume. Certainly the art of conciseness in writing was never carried to a higher or more effective point."—*Boston Saturday Evening Gazette.*

*** *The above five volumes give a connected and complete history of Greece from the earliest times to the death of Alexander.*

EARLY ROME—From the Foundation of the City to its Destruction by the Gauls. By W. IHNE, Ph.D.

"Those who want to know the truth instead of the traditions that used to be learned of our fathers, will find in the work entertainment, careful scholarship, and sound sense."—*Cincinnati Times.*

"The book is excellently well done. The views are those of a learned and able man, and they are presented in this volume with great force and clearness."—*The Nation.*

ROME AND CARTHAGE—The Punic Wars. By R. BOSWORTH SMITH.

"By blending the account of Rome and Carthage the accomplished author presents a succinct and vivid picture of two great cities and people which leaves a deep impression. The story is full of intrinsic interest, and was never better told."—*Christian Union.*

"The volume is one of rare interest and value."—*Chicago Interior.*

"An admirably condensed history of Carthage, from its establishment by the adventurous Phœnician traders to its sad and disastrous fall."—*New York Herald.*

THE GRACCHI, MARIUS, AND SULLA. By A. H. BEESLEY.

"A concise and scholarly historical sketch, descriptive of the decay of the Roman Republic, and the events which paved the way for the advent of the conquering Cæsar. It is an excellent account of the leaders and legislation of the republic."—*Boston Post.*

"It is prepared in succinct but comprehensive style, and is an excellent book for reading and reference."—*New York Observer.*

"No better condensed account of the two Gracchi and the turbulent careers of Marius and Sulla has yet appeared."—*New York Independent.*

THE ROMAN TRIUMVIRATES. By the Very Rev. CHARLES MERIVALE, D.D.

"In brevity, clear and scholarly treatment of the subject, and the convenience of map, index, and side notes, the volume is a model."—*New York Tribune.*

"An admirable presentation, and in style vigorous and picturesque."—*Hartford Courant.*

THE EARLY EMPIRE—From the Assassination of Julius Cæsar to the Assassination of Domitian. By Rev. W. WOLFE CAPES, M.A.

"It is written with great clearness and simplicity of style, and is as attractive an account as has ever been given in brief of one of the most interesting periods of Roman History."—*Boston Saturday Evening Gazette.*

"It is a clear, well-proportioned, and trustworthy performance, and well deserves to be studied."—*Christian at Work.*

THE AGE OF THE ANTONINES—The Roman Empire of the Second Century. By Rev. W. WOLFE CAPES, M.A.

"The Roman Empire during the second century is the broad subject discussed in this book, and discussed with learning and intelligence."—*New York Independent.*

"The writer's diction is clear and elegant, and his narration is free from any touch of pedantry. In the treatment of its prolific and interesting theme, and in its general plan, the book is a model of works of its class."—*New York Herald.*

"We are glad to commend it. It is written clearly, and with care and accuracy. It is also in such neat and compact form as to be the more attractive."—*Congregationalist.*

** *The above six volumes give the History of Rome from the founding of the City to the death of Marcus Aurelius Antoninus.*

EPOCHS OF MODERN HISTORY.

A SERIES OF BOOKS NARRATING THE HISTORY OF ENGLAND AND EUROPE AT SUCCESSIVE EPOCHS SUBSEQUENT TO THE CHRISTIAN ERA.

Edited by

EDWARD E. MORRIS.

Eighteen volumes, 16mo, with 74 Maps, Plans, and Tables. Sold separately. Price per vol., $1.00.
The Set, Roxburgh style, gilt top, in box, $18.00.

THE BEGINNING OF THE MIDDLE AGES—England and Europe in the Ninth Century. By the Very Rev. R. W. CHURCH, M.A.

"A remarkably thoughtful and satisfactory discussion of the causes and results of the vast changes which came upon Europe during the period discussed. The book is adapted to be exceedingly serviceable."—*Chicago Standard.*

"At once readable and valuable. It is comprehensive and yet gives the details of a period most interesting to the student of history."—*Herald and Presbyter.*

"It is written with a clearness and vividness of statement which make it the pleasantest reading. It represents a great deal of patient research, and is careful and scholarly."—*Boston Journal.*

THE NORMANS IN EUROPE—The Feudal System and England under the Norman Kings. By Rev. A. H. JOHNSON, M.A.

"Its pictures of the Normans in their home, of the Scandinavian exodus, the conquest of England, and Norman administration, are full of vigor and cannot fail of holding the reader's attention."—*Episcopal Register.*

"The style of the author is vigorous and animated, and he has given a valuable sketch of the origin and progress of the great Northern movement that has shaped the history of modern Europe."—*Boston Transcript.*

THE CRUSADES. By Rev. G. W. Cox.

"To be warmly commended for important qualities. The author shows conscientious fidelity to the materials, and such skill in the use of them, that, as a result, the reader has before him a narrative related in a style that makes it truly fascinating."—*Congregationalist.*

"It is written in a pure and flowing style, and its arrangement and treatment of subject are exceptional."—*Christian Intelligencer.*

THE EARLY PLANTAGENETS—Their Relation to the History of Europe; The Foundation and Growth of Constitutional Government. By Rev. W. STUBBS, M.A.

"Nothing could be desired more clear, succinct, and well arranged. All parts of the book are well done. It may be pronounced the best existing brief history of the constitution for this, its most important period."—*The Nation.*

"Prof. Stubbs has presented leading events with such fairness and wisdom as are seldom found. He is remarkably clear and satisfactory."—*The Churchman.*

EDWARD III. By Rev. W. WARBURTON, M.A.

"The author has done his work well, and we commend it as containing in small space all essential matter."—*New York Independent.*

"Events and movements are admirably condensed by the author, and presented in such attractive form as to entertain as well as instruct."—*Chicago Interior.*

THE HOUSES OF LANCASTER AND YORK —The Conquest and Loss of France. By JAMES GAIRDNER.

"Prepared in a most careful and thorough manner, and ought to be read by every student."—*New York Times.*

"It leaves nothing to be desired as regards compactness, accuracy, and excellence of literary execution."—*Boston Journal.*

THE ERA OF THE PROTESTANT REVOLUTION. By Frederic Seebohm. With Notes, on Books in English relating to the Reformation, by Prof. George P. Fisher, D.D.

"For an impartial record of the civil and ecclesiastical changes about four hundred years ago, we cannot commend a better manual."—*Sunday-School Times.*

"All that could be desired, as well in execution as in plan. The narrative is animated, and the selection and grouping of events skillful and effective."—*The Nation.*

THE EARLY TUDORS—Henry VII., Henry VIII. By Rev. C. E. Moberley, M.A., late Master in Rugby School.

"Is concise, scholarly, and accurate. On the epoch of which it treats, we know of no work which equals it."—*N. Y. Observer.*

" A marvel of clear and succinct brevity and good historical judgment. There is hardly a better book of its kind to be named."—*New York Independent.*

THE AGE OF ELIZABETH. By Rev. M. Creighton, M.A.

"Clear and compact in style ; careful in their facts, and just in interpretation of them. It sheds much light on the progress of the Reformation and the origin of the Popish reaction during Queen Elizabeth's reign ; also, the relation of Jesuitism to the latter."—*Presbyterian Review.*

" A clear, concise, and just story of an era crowded with events of interest and importance."—*New York World.*

THE THIRTY YEARS' WAR—1618-1648. By Samuel Rawson Gardiner.

" As a manual it will prove of the greatest practical value, while to the general reader it will afford a clear and interesting account of events. We know of no more spirited and attractive recital of the great era."—*Boston Saturday Evening Gazette.*

" The thrilling story of those times has never been told so vividly or succinctly as in this volume."—*Episcopal Register.*

THE PURITAN REVOLUTION; and the First Two Stuarts, 1603-1660. By SAMUEL RAWSON GARDINER.

"The narrative is condensed and brief, yet sufficiently comprehensive to give an adequate view of the events related." —*Chicago Standard.*

"Mr. Gardiner uses his researches in an admirably clear and fair way."—*Congregationalist.*

"The sketch is concise, but clear and perfectly intelligible." —*Hartford Courant.*

THE ENGLISH RESTORATION AND LOUIS XIV., from the Peace of Westphalia to the Peace of Nimwegen. By OSMUND AIRY, M.A.

"It is crisply and admirably written. An immense amount of information is conveyed and with great clearness, the arrangement of the subjects showing great skill and a thorough command of the complicated theme."—*Boston Saturday Evening Gazette.*

"The author writes with fairness and discrimination, and has given a clear and intelligible presentation of the time."— *New York Evangelist.*

THE FALL OF THE STUARTS; and Western Europe. By Rev. EDWARD HALE, M.A.

"A valuable compend to the general reader and scholar." —*Providence Journal.*

"It will be found of great value. It is a very graphic account of the history of Europe during the 17th century, and is admirably adapted for the use of students."—*Boston Saturday Evening Gazette.*

"An admirable handbook for the student."—*The Churchman.*

THE AGE OF ANNE. By EDWARD E. MORRIS, M.A.

"The author's arrangement of the material is remarkably clear, his selection and adjustment of the facts judicious, his historical judgment fair and candid, while the style wins by its simple elegance."—*Chicago Standard.*

"An excellent compendium of the history of an important period."—*The Watchman.*

THE EARLY HANOVERIANS—Europe from the Peace of Utrecht to the Peace of Aix-la-Chapelle. By EDWARD E. MORRIS, M.A.

"Masterly, condensed, and vigorous, this is one of the books which it is a delight to read at odd moments; which are broad and suggestive, and at the same time condensed in treatment."—*Christian Advocate.*

"A remarkably clear and readable summary of the salient points of interest. The maps and tables, no less than the author's style and treatment of the subject, entitle the volume to the highest claims of recognition."—*Boston Daily Advertiser.*

FREDERICK THE GREAT, AND THE SEVEN YEARS' WAR. By F. W. LONGMAN.

"The subject is most important, and the author has treated it in a way which is both scholarly and entertaining."—*The Churchman.*

"Admirably adapted to interest school boys, and older heads will find it pleasant reading."—*New York Tribune.*

THE FRENCH REVOLUTION, AND FIRST EMPIRE. By WILLIAM O'CONNOR MORRIS. With Appendix by ANDREW D. WHITE, LL.D., ex-President of Cornell University.

"We have long needed a simple compendium of this period, and we have here one which is brief enough to be easily run through with, and yet particular enough to make entertaining reading."—*New York Evening Post.*

"The author has well accomplished his difficult task of sketching in miniature the grand and crowded drama of the French Revolution and the Napoleonic Empire, showing himself to be no servile compiler, but capable of judicious and independent criticism."—*Springfield Republican.*

THE EPOCH OF REFORM—1830-1850. By JUSTIN MCCARTHY.

"Mr. McCarthy knows the period of which he writes thoroughly, and the result is a narrative that is at once entertaining and trustworthy."—*New York Examiner.*

"The narrative is clear and comprehensive, and told with abundant knowledge and grasp of the subject."—*Boston Courier.*

IMPORTANT HISTORICAL WORKS.

THE DAWN OF HISTORY. An Introduction to Pre-Historic Study. New and Enlarged Edition. Edited by C. F. KEARY. 12mo, cloth, $1.25.

This work treats successively of the earliest traces of man; of language, its growth, and the story it tells of the pre-historic users of it; of early social life, the religions, mythologies, and folk-tales, and of the history of writing. The present edition contains about one hundred pages of new matter, embodying the results of the latest researches.

"A fascinating manual. In its way, the work is a model of what a popular scientific work should be."—*Boston Sat. Eve. Gazette.*

THE ORIGIN OF NATIONS. By Professor GEORGE RAWLINSON, M.A. 12mo, with maps, $1.00.

The first part of this book discusses the antiquity of civilization in Egypt and the other early nations of the East. The second part is an examination of the ethnology of Genesis, showing its accordance with the latest results of modern ethnographical science.

"A work of genuine scholarly excellence, and a useful offset to a great deal of the superficial current literature on such subjects."—*Congregationalist.*

MANUAL OF MYTHOLOGY. For the Use of Schools, Art Students, and General Readers. Founded on the Works of Petiscus, Preller, and Welcker. By ALEXANDER S. MURRAY, Department of Greek and Roman Antiquities, British Museum. With 45 Plates. Reprinted from the Second Revised London Edition. Crown 8vo, $1.75.

"It has been acknowledged the best work on the subject to be found in a concise form, and as it embodies the results of the latest researches and discoveries in ancient mythologies, it is superior for school and general purposes as a handbook to any of the so-called standard works."—*Cleveland Herald.*

"Whether as a manual for reference, a text-book for school use, or for the general reader, the book will be found very valuable and interesting."—*Boston Journal.*

THE HISTORY OF ROME, from the Earliest Time to the Period of Its Decline. By Dr. THEODOR MOMMSEN. Translated by W. P. DICKSON, D.D., LL.D. Reprinted from the Revised London Edition. Four volumes, crown 8vo. Price per set, $8.00.

"A work of the very highest merit; its learning is exact and profound; its narrative full of genius and skill; its descriptions of men are admirably vivid."—*London Times.*

"Since the days of Niebuhr, no work on Roman History has appeared that combines so much to attract, instruct, and charm the reader. Its style—a rare quality in a German author—is vigorous, spirited, and animated."—Dr. SCHMITZ.

THE PROVINCES OF THE ROMAN EMPIRE. From Cæsar to Diocletian. By THEODOR MOMMSEN. Translated by WILLIAM P. DICKSON, D.D., LL.D. With maps. Two vols., 8vo, $6.00.

"The author draws the wonderfully rich and varied picture of the conquest and administration of that great circle of peoples and lands which formed the empire of Rome outside of Italy, their agriculture, trade, and manufactures, their artistic and scientific life, through all degrees of civilization, with such detail and completeness as could have come from no other hand than that of this great master of historical research."—Prof. W. A. PACKARD, Princeton College.

THE HISTORY OF THE ROMAN REPUBLIC. Abridged from the History by Professor THEODOR MOMMSEN, by C. BRYANS and F. J. R. HENDY. 12mo, $1.75.

"It is a genuine boon that the essential parts of Mommsen's Rome are thus brought within the easy reach of all, and the abridgment seems to me to preserve unusually well the glow and movement of the original."—Prof. TRACY PECK, Yale University.

"The condensation has been accurately and judiciously effected. I heartily commend the volume as the most adequate embodiment, in a single volume, of the main results of modern historical research in the field of Roman affairs."—Prof. HENRY M. BAIRD, University of City of New York.

IMPORTANT HISTORICAL WORKS.

THE HISTORY OF GREECE. By Prof. Dr. ERNST CURTIUS. Translated by Adolphus William Ward, M.A., Fellow of St. Peter's College, Cambridge, Prof. of History in Owen's College, Manchester. Five volumes, crown 8vo. Price per set, $10.00.

"We cannot express our opinion of Dr. Curtius' book better than by saying that it may be fitly ranked with Theodor Mommsen's great work."—*London Spectator.*

"As an introduction to the study of Grecian history, no previous work is comparable to the present for vivacity and picturesque beauty, while in sound learning and accuracy of statement it is not inferior to the elaborate productions which enrich the literature of the age."—*N. Y. Daily Tribune.*

CÆSAR: a Sketch. By JAMES ANTHONY FROUDE, M.A. 12mo, gilt top, $1.50.

"This book is a most fascinating biography and is by far the best account of Julius Cæsar to be found in the English language."—*The London Standard.*

"He combines into a compact and nervous narrative all that is known of the personal, social, political, and military life of Cæsar; and with his sketch of Cæsar includes other brilliant sketches of the great man, his friends, or rivals, who contemporaneously with him formed the principal figures in the Roman world."—*Harper's Monthly.*

CICERO. Life of Marcus Tullius Cicero. By WILLIAM FORSYTH, M.A., Q.C. 20 Engravings. New Edition. 2 vols., crown 8vo, in one, gilt top, $2.50.

The author has not only given us the most complete and well-balanced account of the life of Cicero ever published; he has drawn an accurate and graphic picture of domestic life among the best classes of the Romans, one which the reader of general literature, as well as the student, may peruse with pleasure and profit.

"A scholar without pedantry, and a Christian without cant, Mr. Forsyth seems to have seized with praiseworthy tact the precise attitude which it behooves a biographer to take when narrating the life, the personal life of Cicero. Mr. Forsyth produces what we venture to say will become one of the classics of English biographical literature, and will be welcomed by readers of all ages and both sexes, of all professions and of no profession at all."—*London Quarterly.*

VALUABLE WORKS ON CLASSICAL LITERATURE.

THE HISTORY OF ROMAN LITERATURE. From the Earliest Period to the Death of Marcus Aurelius. With Chronological Tables, etc., for the use of Students. By C. T. CRUTTWELL, M.A. Crown 8vo, $2.50.

Mr. Cruttwell's book is written throughout from a purely literary point of view, and the aim has been to avoid tedious and trivial details. The result is a volume not only suited for the student, but remarkably readable for all who possess any interest in the subject.

"Mr. Cruttwell has given us a genuine history of Roman literature, not merely a descriptive list of authors and their productions, but a well elaborated portrayal of the successive stages in the intellectual development of the Romans and the various forms of expression which these took in literature."—*N. Y. Nation.*

UNIFORM WITH THE ABOVE.

A HISTORY OF GREEK LITERATURE. From the Earliest Period of Demosthenes. By FRANK BYRON JEVONS, M.A., Tutor in the University of Durham. Crown 8vo, $2.50.

The author goes into detail with sufficient fullness to make the history complete, but he never loses sight of the commanding lines along which the Greek mind moved, and a clear understanding of which is necessary to every intelligent student of universal literature.

"It is beyond all question the best history of Greek literature that has hitherto been published."—*London Spectator.*

"With such a book as this within reach there is no reason why any intelligent English reader may not get a thorough and comprehensive insight into the spirit of Greek literature, of its historic development, and of its successive and chief masterpieces, which are here so finely characterized, analyzed, and criticised."—*Chicago Advance.*

TRANSLATIONS OF PLATO.

THE DIALOGUES OF PLATO. Translated into English, with Analysis and Introductions. By B. JOWETT, M.A., Master of Balliol College, Oxford. A new and cheaper edition. Four vols., crown 8vo, per set, $8.00.

"The present work of Professor Jowett will be welcomed with profound interest, as the only adequate endeavor to transport the most precious monument of Grecian thought among the familiar treasures of English literature. The noble reputation of Professor Jowett, both as a thinker and a scholar, is a valid guaranty for the excellence of his performance."—*New York Tribune.*

SOCRATES. A Translation of the Apology, Crito, and parts of the Phædo of Plato. Containing the Defence of Socrates at his Trial, his Conversation in Prison, with his Thoughts on the Future Life, and an Account of his Death. With an Introduction by Professor W. W. Goodwin, of Harvard College. 12mo, cloth, $1.00; paper, 50 cents.

TALKS WITH SOCRATES ABOUT LIFE. Translations from the Gorgias and the Republic of Plato. 12mo, cloth, $1.00; paper, 50 cents.

A DAY IN ATHENS WITH SOCRATES. Translations from the Protagoras and the Republic of Plato. Being conversations between Socrates and other Greeks on Virtue and Justice. 12mo, cloth, $1.00; paper, 50 cents.

"Eminent scholars, men of much Latin and more Greek, attest the skill and truth with which the versions are made; we can confidently speak of their English grace and clearness. They seem a 'model of style,' because they are without manner and perfectly simple."—W. D. HOWELLS.

"We do not remember any translation of a Greek author which is a better specimen of idiomatic English than this, or a more faithful rendering of the real spirit of the original into English as good and as simple as the Greek."—*New York Evening Post.*

CHARLES SCRIBNER'S SONS,
743 and 745 Broadway, New York.

www.ingramcontent.com/pod-product-compliance
Lightning Source LLC
Chambersburg PA
CBHW030314240426
43673CB00040B/1160